ROUND UP THE USUAL SUSPECTS

ROUND UP THE USUAL SUSPECTS

CRIMINAL INVESTIGATION IN *LAW & ORDER,*
COLD CASE, AND *CSI*

Raymond Ruble

Westport, Connecticut
London

M

Library of Congress Cataloging-in-Publication Data

Ruble, Raymond S.
    Round up the usual suspects: criminal investigation in Law & order, Cold case, and CSI/Raymond Ruble.
        p. cm.
    Includes bibliographical references and index.
    ISBN 978-0-275-99512-6 (alk. paper)
    1. Criminal investigation—United States—Case studies. 2. Forensic sciences—United States—Case studies. 3. Crime scene searches—United States—Case studies. 4. Law & order (Television program) 5. Cold case files (Television program) 6. CSI: crime scene investigation. 7. Mass media and crime. I. Title.
    HV8073.R79   2009
    363.250973—dc22   2008033450

British Library Cataloguing in Publication Data is available.

Library of Congress Catalog Card Number: 2008033450
ISBN: 978-0-275-99512-6

First published in 2009

Praeger Publishers, 88 Post Road West, Westport, CT 06881
An imprint of Greenwood Publishing Group, Inc.
www.praeger.com

Printed in the United States of America

The paper used in this book complies with the Permanent Paper Standard issued by the National Information Standards Organization (Z39.48–1984).

10   9   8   7   6   5   4   3   2   1

Major Strasser has been shot. Round up the usual suspects.

—Captain Renault, *Casablanca*

CONTENTS

PREFACE

In the last twenty years, TV detective shows have ventured into previously underexplored territories. The robbers are up to their old tricks all right—thankfully this has not changed—but the cops have developed new ways of dealing with the rascals.

Three TV series—*CSI: Crime Scene Investigation, Cold Case,* and *Law & Order*—are at the forefront of these changes in the popular culture of small-screen crime fighting. Each of these shows is anchored in its own model of crime fighting. *CSI* has the "forensic science" model of criminal detection in which good detective work involves the combination of biology, chemistry, and physics lab sciences. *Cold Case* offers the "memory romance" model of criminal detection, which sees the detective as a sort of fairy godmother fulfilling the victim's heart-felt longings. *Law & Order* presents the "legal cooperation" model of criminal detection, according to which successful crime fighting is an outcome of bureaucratic efficiency (except with the Feds!) and properly playing by the rules.

Pity the poor old TV gumshoe; he's been transformed into an organizational bean counter, a lab rat, or a devout sentimentalist! Where are you now, Joe Friday? A la Joe DiMaggio, gone, gone away.

Like a good cookbook, a criminal detection model is a type of blueprint that comes with its own unique set of operating instructions. It tells the members of the criminal justice system how to proceed as a crime is discovered, evidence is collected, and suspects are found, interrogated, and prosecuted. Each of these model "cookbooks" is significantly different from the others, yet they all have the same purpose: to round up the usual suspects.

This is a book about these TV detective series and the different crime-fighting models that distinguish them. To understand the three main models of criminal detection even further, two additional TV series will be explored—*Boomtown* and *Without a Trace. Boomtown's* crime-fighting model is the "points-of-view" model in which truth and justice are quilts stitched together out of many separate and divergent patches. *Without a Trace* is based on the "essential self" model of criminal detection, according to which detective work seeks to uncover the hidden true identity of the victim.

All five of these series embody uniquely sculptured formats that differ from each other just as a cookbook with crockpot recipes differs dramatically from one with recipes for grilling. Each aims at producing a nourishing meal, but each completes its objectives in distinctly different ways.

The pages below discuss a number of interesting philosophical issues raised in the popular TV police procedural series *CSI* (debut 2000), *Cold Case* (debut 2003), *Without a Trace* (debut 2002), *Boomtown* (debut 2002), and *Law & Order* (debut 1990); these issues make each series the informative and entertaining vehicle that it is. As spinoff series, *Law & Order* produced *Law & Order: Special Victims Unit* (debut 1999), *Law & Order: Criminal Intent* (debut 2001), *Law & Order: Trial by Jury* (which debuted in 2005 but was cancelled after thirteen episodes), and *Law & Order: London*, set to debut in 2009. *CSI* produced two spinoff series, *CSI: Miami* (debut 2002) and *CSI: New York* (debut 2004). *Cold Case* and *Without a Trace* have yet to produce a spinoff series. *Boomtown* went bust early in its second season. Each of these series except *Law & Order: Trial by Jury*, produced more than twenty episodes a season and each of them except *Boomtown* is still in production at the time of this writing.

CSI's spinoff series are, quite appropriately, clones of their parent, so no attempt will be made here to pursue the nuances offered by these replicates. *Law & Order*'s spinoff series differ from their parent in that *Special Victim's Unit* and *Criminal Intent* fail to give the sort of attention to that which is really unique about the parent series—the prosecution of the defendants uncovered by the detectives in the first half of each episode and the resulting cooperation between the police detectives and the DA's office.

No matter. The parent series *CSI* and *Law & Order* are thriving. Well over 500 of these parental episodes are currently enjoying a robust afterlife in the immortal world of TV reruns. Few viewers have seen all of these episodes or can remember many of their plot lines. Fortunately, for the avid fan, many seasons' worth of these shows are readily available on DVDs, at NBC's or CBS's network Web pages, and at such generic websites such as TV.com, which list all of these episodes and their plot lines. This text will briefly discuss several episodes from each series, morsels selected for the flavor they add to the meal we are cooking here. Each series has its unique style, which, to overcook the metaphor, makes it equivalent to the soup, the salad, the meat, the potatoes, or the dessert of a full-fledged dinner. For readers who have not seen or cannot remember a particular TV episode discussed in the text, enough of the episode's plot line is included to make sense of the conclusions drawn from it. Occasionally, passages cited from series' episodes have been compressed or slightly rearranged in order to clarify their meaning. To that end, the practice of using ellipsis points (...) to separate quotations has been omitted so as not to stifle the smooth flow of dialogue so essential to the broadcast medium. The sheer volume of available episodes makes it impossible to cite much of the broadcast material in each episode examined in the text or even to discuss most of the episodes in anything short of an encyclopedia. To the reader who is disappointed that his or her favorite episodes are not included in this discussion, there is always the solace of Internet chat rooms and blogs, the endless supply of which more than make up for the limitations imposed on this text for brevity's sake. But the flavor of the meal lies in the tasting, and the tasting lies in the interesting points suggested by the raw ingredients of the episodes contained in these series. The reader ought to be able to extract the issues from the examples presented in the text and apply their lessons as "cooking instructions" to the vast bulk of the episodes of these series for which spatial limitations prevent discussion.

Sharp-eyed and sharp-eared readers and TV viewers may uncover a few errors regarding the names of the legion of minor characters that populate the many episodes cited in this text. All citations are taken from the broadcast episodes themselves. Citation errors are solely the responsibility of the author. It is my hope that there are no such citation miscues, but it would be a case of rank hubris to claim to succeed in accurately naming every minor character in each of these dramas, especially when a name is not specifically or unambiguously attached to a character in the course of a given episode.

A final wash up before dinner time: These five models of criminal detection—forensic science, memory romance, the essential self, points of view, and the legal cooperation model—are cookbooks for preparing many more dishes than just the criminal detective show. These models can produce equally well dramatic thrillers, action movies, science fiction tales, romances, war stories, histories, documentaries, or what have you. The list can be extended to any storytelling subject because each of these models embodies a component of how we humans understand the world we live in, which leads to the point of the Introduction.

INTRODUCTION: POLICE PROCEDURALS AND THE HUMAN NEED FOR STORIES

Human beings are the only critters we know of who possess the desire and the capacity to engage in the art of storytelling. The telling of and listening to stories runs so deeply within us that it is inconceivable that human culture could exist without this art form. Why is storytelling so important to us? Storytelling fulfills a number of basic human needs: 1) the need for information, 2) the need for enlightenment, and 3) the need for entertainment.

The need for information is basic to human existence. Humans are born with little, if any, innate knowledge, and therefore our very ability to live depends on our capacity to gather, store, and recollect accurately information about our ever-changing environment. Survival needs present us with some unavoidable complications. There is almost always too much information from which to select. Ways must therefore be devised to sift relevant and important data from the sheer mass of stuff out there in order to find the small needle in the large haystack. But our information-sifting strategies may be inefficient or incapable of getting the job done at all or getting it done quickly enough. Even worse than this, we may mistakenly believe we have the right answer to a situation when we do not have it, and this sort of mistake frequently leads to undesirable outcomes. How do we know that we have gathered the right evidence and that we have interpreted that evidence correctly? These are perpetual perplexities.

Second, humans have a need for what may be termed "enlightenment satisfaction." This concept means that we wish to know valuable and significant things about the nature of the world and our proper place in it. As a species, we are not mere animals; we are also philosophers. We are not content to simply live in the world. We are self-consciously aware of the world's existence and our place in it, and we have the human drive to wonder about this. We have the self-reflective capacity to be *concerned* with our existence. We naturally ask questions such as: "Are we right about thinking such and such?" "Are these things really important?" "How important are they?" Possible answers to these questions are in turn subjects for further reflection and second-guessing. Questions and reflective answers there will always be.

Finally, we humans have a deep-seated desire for entertainment. Life can be full of drudgery, tedium, and danger. These factors wear us out, and our existence can be more or less consumed by them. The English philosopher Thomas Hobbes famously likened this to a state of nature in which our lives are "solitary, poor, nasty, brutish, and short." We want to experience during our lifetimes not a mere brutish existence, but a joyful existence. We want to have some plain old fun.

One form of entertainment is the telling of and listening to (or viewing of) stories. These stories may be completely true, completely fictitious, or somewhere in between, but in any event, some of them must be entertaining, whether or not they are also informative or enlightening. What is experienced as entertaining, of course, varies across cultures, within a culture, between individuals, and even within a given individual himself depending on his mood. What someone finds entertaining at one time may be experienced as uninteresting or even boring the next time around.

Storytelling is not just for fun however. Stories also give us information about the world. Whether it's grandpa telling us about his adventures in the Big War or students explaining how it is that the computer dogs ate their homework, stories pack in a great deal of information. Some of this information is designed to provide answers both informative and enlightening. When Chief says to the kids in *South Park*, "Children, there's a time and place for that and it's called college," he was not only attempting to give the kids information, he was also giving them important advice about the ways of the world and the proper manner to live within it.

For more than a century, detective stories have been instrumental in satisfying audiences' need for information, enlightenment, and pure entertainment. From their comic-book-type origins through Victorian novels into radio, TV, and film, and now finally into the Internet, detective stories have become a popular cultural staple. In the history of TV alone, hundreds of series can properly be labeled as detective shows. But TV detective show audiences too commonly have seen these series as pure entertainment when in fact they offer much more. TV detective shows are cultural weathervanes of enlightenment. They focus on more than just the "whodunit." They also exemplify the issues that are judicially important to our culture. An issue could not become judicially important if it were not already seen as culturally important. In a nutshell, TV detective stories are chock-a-block with value-packed information and (supposed) enlightenment. The old saying, "Crime does not pay!" is just one obvious example of TV detective enlightenment that purports to make us an offer "we cannot refuse."

On Problems and Puzzles

Life is full of problems. Problems are situations that are difficult to deal with or understand. Problems like what to eat for dinner or how to get to work every day are handled by routine activities that solve these recurring problems in a similar manner each and every time they happen. Other problems are infrequent or dramatic enough to outstrip everyday routines. These call for special attention, attention that can be frustrating and time-consuming at best, futile at worst. Murder and mayhem fall into this latter category. Ordinary folk have no occasions for dealing with these sorts of traumatic encounters and are completely flustered when they do occur. We have developed no individual resources with which to respond to them adequately. For these sorts of cases, we have created police departments and courts of law. In order to operate, however, police departments and courts of law have to treat murder and mayhem as themselves subject to an array of problem-solving routines. The legal system has to devise a series of problem-solving routines that allow it to handle smoothly what the ordinary public finds so disruptive.

A *police procedural* is the name given to a type of detective story that presents cases of murder and mayhem as they are routinely handled by police departments and the judicial system. A procedural focuses on how the police and the courts apply their problem-solving skills and technical routines to the case at hand. But police routines, like the routines of the everyday person, are not static, fixed, and unmoving. Times change and with changing times come the development of new procedures as old ones are allowed to fade away into obsolescence. DNA fingerprinting is all the current rage. Phrenology, the analysis of criminal character by studying the bumps and lumps on the skull, is not only passé, it is downright hilarious. How could anyone ever think that the shape of someone's lumpy skull would offer important clues about that person's supposedly criminal behavioral tendencies? But in the last half of the nineteenth century, phrenology was all the rage among the European intellectual elite. How times change.

Some problems, however, defy solution even by the techniques ordinarily applied in police procedurals. When this happens, it is called a *puzzle*. A puzzle is a problem that routines cannot solve easily or cannot solve at all. Some puzzles tickle our need for information, others invoke the need for justice, and still others are merely entertaining. Stumbling over puzzles also provokes a range of responses. To the person charged with solving the puzzle, a common response is increased interest in the case, frequently followed by surprise and frustration. Why are the routines not working like they ought to? How can we make them work? Do we need new routines? If so, what are they? To the victim and the victim's family and friends, the puzzling lack of results can be very unsettling. To them this is not a mind-game. Their problems literally cry out for resolution. Do something! Why can't you solve this? This is commonly deemed the victim's need for *closure*. The puzzle of Amelia Earhart's fate fascinates us still, even though she and her airplane went missing more than seventy years ago. Sometimes closure is so far off the radar screen that it seems but a hopelessly romantic ideal.

While the real-life victim needs a quick and decisive resolution of her situation, to the TV viewer at home or the reader of the mystery novel, puzzles are the meat and potatoes of storytelling because they simultaneously fulfill our needs for information, enlightenment, and entertainment. Got a nifty puzzle? Excellent! Now that is an interesting story. If it is not your own ox being gored, then in some ways the worse the puzzle the better. This comes with one caveat, however: There must be a solution or resolution to the problem at the end of the book or the movie. Do not tell the reader or the viewer, "We do not know whodunit. We will never figure it out." There are plenty of unsolved cases, but unless they appear for further resolution in episodes of *Cold Case*, audiences don't want to hear much about them. They are not sufficiently informative; therefore, they are neither enlightening nor entertaining. They are just frustrating. In popular culture, frustration is the kiss of death.

The Willing Suspension of Disbelief

This is a book about police procedurals. It is about the problem-solving routines devised by the legal system as these routines are mass marketed by TV drama. TV audiences gobble up detective series. As soon as one series becomes shopworn, two more arise to take its place. But something strange is going on here. While particular episodes of any of these series may be based on actual crimes, each episode is a work of fiction. It is understandable why audiences would find actual criminal cases such as those of O. J. Simpson or Scott Peterson interesting, but why do we find fictitious criminal cases interesting? After all, they are not real; they never happened. Indeed, fictitious cases are often far more interesting for audiences then real-life cases. Why is that? It is because the human need for information, enlightenment, and entertainment can be satisfied equally well by examining reality or by imagining the fictitious to be "factual." Ironically, fictitious "information" is just as important to audiences as knowledge of factual events. Humans have an amazing ability to suspend belief concerning the authenticity of cases they are viewing in favor of what makes sense to them at the time, regardless of the fictitious nature of the issue in question. This is a capacity akin to color vision. Surely, we could see the world strictly in terms of black and white, that is, we could stick to actual events and real people. Nancy Grace on *Court TV* tries to do just that. Sometimes, as the saying goes, truth is stranger than fiction. But not often, or not often enough for the many TV channels broadcasting twenty-four/seven. Our world is ever so much more rich and interesting when seen through the colored lenses of fiction too. For us, fiction can be even more "realistic" than reality itself. Fiction *colorizes* fact more than Ted Turner colorizes old black-and-white movies.

This apparently weird preference for the realistic over the real can be resolved by understanding the TV audiences' willing suspension of disbelief. Like all successful TV programs, police procedurals rest on the audiences' willingness to accept certain fictions at face value while still knowing that they are fictions. Because of the limitations of commercial production, TV storytelling must make many assumptions, which the audience must take for granted. For example, successful TV dramas must compress a large number of factors into a simplified format. The forty-four-minute time frame and the number of actors involved in a drama must be packaged in such a manner that the audience does not lose track of the story line because of data overload. Scene changes must be orderly and limited in number for the same reasons. Individual roles must be integrated into the story line so that the identity and the motives of the characters can be easily and quickly recognized. But the real world is never so tidy. The audience knows this and is generally willing to go along with the story line for the purposes of the drama as long as the story line is "realistic." As was the case for *Boomtown*, poor ratings are frequently the result of the audiences' unwillingness or inability to let the storyteller tell a particular story in the manner of her choosing. The audience may decide that the story line is too poorly integrated to be interesting or simply too silly to be believable.

However it happens, TV detective show audiences have to be ready, willing, and able to suspend some pretty basic beliefs about the way the world runs in order to enjoy the materials TV presents. After all, these shows are all more or less complete fictions. But why should mere fictions engage the audience in the first place? Because audiences do not see these events as mere fictions. Each *Law & Order* episode opens with a supposed location and time and the trademark "chung chung" sound accompanying the queue card, which signals to the viewers that the scene is to be understood as taking place in the location and the time indicated, and not in some other locale at some other time. Law & Order is filmed on location in New York City, yet there are usually no actual specific locations in New York City proper as indicated by these cards. It is ironic that these fictions give the scenes such a great sense of reality. In essence, these are unreal, but realistic.

There is another, even stranger, problem with TV detective series. Their stories focus on unfortunate events that happen to people. Woes and misery are their bread and butter. To succeed in the public arena of popular entertainment, TV shows must produce a great deal of audience satisfaction. But how can audiences obtain satisfaction by watching the misfortunes of fellow humans? Seemingly the wretched events depicted would produce a negative response on the part of the audience, and TV shows cannot succeed if they produced such negative reactions. What is going on here? Why does an audience allow a storyteller to get away with depicting "a series of unfortunate events"? It would seem that viewing misfortune would insult the audiences' sensibilities just as much as would an illogical plot line. It is an old story that, contrary to what may logically be expected and humanely hoped, stories filled with "unfortunate events" may be all the more popular simply because of that fact. After all, the ancient Greeks seemed to have thoroughly enjoyed watching Oedipus strut on stage after spiking out his own eyes or seeing Medea murder her own children out of pure cussedness. The answer for the weird popularity of misfortune as depicted by TV detective dramas rests on the voyeuristic human tendency to take perverse intellectual and emotional satisfaction out of watching others suffer.

Maybe Christianity has it right—it is our fallen natures. Original sin has not only poisoned our ability to act correctly, it has poisoned our ability to condemn fully the wanton actions of others. Yet the humanist is more optimistic. We generally do display compassion at the suffering of others; we are often willing to extend our kindness to strangers. Humans can display a high degree of empathy and sympathy for those who are the victims of misfortunes or natural disasters; therefore, it seems a strange thing that audiences should take such a delight in being entertained by scenes of carnage and suffering.

The Greek philosopher Aristotle had a famous answer to this age-old perplexity: We get pleasure by watching certain sorts of horrific events because these events arouse within us fear and pity for the victim, a sort of "There but for the grace of the gods go I" effect. In turn, the fear and pity aroused in us serve as a catharsis, a release, for our own internal anxieties, and this catharsis, this release of tension, is experienced as pleasurable. Thus we paradoxically experience pleasure by viewing certain sorts of sordid and painful subjects. But the victims of these events cannot be too badly abused, by which Aristotle meant that the victims could not be too morally good, because it would simply horrify us if really good people had really terrible things happen to them. Nor could the victims of great misfortunes be too evil, because then the audience would not care enough about their wretched fate to shed any tears. Nor can what befalls the victims be too wretched, because that would simply horrify the audience and not produce the requisite catharsis. For example, great care must be taken when representing children as victims, as their innocence makes their destruction particularly harsh for an audience to behold. What Medea did to her own kids was pretty heavy stuff even way back then.

The Scottish philosopher David Hume had a different explanation for the apparently contradictory phenomena of experiencing pleasure while viewing the misfortunes of others. Hume claimed that pleasure and pain are human affections that are closely related both as felt experiences and in their causal origins. Essentially the TV viewer sees the victim's fate as a fiction. It is unreal, though realistic. But contra Aristotle, the viewer does not too closely identify herself with the victim's fate, whether the victim be of good or bad character. Quite the contrary, the viewer is pleased not to be too closely identified with the victim's misfortunes. The victim is seen as distant from the viewer, indeed, as safely distant, and that distance carries with it the corresponding pleasant feeling of safety for the viewer. Coupled with this distancing propensity, which keeps the unfortunate victim at arm's length, Hume noted the human desire for novelty in explaining the popularity of viewing the pain and suffering of others. What was seen as emotionally moving in the past becomes merely humdrum when repeated too often in the future. Familiarity breeds boredom. Hence those who write TV story lines are continually forced to push the envelope. Mere skeletal remains do not get the job done any more. Far more sensational special effects are required. Thus succeeding *CSI* seasons become increasingly flooded with yucky data ever more voyeuristically viewed. We do not just have killers, now everybody and her sister is a *serial killer.* If Hume's analysis is correct, future seasons of shows like *CSI* will bring us even more sordid and complex puzzles for viewers to put together. We have not yet reached the end of the slime line.

The TV Series

While hundreds of detective series pepper the history of TV, attention will primarily be paid to five of them here: *CSI, Cold Case, Without a Trace, Boomtown,* and *Law & Order.* These shows have been chosen because they are exceedingly popular with TV audiences and TV critics. (*Boomtown* was not popular with the TV audience, but it was very popular among the TV critics.) These series were also chosen for the high quality of their productions, acting, plot lines, and story locations. Primarily, however, these series were selected because they represent distinctly different models of police procedurals and storytelling techniques. They succeed as entertainment because, by incorporating their unique problem-solving methodologies, they supply their audiences with a great deal of information, enlightenment, and entertainment.

CSI presents a radically different model of police procedurals than any that have gone before it. While other TV police procedurals occasionally use forensics as a minor problem-solving tool in tracking down whodunit, *CSI* is all about the gathering of forensic evidence and the procedures used to extract it. *CSI* "criminalists" operate in the same manner as airplane crash investigators. Their job is to gather evidence objectively and explain it accurately so that the police and the courts, as well as the shows' audiences, may have a scientifically accurate understanding of what took place at the scene of the crime. The theory of the *CSI* format is to show that the "howdunit" is the only appropriate way to determine "whodunit." Because *CSI* focuses its laser-like intensity on the empirical evidence of crimes, evidence that exists solely for the purpose of being available for forensic examination, it pays little attention to the personal lives of the people who populate the Las Vegas crime lab, let alone the personal lives of the criminals and those of the victims it puts on the autopsy table. Each of its main characters is of interest primarily because of his or her ability to process evidence quickly, accurately, and thoroughly. Blood will tell; murder will out. Forget the eyewitness. Bring on the damned spots. They will always be there in the black light, glowing in the dark.

CSI is the paradigm case of the "forensic science" model of criminal detection.

Cold Case, on the other hand, presents a radically different crime-fighting model from that of *CSI*. *Cold Case* focuses on closure. Closure is achieved not simply for the relatives of the murder victims around whom the episodes unwind, but more importantly, for the dead persons themselves. *Cold Case's* unique procedural focus provides a compelling contrast to the format of *CSI*. *Cold Case* focuses on the human faculty of memory. Bring on the eyewitness; forget the black light. While cooperation among different members of the crime-fighting team and the use of objective, scientific, forensic evidence are components of the *Cold Case* methodology, they play insignificant roles relative to the memory of those who were present long ago when the events under examination originally occurred. These memory beliefs are hardly ever questioned during each episode. An episode's case study unfolds as witness after witness presents his or her recollection of how events surrounding the murder transpired without ever contradicting each other. Instead, each new witness's recollections collaborate and amplify the testimony of each of the others until all the relevant missing puzzle pieces are correctly assembled, forming a seamless picture of the crime in question and completing the romantic story of the forgotten victim.

Cold Case is the paradigm case of the "memory romance" model of criminal detection.

Without a Trace presents crime fighting from a federal point of view. Unlike the other police procedurals discussed in this book, *Without a Trace* is a TV series devoted to federal law enforcement, specifically to the narrow issue of missing persons, persons who may have been kidnapped. In *Without a Trace*, the series' hook is seemingly in the time line. If a missing person is not located within forty-eight hours, the chances are he is "gone for good." Each scene change is accompanied by a marker to show how long the missing person has been missing, but the vaunted time line is not what makes this TV series unique.

This police procedural is unique because the missing person can be located only by discovering that person's hidden essence—only by discovering what really made that person tick. The search for the missing person is all about discovering the specific essence of that missing person, her essential self, as that essential self is manifested by her underlying dynamic emotional tensions and their satisfaction and release. In a nutshell, that is the problem-solving strategy of *Without a Trace*. A person is missing because of a specific essential characteristic that uniquely shapes her identity. Each disappearance is linked to secret emotional factors and deeply felt emotional desires, which are either completely hidden from that person's friends, family, or co-workers, or are at most known to very few others. These secret emotional desires give that person her identity, and they account for why that person is missing. Find the missing person's secret emotional focus; find the missing person.

Without a Trace is the paradigm case of the "essential self" model of criminal detection.

Boomtown was a completely different kettle of fish. *Boomtown's* essence lay in its treatment of the storytelling arc. It shattered it. Ordinary storytelling starts at the beginning, goes to the middle, and finishes at the end. *Boomtown* did none of these things. Like being dealt a series of cards, the TV audience was dealt a series of different perspectives about the same event from various points of view, and then was required to put these pieces together to form a coherent hand. *Boomtown* was a TV police procedural that demanded audience participation to make it tick, to form the completed Rubik's Cube out of the story line bits and pieces. Because "perspectivism" ruled this series, the internal thought processes of its chief characters wrestling with the case as well as with each other received pride of place over the presentational logic of the story line. The audience did not see whodunit; the audience saw the main characters seeing whodunit and seeing each other seeing whodunit. It was all delightfully rich, but also delightfully confusing. Unfortunately for its longevity, to most of its audience it was simply too confusing.

Boomtown was an odd fellow, to say the least. Though it was a hit with the critics, it was not a popular success. It was cancelled in the fall of 2003 after only two episodes of its second season. Yet *Boomtown* presented an interesting experiment in police procedural storytelling. Of the shows discussed in this book, it is the only series that presented, in each of its episodes, criminal detection and apprehension from the point of view of the uniformed street cop, the plainclothes detective, the DA's office, the emergency medical responders, and a newsperson. *Boomtown* provided its viewers with such a rich diet of perspectives, they choked on it. The fundamental flaw in *Boomtown*, however, was not that it offered the viewer an overly rich diet of regular characters, it was that it could not put together its storytelling arc in a manner that was not confusing to the average viewer.

Boomtown is the paradigm case of the "points-of-view" model of criminal detection.

Law & Order focuses on police and judicial routines, which are embedded within the law enforcement community. This series sees crime fighting primarily as institutionalized within two different collectives, the detective force, whose job it is to apprehend suspects, and the judicial system, whose job it is to dispense justice to those enmeshed within the police network. The *Law & Order* franchise is unique in TV detective land not simply because it is still going strong after nineteen seasons, but because it devotes a significant amount of time within each episode to the criminal trials of those apprehended by the detective side of the show. Cooperation and smooth sailing are the watchwords of the *Law & Order* franchise. Each episode concludes with executive assistant district attorneys (EADA) Ben Stone or Jack McCoy vigorously prosecuting the offenders identified and arrested by the likes of Detectives Mike Logan, Lennie Briscoe, Rey Curtis, and Ed Green. While this format can be called the classical approach to the police procedural in so far as it relates to the first half of each episode, namely that part in which the detectives get their man, it stretches the traditional format by adding the prosecution of the offenders by the EADAs to the second half of the episode. Without interinstitutional and intrainstitutional cooperation between these two "equally important, yet distinct halves of the criminal justice system," as the series opening voiceover puts it, successful crime fighting would be impossible. Every episode in these series presents the crime fighters as freely and gladly cooperating with each other to achieve the stated goal, that is, to find and convict the persons responsible for the carnage involved in that episode. *Law & Order* is the paradigm case of the "legal cooperation" model of criminal detection.

In the following five chapters, each of these TV series and its embedded crime-fighting methodology and viewpoint about human nature will be examined in detail so that an understanding of these models may become evident. Each series provides the TV viewer with a different crime-fighting model and with a set of interesting characters involved in various sorts of murder and mayhem. Like the dishes of a fine meal, each of these series comes together to make quite a handsome dinner.

And what is on the menu? What is for dinner? Only the most central issues pertaining to human existence, the issues that philosophers, story writers, and sharp TV producers were destined to create. Is there a distinctly human nature? Does the individual herself have a fixed personality, and if so, what events made her the person that she is? How do we really know anything about anyone anyway? Are there rational formulas based on scientific reasoning principles that can be applied successfully to solve the problems of human conduct that confront us and answer the questions about those problems that confound and puzzle us? Can crime fighting really be reduced to a science? And finally, what is the right response to those who have been convicted of criminal activities? What should we do with the rogues and rascals living among us? In short, why do people do the bad things they do, how can they be apprehended and convicted, and what is to become of them after their convictions? That's what's for dinner.

The items on the menu may all be imaginary—these are after all fictional TV shows—but to be tasty they must be realistic enough to be edible. They must tweak the TV viewers' taste buds enough to cause them to salivate: to be informed, to be enlightened, and most of all, to be entertained.

Eat! Enjoy!

Suggested Reading

Aristotle's theory of tragedy is found in his *Poetics*, Chapter 6 (*circa* 340 BCE), reprinted in *Poetics* (Penguin Classics), translated by M. Heath, 1997.

Thomas Hobbes's views on human nature are found in his *Leviathan* (1656), reprinted in *Leviathan* (Penguin Classics), edited by C.B. MacPherson, 1982.

David Hume's views on tragedy are found in his essay, "Of Tragedy," in *Essays Moral, Political and Literary* (1748), reprinted in *Selected Essays* (Oxford World's Classics), edited by S. Copley and A. Edgar, Oxford University Press, 2008.

CHAPTER 1

CSI: CRIME SCENE INVESTIGATION, A CARTESIAN HYMN

Blame it on O. J. Ever since the O. J. Simpson trial fiasco, the American criminal justice system has been looking for a way to remove what has been perceived to be an unwarranted subjectivity within the legal system. Television has kept pace with this paradigm shift. While shows such as *Law & Order* and its various spinoffs represent standard police procedurals, *CSI* and its two offspring, *CSI: Miami* and *CSI: New York*, have established an entirely new paradigm in the popular vision of crime fighting. Hunter and Columbo are long gone. TV crime fighters entered a new day at the start of the new millennium, that of the police procedural *CSI* style—team-player technicians with tons of equipment and know-how and precious little personality or personal lives to match. Goodbye subjectivity; hello objectivity. *CSI* must be doing something right. It has swept the TV ratings for much of this century's first decade.

The desire for an impersonal, purely objective, and scientific crime-fighting methodology is not new to the twenty-first century. Its origins stem back to the development of modern science in the seventeenth century. No one was more instrumental in this development than René Descartes. Descartes was a French mathematician renowned for inventing analytical geometry and the X/Y axis graphing system, also known as the Cartesian coordinate system. Descartes was equally important in the development of the philosophical and scientific culture of the Western world with his search for a completely objective problem-solving methodology. Most famously, in his *Meditations* (1641), he set out to "establish a firm and permanent structure for the sciences" by discovering the absolute foundation of all possible knowledge. This foundation would consist only of ideas and principles that were true and knowable beyond the shadow of all possible doubt. Indeed, Descartes went so far as to conjure up one of the most famous thought experiments in Western philosophy when he speculated on the existence of an all-powerful evil genius who desires to fool us about everything. Imagine the criminal justice system's worst nightmare—criminals and defense attorneys who are all-knowing and all-powerful! In Descartes' philosophy, the only adequate foundation for science is one that gives us knowledge that even this evil genius bogeyman bad guy cannot over-turn. This "Cartesian hymn" to knowledge forms a system based on clear and distinct ideas and indubitable and certain first principles. This hymn is alive and well in our new millennium. Its perspective lays the cornerstone for *CSI*.

Descartes' description of this problem-solving system employed a building metaphor. Like an intellectual slum, prevailing ramshackle opinions and beliefs about information processing must first be ruthlessly bulldozed out of the way to clear the mental landscape of all detritus and debris. Once the ground is cleared, the edifice of real scientific knowledge can be constructed. The applica-tion of these first principles allows the systematic construction of sciences such as physics, chemistry, and biology, which are based on mathematical principles, principles that necessarily support all of the laws of nature. In turn, these laws of nature apply to all empirical examples, rendering these examples clearly understandable through the light of nature. Once established, these scientific laws would provide support for a full-fledged subject area, a *science*, a total sys-tem of knowledge with a place for everything and everything in its place. In due course, this science would naturally generate a host of technological appli-cations of its first principles. The whole of human life could then be completely redrawn according to these immutable first principles. The gateways would now be opened to the establishment of an objective, scientific criminal detection and problem-solving system based on the rigorous application of known scien-tific laws to the vicissitudes of criminal machinations. *CSI*, TV's Cartesian hymn, stepped right through that gateway.

Needless to say, Descartes' building metaphor has had an enormous influ-ence on subsequent human history. *Foundationalism*, as it is called, provides the worldview for modern criminal science. Central to TV programs such as *CSI* and its various replicates is the application of this scientific methodology to the criminal justice system. Behold the birth of the *criminalist*. The Carte-sian methodology supplies the criminalist with a set of problem-solving algo-rithms that can swiftly, accurately, and infallibly achieve the desired result, in this case finding out "whodunit." An algorithm is a problem-solving principle like a mathematical formula. As long as no counting mistakes are made in their application, algorithmic principles will always yield absolutely true and objective results.

A perfect example of this perspective is presented in *CSI's* "Burden of Proof" (Episode 38). Criminalist Warrick Brown searches for the correct algo-rithm to refine a blurry photographic image of a twelve-year-old incest victim. The successful completion of this task plays a key role in uncovering the iden-tity of the photographer, who happens to be the depicted girl's own father. The clarification and enlargement of the image reflected on the victim's cornea allows the team to identify the crime scene, which happens to be the victim's father's boat. Without the application of the correct algorithm, the original photograph would remain too blurry to be of any use as evidence and the case would not be cracked.

From the Cartesian viewpoint of *CSI*, TV shows such as *Law & Order* and *Cold Case* are still mired largely in the old-fashioned use of crime-fighting heuristics. Heuristics are mere rules of thumb, or tips that indicate to the criminal investigator promising avenues of approach when applied to the case in question. But these procedural tips may prove futile. Even worse, they may give investigators subjective reasons to believe incorrectly that they have solved the case when they have in fact failed to do so. *Law & Order's* episode, "Monster," provides an example of this when Detectives Lennie Briscoe and Rey Curtis incorrectly believe they have apprehended the assailant of a ten-year-old girl. They mistakenly grill the wrong man because he is a pedophile. At best the old-fashioned heuristics that Briscoe and Curtis apply only work some of the time. They are rather hit and miss in their results. Too many criminals get away with their crimes; too many innocent people are incorrectly arrested and convicted using these heuristic procedures. Real criminalists like *CSI's* Gil Grissom and Catherine Willows can offer ironclad guarantees of success for their cases, not just the cross-your-fingers, full-steam-ahead approach of *Law & Order's* Briscoe and Curtis or the dreamy-eyed romances of *Cold Case's* Lilly Rush and her crew of fairy godmother wannabes.

Central to this newfangled methodology of criminal detection algorithms is the holy trinity of data, theory, and technology. In a living language, the rules of grammar, definitions, and linguistic customs all interact to bring life to that language. Similarly, in scientific investigations, data (or evidence), theories, and technology all interact to make sense out of the problems the investigations seek to solve. No other scientific criminal justice system is conceivable.

Although evidence, methodology, and technology are different threads in the crime-fighting fabric, in practice, these components all interweave to form the tapestry which is that fabric, the *scientific* explanation of the crime under consideration. A *CSI* investigation is not a matter of first gathering evidence, then using technology, and then applying theory. All three components are present simultaneously. To understand the criminalist's Cartesian methodology, however, it is helpful to separate the strands of the crime-fighting fabric, the better to see how each one contributes to composing the whole cloth of the criminal investigation.

On Evidence

A scientific understanding of a crime scene involves the collection of data, also known as evidence or clues. Why is evidence so important? The answer to this question is quite simple. In the absence of evidence, there would be no science, no problem solving, and no criminal detection at all. No evidence? Then there would be no clues; literally, no *stuff* with which to work. Evidence provides the pieces of the shattered puzzle the crime scene investigator is trying to reconstruct. There must be evidence to find and identify and assimilate because understanding what happened amounts to understanding the evidence.

CSI presents a paradigm shift in the gathering of crime-fighting evidence. Older popular culture crime fighters, from the fictitious Sherlock Holmes to those of the real-life O. J. Simpson case, employ the heuristic of eyewitness testimony as the bedrock paradigm of forensic evidence. *Law & Order* and *Cold Case* still cling to this approach. The inept Simpson trial helped to show the folly of all that. Eyewitness testimony is frequently untrustworthy. It fails because it is unable to provide "conclusive includers" or "conclusive excluders," that is, algorithms by means of which evidence conclusively rules in or rules out a particular suspect as the sought-after criminal. It must be noted here that for the purebred Cartesian, "conclusive" means known beyond the possibility of all rational doubt. In a court of law, "conclusive" means known beyond the possibility of reasonable doubt. According to *CSI*'s standards, the excluders and includers of shows like *Cold Case* and *Law & Order* are not objectively conclusive algorithms; they are only subjectively non-inclusive or nonexclusive heuristics. Eyewitness testimony, the old-fashioned criminal justice paradigm, is simply too vulnerable to counterattack by clever, evil-genius–like defense attorneys; to lies told by self-serving suspects and witnesses; and to alternative understandings of the evidence. Eyewitness testimony can never be conclusive in the required scientific sense. Absolutely reliable tools of exclusion and inclusion are needed, and *CSI*'s forensic techniques such as DNA fingerprinting purport to do just that. This lies at the heart of the *CSI* revolution. It is a paradigm shift in evidence.

These points are illustrated nicely in "Too Tough to Die" (Episode 16). Detectives Catherine Willows and Warrick Brown are asked to conduct a quick review of a case in which a woman claims to have seen her husband's murder. Her testimony, however, does not align with the forensic evidence. Saying, "I want to be certain," Brown dismisses her claims because, like the typical eyewitness, she "saw what she wanted to see, and not what really happened." In "A Bullet Runs Through It, Part One" (Episode 124), the teams use scientific law to determine beyond the shadow of a doubt that the bullet that kills Officer Danny Bell in a wild shootout was fired by the gun of Jim Bass and not the gun of Sophia Curtis, even though she is subjectively certain that she accidentally shot Officer Bell during that mêlée. Shaky subjective evidence such as Curtis's traumatic recollection of the shootout is replaced by the rock-bottom evidence of bullet ballistics. "Physical evidence cannot be wrong. It is not influenced by emotion or prejudice," Grissom says in "A Bullet Runs Through It, Part Two" (Episode 125) in reference to the events surrounding the shootout.

Integral to every *CSI* episode is a protracted search for evidence. *CSI* devotes a large share of its screen time in each episode to the search for evidence, and essential to this search is the application of the experimental scientific model of criminal detection. The crime scene must be exhaustingly searched for clues. After the opening reenactment of the crime, each episode really begins with the arrival of the investigative team. At the crime site, they collect and initially process the evidence, some of which goes back to the lab for further analysis. This analysis involves the application of the experimental method to the data to determine exactly what manner of data has been collected. If there is the suspicion that blood has been spilled at the scene and later cleaned up, the team members can apply the well-known Luminol test. Luminol sprayed on a suspected blood stain will show up in a rich shade of blue when seen through ultraviolet light, indicating the presence of hemoglobin. The failure to see this unique color means conclusively that any stain in question is not a blood stain. Another common field test of suspected blood stains used repeatedly in *CSI* involves taking a sample of the stain with a cotton swab and applying a solution of phenolphthalein and then a solution of hydrogen peroxide to the swab. If the swab turns red, blood is present.

The collection of evidence does not cease with the examination of the crime scene itself. Often pieces of evidence collected at the crime scene are brought back to the lab for further examination. Was the blood found at the crime scene human? A gel diffusion test can determine whether the blood in question is human or belongs to some other animal. Latent prints on an object can be revealed by heating it in an enclosed container containing super glue. The glue fumes will adhere to the prints, making them visible to the naked eye. The prints can then be put through the Automated Fingerprint Identification System (AFIS) for identification purposes. Semen stains become visible by applying black light to the crime scene.

CSI's bag of tricks is a large one. Sometimes evidence is too complex to process on site. A motor vehicle containing a dead person might be brought back to the lab so that the vehicle can be disassembled to determine what events transpired in it. Grainy security tapes are often enhanced for clearer viewing in the lab by technical assistant Archie Johnson. Lab technician Bobby Dawson frequently handles gun tests for the lab, and tech Mia Dickerson works with DNA samples now that former lab assistant Greg Sanders has become a field operative.

Autopsies are the bread and butter of the series' technical analysis. Rare are the *CSI* episodes without human wreckage on display at the autopsy table, awaiting the loving attention of Dr. Al Robbins and his assistant David Phillips. Many are the bloody body parts held up for display like gruesome renditions of Yorick's skull hoisted by Hamlet.

There is an interesting issue at play in *CSI*. *CSI* aims at modeling absolutely objective evidence for the application of its Cartesian crime-fighting methodology. As a vehicle of popular entertainment, however, *CSI* uses two types of data, which can be labeled emotionally neutral data and emotionally laden data. Emotionally neutral data consist of things such as DNA samples, fingerprints, tire impressions, bullet ballistics, and so forth. Such data form the heart and soul of scientific evidence. Emotionally laden data consist of things such as complex computer-generated graphics of the human body as it is being violated by bullets or knife blades (usually accompanied by weird sound effects!), blood splatter patterns, "picturesque" body autopsies, and so forth. Emotionally laden data are those purposely placed into the *CSI* program to titillate or gross out the audience. While data serve a necessary crime-fighting function, strictly speaking, the *CSI* paradigm only requires the gathering of emotionally neutral data. Yet most *CSI* episodes contain large servings of emotionally laden data. Each class of data gives rise to a further question. Why are emotionally neutral data interesting to the viewing audience at all? And why do emotionally laden data, which are often highly charged with negative emotions, make *CSI* and its spinoffs such hit series? Emotionally laden data are hardly needed to satisfy the reigning algorithmic methodological paradigm of *CSI*. Why include any of them in the series, let alone so many? Is *CSI* at cross-purposes with itself?

As the creators of a popular TV series, the *CSI* producers are presented with a dilemma. Few scientific data grab the scientists on the emotional level. Indeed, it is one of the bragging points of Cartesian science that it is an objective, unemotional, value-free analysis of data. Grissom's whole demeanor testifies to this approach, and he is the lead criminalist for this show. He sets the height of the bar for all the others. Yet if all of the criminalists shared Grissom's stolid demeanor, the episodes would not be much fun to watch. How can a TV series succeed as entertainment if it incorporates so much emotionally neutral data discovered by emotionally vacant scientists? And how can a TV series be true to the ideals of pure science if it incorporates so much emotionally laden data, especially if those data are analyzed by emotionally intense investigators?

The answer to both of these questions, from the scientific paradigm point of view, is that human beings are problem and puzzle solvers. *CSI* works at its best by showing how its investigators (re)assemble the data bits into coherent pictures. Every episode contains periods during which specific investigators take fragments (of a bomb, a body, a piece of cloth, or a 9-1-1 call) and make them whole again, if you will. No member of the audience can do this, but we enjoy watching others do it. It is a form of spectator sport.

Every episode of *CSI* gives the TV audience a bird's-eye view of the team members ingeniously putting Humpty Dumpty back together again. In "Got Murder?" (Episode 58), an eyeball found in a bird's nest prompts a search of a whole garbage dump. In "Who Are You?" (Episode 6), conflicting eyewitness accounts are settled by crucial excluders. The skeletal remains of Fay Green are discovered embedded in the foundation of a house. Grissom employs the services of forensic paleontologist Teri Miller to reconstruct the dead woman's face, which is then identified as that of Fay Green after her reconstructed image is shown on the local TV news. In "Fahrenheit 932" (Episode 12), Grissom clears Frank Damon, who has been wrongly accused of arson. It seems that Damon and his wife have an argument, during which his wife throws a kerosene lamp at him. The lamp shatters, resulting in an accelerant-splattered closet fire that quickly engulfs the entire house. In "To Have and To Hold" (Episode 14), a dog fetching a stick turns up with a human tibia instead. This prompts the team to employ a squad of police cadets to search many square miles of desert for the rest of the skeleton. In "The Accused Is Entitled" (Episode 48), Grissom's former mentor, Dr. Philip Gerard, is hired by the defense to find apparent forensic mistakes in a previous data analysis made by the lab. As nitpicky as Gerard's complaints against each of the *CSI* team members may be, Grissom's team is forced to go back over the evidence with a fine-tooth comb to establish that Tom Haviland did indeed murder Kim Hsu.

Why even use so much emotionally laden data in the first place? In itself, it has nothing to do with the purely objective problem-solving scientific algorithms so heralded by *CSI*. The answer to this question is simple—because *CSI* is a TV show and the pure objectivity of scientific problem solving is insufficiently entertaining by itself to most viewers. Since its inception, *CSI* has centered on emotionally laden data, voyeuristically bringing the viewer inside the otherwise hidden body or presenting the normal body as hideously deformed by violent or natural causes following death (e.g., being "microwaved" in a duffle bag for two months while sitting in the hot Nevada sun, being eaten by a hoard of fire ants, or rotting on a body farm). Yucky data has always been a staple of this series. Why does this have viewer appeal? It has no scientific appeal per se. Aristotle had a famous answer to this question. We get pleasure by watching certain sorts of horrific events because these events arouse within the viewer fear and pity for the victim—a sort of "There but for the grace of the gods go I" effect. Hume's answer to this question was that pleasure and pain are human affections, which are closely related both as felt experiences and in their causal origins, and that there is an innate human desire for novelty. But both of these answers only go so far.

Neither Aristotle's theory nor Hume's can explain what is inexplicably missing from all of the emotionally laden data that seep through the corpse of *CSI*, namely the virtual lack of the depiction of the emotional effects crime has on its survivors. Real crimes, murders, robberies, and rapes frequently devastate their surviving victims and the friends and relatives of those who do not survive. But rarely in *CSI* does the viewer see these sorts of effects. Doing so would provide a distraction to this show's viewpoint. The voyeurism of the crime scene investigator encourages voyeurism in its audience, but not all manners of voyeurism. The audience is encouraged to see the crime scene as the criminalist sees it: a shattered jigsaw puzzle of evidence to be dispassionately reassembled. It does not generally encourage the audience to see the shattering effects crime has on its victims and its survivors. That would be too painful.

In "Face Lift" (Episode 17), the Marlowe family's five-year-old daughter, Melissa, was kidnapped twenty years ago. Forensic evidence puts her at the scene of a recent robbery in which her "father," Joseph Felton, is murdered. Her actual biological parents are so overjoyed to see her again that they mortgage their house to free her on bail when she is charged with Felton's murder. Melissa, who claims to have a dual personality named Tammy, willfully displays both of her personas to Catherine Willows before making bail, proving that she is indeed quite the con artist. After she skips bail, her biological parents still maintain to Grissom their belief in her innocence, even though they are then arrested as accessories to murder. Their faith that Melissa is still an innocent five-year-old is unshaken by the blatant evidence that she is guilty of robbery, murder, and skipping out on her bail. For her parents, faith trumps evidence. The evidence against Melissa is not too painful to examine because to them it is not real evidence in the first place.

Sara Sidle plays the emotional counterpart to the staid Gil Grissom. She is a tough cookie, but she has her tender side too. In "Too Tough to Die" (Episode 16), the usually tough-minded Sidle has to uncover the identity of a Jane Doe found shot in the head along a lonely roadside. The shooting victim, Pamela Alder, survives the head wound only to fall into a persistent vegetative state, a fact that her husband, Tom, seems emotionally unable to comprehend.

Sidle believes Tom is so delighted his wife is alive that he fails to comprehend that she will spend the rest of her life in a hopeless coma. But Sidle does comprehend Pamela's fate, and she is deeply disturbed by it because she can identify with Pamela, who is about her own age.

In "Chaos Theory" (Episode 25), a case is not solved in the eyes of the victim's shattered parents because the team's explanation of Paige Rycoff's death seems too absurd to be believed. According to Grissom, college student Paige Rycoff's death is the result of a series of bizarre coincidences. Prior to dropping out of college, she decides to clean up her room one dark and stormy night. As luck has it, she accidentally drops her garbage can down the trash chute. Seeking to recover it, she goes out into the night to search the dumpster. As she is poised on the lip of the dumpster, a taxi, blinded by the driving rain, accidentally runs into the dumpster, crushing Paige between it and an adjoining building. Paige's body falls into the dumpster, where it is covered by a further accumulation of trash.

The team is stuck for a solution of Paige's whereabouts for most of the episode. After exhausting all other reasonable solutions, Catherine and Gil discover Paige's body in the dumpster because it is the only place they had not yet looked. When they present to the Rycoffs the explanation for what happened to their daughter Paige, the Rycoffs reject it out of hand. They cannot believe that such a ridiculous series of events led to the death of their beloved daughter. They vow to find others to help pursue the evidence. Grissom cannot understand the Rycoff's refusal to accept the results of their investigation. "We told them what happened," he said. Catherine Willows replied, "Yeah. But we didn't give them what they needed, closure." A perplexed Grissom believes that "Truth brings closure." Sadder and wiser, Willows responds, "Not always." Knowing the truth, at least as far as the team could determine it, did not set the Rycoffs free.

On Technology

Before the rise of modern science, the human senses generally seemed sufficient for gathering the data necessary for satisfying most human needs. But the information readily available to unaided human senses is limited in scope, incomplete, and fragmentary. Often the senses present us with information that is irrelevant to our concerns and full of well-known blind spots. Technological devices were developed to fill in these blind spots, devices such as clocks and eye glasses, telescopes, and microscopes. Then an interesting thing happened. The more these simple technological devices were improved, the more data were discovered. While solving some problems, these devices themselves created even more problems by so enlarging the data pool that new means had to be created to understand the newly discovered data. In turn the enlarged data pool created a feedback loop that led to the development of further technology such as electron microscopes and infrared telescopes, which in turn enlarged the data pool even more. Such is the logic of technology. Such is the logic of scientific development.

One of the signature components of the *CSI* series is its emphasis on the role technology plays in criminal investigations. Viewers of the series regularly see the investigators arrive at a crime scene with their mini-toolkits designed both to collect and field test evidence such as blood samples or tire impressions. It all begins with the simple flashlight. Many *CSI* episodes take place at night (the investigators are, after all, the night crew of the Las Vegas Police Department), so it was natural for the show's producers to give each investigator a flashlight to "bring the evidence into the light." Like Sherlock Holmes and his famous magnifying glass, the *CSI* investigator must see the data. The symbol of the flashlight is taken to such extremes that even when episodes occur in bright daylight or indoors, artificial means are used to make the surroundings gloomy enough to allow the investigator the occasion to utilize that all-important flashlight. Goethe would have made a fine teammate of the *CSI* criminalists. "Light! More light!" were his dying words.

Evidence collected at the crime scene is sent back to the lab for fingerprint or DNA work-up, autopsy, trace analysis, firearm forensics, and so forth. Commonly, the lab analysis consists of the team member viewing a special computer or other piece of equipment as fingerprints are run (almost always arriving at a positive identification). A lab technician may pick a sheet of paper out of a machine, which not only analyzes a DNA sample, but also identifies whose DNA it is. Tire or shoe prints, fiber analysis, chemical residues, and soil samples are also analyzed quickly, routinely, and successfully in this manner. Every piece of equipment *CSI* so casually showcases is real. The Las Vegas crime lab is actually one of the best equipped crime labs in the country.

But in one way the methods employed by the *CSI* team are fictitious. It is the investigator, not the machine, who makes the judgment that the data samples match. Identification is a human judgment, not a mechanical process.

Even if the machine being used to run prints through AFIS says "MATCH," for example, that match is the result of the efforts of a human computer programmer who wrote the machine's code to indicate when certain characteristics would count as a match. But to highlight the algorithms involved in solving the problem of criminal identification, the show makes it seem as though the machinery itself is doing the investigating. Though it is true that without the technological wizardry many of the investigations would be stopped dead in their tracks and there would be no plot lines to follow, real human programmers are the wizards, not mere machines. Computer comparisons no more identify matches than the ubiquitous flashlights recognize evidence. Real live humans use both tools—flashlights and computers—as implements for making real-life problem-solving decisions.

Consider, for example, the apparently straightforward job of identifying fingerprints found at the crime scene, a staple of criminal investigations for well over a century. Most fingerprint samples run for identification purposes are known as *partials*. This simply means that the print sample does not contain complete fingerprint patterns for each of the ten fingers (counting the thumbs as fingers). Many fingerprints lifted from a crime scene do not have prints for each of the ten fingers. Only some of the fingers may have left their prints. Or equally likely, a given fingerprint may contain only part of the finger's surface. So how does the investigator identify which fingerprints she has? And if a print is only part of a finger's print, which part is it? The left side? The right side? The top? The bottom? More than one person may have left prints in the same location at the crime scene. Criminalists do not want to mix and match prints from different persons as if they all belonged to the same person. That would mess up the analysis nicely. Also, many fingerprint samples are smeared, as they were applied to the surface in question via some sort of wiping motion. When this occurs, the smeared picture must be focused in order to produce clear prints. So many variables are involved in identifying fingerprints that the *CSI* producers would give the viewers migraines just presenting them. No wonder they decided just to let the computer screen say "MATCH" and be done with it. The same problems apply to ballistics, tire identification, shoe prints, and so on.

Furthermore, for a computer to find a match of fingerprints, it must be coded to produce and store in its memory a series of electronic pulses that represent, in this case, the specific set of fingerprints. Then the new print sample must be encoded into the machine using the same coding instructions. The machine actually compares electronic patterns, not little pictures of fingerprints. DNA sample comparisons make this notion easier to visualize. Extracting usable DNA from an organic sample is a long and technically complicated process. Identifying that sample is just as complicated. No episode of *CSI* could possibly go through the ins and outs of these processes without totally confusing the audience. Look at what it did to the O. J. Simpson jury, for example. It is a far simpler thing to just let Greg Sanders pull a piece of paper out of a machine that identifies the person whose DNA was tested. "Bing, bing," like a Vegas slot machine, the show's plot can move along again nicely, thank you.

All those bells and whistles only work because of an intellectual move called *reductionism*. Reductionism is a method of analysis that seeks to understand macrophenomena by seeing them as made up of "micro" components. Consider the phenomenon of lightning. We are all aware of the big light and sound show in the sky that we call thunder and lightning. The ancient Greeks considered these occurrences to be manifestations of Zeus's anger. It took Benjamin Franklin's famous kite experiment to demonstrate that lightning is actually electricity, as is the Mini-Me version of lightning, static electricity. And what is electricity but just a lot of electrons and protons with an attitude problem? So a proper scientific understanding of the macrophenomenon of lightning reduces it to the microphenomenon of "electrons gone wild." Reductionism represents another triumph for Cartesian methodology. The notion that lightning is produced by electricity becomes the claim that lightning is really electricity. The notion that electricity is a product of electrons and protons becomes the claim that electricity is really an energy flow between electrons and protons. In this manner, reductionism translates a host of events, which are subjects of everyday experiences, into manifestations of tiny particles known only to the select few who have the training to be able to understand them. In a word, criminalists must now become highly trained professionals. To use a common slang term for this, criminalists must become rocket scientists.

These technological devices allow the highly trained professional investigators to identify and distinguish minute pieces of conclusive evidence of guilt or innocence readily and easily. Investigators can only do this by translating overt public empirical evidence into its teeny-tiny subcomponents, which only they can understand. During the course of every episode various suspects are first shown to the audience to be plausible culprits, but they are later conclusively cleared because some key piece of reductionist data does not fit their circumstances. The innocent suspects are innocent because they possess the wrong fingerprints, DNA, shoe tread pattern, vehicle make and model, paint fragments, blood spatter patterns, etc. They are never, ever cleared because of overt public inspection—they do not look like the bad guy—or because they have an alibi in the traditional sense of the term—they were having dinner with thirty-seven other people at the time of the murder. *CSI* does not work that way. Eyewitness identifications and alibis are *persona non grata* in this series. Only bits and pieces of materials from the world of the very minute nail the culprits.

In a way, *CSI*'s criminalists are the high priests of technology. They serve functions that have been traditionally attributed to esoteric religious personnel. Like the high priest, they serve one chief, albeit hidden, god, Truth. Truth is a hidden god, and will remain so without the criminalists' intercessions.

Only they can uncover Truth's messages. After all, "Ye shall know the truth, and it shall set you free" or send you straight to the slammer. The team members labor mightily in that service. Laypersons are helpless before it, for laypersons do not know the hidden means necessary for accessing this god. Like the priests at the altar, the criminalists present their offerings, their sacrifices, to the altar of technology and wait to see if they will find favor with the god of AFIS (whom we have already met), the god of CODIS (Combined DNA Index System), the twin gods of NCAVC (National Center for Analysis of Violent Crime) and NCIC (National Crime Information Center), or demigods such as GC/MS (gas chromatography/mass spectrometer), BSP (blood splatter patterns), PCR (polymerase chain reaction), or CVSA (computerized voice stress analyzer). *CSI* clergy attend to many, many gods. None of these gods speaks to mere laypersons. Access to them is confined to the anointed.

The series audience can only watch in wonder as the criminalists work their reductionist problem-solving antimiracle miracles. They are not real miracles because real miracles only take place in violation of the Cartesian laws of nature, and *CSI* is all about the laws of nature. The unsuspecting recipients of their antimiracle efforts are either already dead (and who better to work with the dead than the high priests?), or they are still living criminal victims who have been ensnared in the priestly domain, only to have their precious secrets laid bare for all the world to see. "Behold, it's an antimiracle!"

Just how did the *CSI* criminalists get to be the anointed high priests of technology? What were the pathways to their exulted positions? For a show that is so thoroughly grounded in the metaphysics of materialistic reductionism, the series is curiously silent about the training of these technocrats. We know precious little of their pedigrees. Mere bits and pieces of the background and training of each major character come out as the series unfolds. Sara Sidle met Gil Grissom in San Francisco at a conference; Catherine Willows, who is Sam Braun's illegitimate daughter, grew up in Vegas and was a pole dancer before she earned her degree at the fictitious West Las Vegas College. Captain Jim Brass is from New Jersey and in the pilot episode he was the head of the lab. Warrick Brown, Nick Stokes, and Greg Sanders, like Athena, might well have sprung full grown from the head of Zeus, degrees and all, as far as *CSI* is concerned. Viewers hungry for details about the characters' lives prior to the series will not find much to go on in the series itself. Instead, they will have to consult coffee table books such as *CSI: Crime Scene Investigation Companion* and *Ultimate CSI: Crime Scene Investigation* to get the lowdown on who's who in the forensic theology zoo.

Because of the materialistic methodological reductionism that supplies the foundations for this series' crime-fighting modus operandi, not just anyone is qualified to lead an investigation or to gather evidence. Columbo and Hunter could not work on this A-Team. *CSI* personnel serve the role of investigative high priest gatekeepers. Gatekeepers traditionally serve the function of determining who will be admitted into the estate. In this case the estate is the field of criminal forensic science. Not just any person is qualified to lead investigations or gather evidence at a crime scene. Criminalists must undergo extensive training in this discipline to become an expert. The members of the *CSI* team are all supposed to be highly trained specialists in their fields. Gil Grissom, for example, is a specialist in entomology, especially the study of the sequences at which insects arrive at a body. In "Living Doll" (Episode 165), it is claimed that Grissom has twenty-two years of forensic experience and worked more than 2,000 cases, although none of these cases quite affected him as much as that of Natalie, the Miniature Killer of this and previous episodes.

In "Burden of Proof" (Episode 38), Grissom is presented with a puzzle concerning a murder victim whose body was "hidden" in plain sight at a body farm disguised as one of the farm's experimental "subjects." This victim appears to have a particular form of larvae attached to it, larvae that normally are found only in cattle. In addition to the problem of the contamination of the victim's corpse by insects and other creatures found at the body farm itself, Grissom has to explain the presence in the corpse of this unique insect. He succeeds by cleverly showing that the dead man was murdered by a bullet made from frozen ground beef, beef that contains the egg of an insect uniquely found in cattle. The ground beef bullet comes from the gun of Russ Bradley, a jealous ex-husband of the dead man's fiancée. Bradley happens to own a chain of grocery stores and practices reloading his own spent hand gun ammunition. His nifty meat bullet meets its match in the wiles of Grissom's entomological expertise.

"Sex, Lies, and Larva" (Episode 10) also turned on Grissom's expertise. Regarding a bug-ridden corpse shown at the beginning of the episode, Grissom says to Sidle, "They're our first witnesses to the crime." Later in the episode, by wrapping a pig's carcass in a blanket and exposing it to insect infestation in the *CSI* parking lot, Grissom succeeds in showing that Kaye Shelton, the victim, has been dead for five days before her body was discovered, not for three days as originally thought.

It is a curious omission for this series that Catherine Willows, Sara Sidle, Nick Stokes, Warrick Brown, and Greg Sanders, the other lead criminalists, have no specific scientific expertise akin to Grissom's. They must have such credentials. Not only does the whole series framework demand it, each episode presents many of them using components of esoteric scientific technology with a degree of easy familiarity. They must have this training in order to do their jobs. The series simply fails to explain exactly what that training is and how they got it. Given the irreplaceable role technology has for this series' crime-fighting format, the failure to explicate their credentials as certified, orthodox high priests of technology remains a curiously unfulfilled promissory note, a puzzle about the puzzle solvers.

On Theory

The term "theory" refers to the intellectual framework that makes possible evidence gathering and identification. Included under this umbrella notion are the ideas of a manifold of rudimentary concepts such as fingerprints and DNA, more general notions such as hypotheses, scientific theories, and laws of nature, as well as methodological operating principles such as Locard's Exchange Principle, all of which tell the investigators how to assemble puzzle pieces to form coherent pictures. Without these intellectual components, evidence could not be recognized as evidence at all; nor could the investigator assign any sort of meaning to the evidence. In short, no *investigation* would occur. As Grissom dispassionately says in "Too Tough to Die" (Episode 16), regarding a gunshot and rape victim found on a deserted road where her assailant had left her to die, "Locard's principle. He took a piece of her away with him and he left a piece of himself here. We get to find it."

When the investigators arrive at the scene of the crime, they are there to gather evidence. But they do not use a bulldozer to do so. Rather, their job is highly selective (remember that trusty flashlight). Their job is to gather just the *right* evidence. But what constitutes the right evidence, given that the sheer volume of evidence is almost always overwhelming? Here is where theory comes into play. By knowing the concepts of fingerprints, DNA, shell casings, etc., the investigators know what sort of evidence to look for a priori, that is, prior to even arriving at the scene. In other words, they already know conceptually how to separate the evidential wheat from the chaff. The unfolding of the episode has the viewer following the *CSI* investigator's application of this specific, single-minded, a priori problem-solving process.

They are at the crime scene only to gather material evidence. They are not there to delve into psychic auras, karmic calamities, or feng shui faux pas. In "Spellbound" (Episode 136), when Sanders casually lays claim to some sort of psychic sixth sense inherited from his Nana Olaf, Grissom asks him to read his mind. Sanders hopefully claims that Grissom was thinking about giving him a big promotion, but Grissom brings Sanders down to earth by saying, "I'm thinking that you should focus on your other five senses." Claims about ESP and other nonmaterial data have no place in this series. Sanders may think "You can believe [psychic predictions] and still be a scientist," but Grissom counters that "The problem begins when people mistake their beliefs for science."

CSI's criminal problem-solving format is so materialistically oriented that it does not even incorporate a recognized branch of criminal justice system, forensic psychiatry. Unlike *Law & Order*, *CSI* does not employ a forensic psychiatrist on its staff. Suspects are never sent to a Dr. Elizebeth Olivet or a Dr. Emil Skoda to get their heads shrunk. To do so would be to acknowledge that there was a possible area of criminal investigation that was immune to the reductionistic, materialistic methodology of the Cartesian method, namely that part having to do with what motivates people to act as they do. Concerns about motives and other methods of madness have no place in *CSI*. It is a series devoted to "howdunit," not "whydunit."

"Invisible Evidence" (Episode 76) presents a typical example of the investigation process in this series. Untypical for this series, it begins in a courtroom where evidence presented to show that Michael Fife had raped and murdered his neighbor, Rachel Lyford, is thrown out of court because Warrick Brown failed to secure a search warrant prior to discovering a bloody knife in Fife's car. The blood on the knife matches the victim's blood, but the failure to secure a search warrant prior to the knife's discovery renders it legally inadmissible. Rather than give up on the case and let a murderer get away, Gil Grissom invokes the principle that no matter how thorough the search, there is always more relevant evidence out there awaiting discovery. The chase is on! The rest of the episode follows this chase for further evidence. An autopsy of the victim discovers a waxy substance on her body and a strange ligature-like mark around her neck. The mark was caused when the killer ripped off of Lyford's neck a set of her father's dog tags that Lyford wore, and the waxy substance turns out to be a form of expensive commercial car wax. In Lyford's apartment, a semen-stained fingerprint is found on her toilet flush handle. DNA analysis of the stain fails to match the suspect, Michael Fife. The wax is traced to a carwash where Fife had his car cleaned on the day of the murder. Broken pieces of taillight matching Fife's car are found in the carwash drain. Subsequently, Gary Quinn, one of the carwash attendants, is discovered to be wearing the dog tag chain taken from Lyford's neck as a sort of souvenir of the crime. His DNA proves to match the DNA from the semen sample from the toilet flush handle. He is then charged with the murder of Rachel Lyford, and Michael Fife, the original suspect in whose car Quinn stashed the bloody murder weapon during the carwash, is freed from suspicion.

Justice was served in this case thanks to the "technogeniuses" of the team applying the Cartesian scientific methodology. No other method could have provided the conclusive includers that infallibly showed that Gary Quinn had in fact raped and murdered Rachel Lyford. No other system could have provided the conclusive excluders that showed infallibly that Michael Fife had in fact not raped and murdered Rachel Lyford in spite of the presence of the murder weapon in his car.

As illustrated in this case, observational knowledge is the product of the application of theory to experience. Theory here means the concepts, rules, laws, and paradigms that go into the makeup of a discipline. In baseball, the home plate umpire cannot call a pitch a strike without applying the notions of pitch, batter, swing, etc., and these notions are embedded in the game of baseball, which is a rule-governed activity. The same holds true for criminal investigators. As Thomas Kuhn points out in *The Structure of Scientific Revolutions*, in reference to the activities of collecting, counting, and sorting, grouping in accordance with the material laws embodied within the discipline makes scientists *scientists*, and not just amateur collectors of trivial information.

CSI investigations are governed by the rules of problem solving as established by the game of science itself, or in this case, by the game of scientific criminal investigations. As in baseball, so too in "crime ball." It takes more than mere equipment to play the game. It takes an understanding of the set of rules that govern game behavior and the application of these rules to the playing field that distinguishes playing the game from merely playing at playing the game.

The game of scientific crime fighting, *CSI* style, is very different from the crime-fighting models depicted by Rick Hunter or Columbo. Their model is intensely personal. Hunter is angry at the criminals; nay, he is outraged with them. Criminals are scumbag, dirt balls who deserve to be literally sponged off the world. For Hunter crime fighting is a civic cleansing crusade. For Columbo, crime fighting is a matter of dogged determinism aimed at defeating the smug.

Criminals are those who thumb their noses at society, thinking that they are above it all. Nailing them is a matter of wiping the smile off their faces.

For Gil Grissom and his team, crime fighting is an intellectual exercise akin to Sudoku. One and only one answer fits correctly into each cell or block. An understanding of chemistry, biology, and physics provides the essential scientific theories needed to fill in the blanks correctly in the problem that is the case at hand. Unlike Hunter, Grissom is not outraged at the criminal any more than he is outraged at the fire ants that devour Randy Traschel's body in "Snuff" (Episode 54). Indeed, by removing the victim's flesh, the fire ants actually help Grissom find his killer. When it was necessary to wipe out the ant colony to get to Traschel's body, the dead ants become "martyrs to science." Unlike Columbo, Grissom will not badger the suspect in an apparently bungling manner until the suspect commits an indiscretion sufficient to hang himself. Grissom only confronts a possible suspect when he already has irrefutable forensic evidence concerning some aspect of the case, evidence that only the application of the scientific method can disclose. There is no appearance of bungling here. Bungling is bad science; bunglers are bad scientists.

The *CSI* team arrives on site, dressed in their professional garb, ready to investigate a crime scene. They are scientists. They are professionals. They are not there to be angry or bungling. They are there to be scientists. While this may be stating the obvious, it is a point well worth making. The team is called out of the office to visit places in which there have been apparent violations of the law, which have produced one or more victims. As illustrated by the events surrounding Rycoff's death in "Chaos Theory," it does not follow that all missing or dead persons are the victims of criminal actions. Accidents do happen, even weird ones like those surrounding Rycoff's death. The presence of a mangled corpse in a garbage dump does not necessarily entail murder. Death by natural causes can be pretty gruesome too. The dispassionate application of the Cartesian methodology by the highly trained expert criminal investigators will soon distinguish the murder victim from the accidentally dead.

In one of the mini-dramas that make up the compound crime scenes of "Toe Tags" (Episode 144), the team investigates just such a case, the death of supermodel Rebecca McGill. McGill dies because she fell to her death, literally bashing her brain clean out of her head in the process. But is her fall an accident, is it suicide, or is it homicide? She is standing at the edge of a cliff before she falls. Initially it looks like a tragic accident: She is backing up to focus a picture on her cellphone and—oops—over she goes. Upon questioning, her husband, Gavin McGill, insists in a chagrined manner that her death is no accident but suicide. When Warrick Brown asks why he did not inform them of this fact earlier in the investigation, Gavin responds, "How would you like it if your wife preferred to be dead in the next minute than to be with you?" But it turns out that Gavin is mounting a clever lie, because a closer examination of Rebecca's cellphone video records show pictures of Gavin struggling with her as he pushes her over the cliff. As Grissom says to a group of student criminalists about this sort of situation, "First opinions are crucial, but if the evidence changes, so must the theory."

The team's first opinion on arriving at a death site is naturally to adopt the position that any death they are called on to investigate is a case of criminal misconduct. Accordingly, while Warrick might come to believe after he processed the case that Rebecca jumped to her death, his initial prejudgment is that she is a murder victim. That is why he kept digging at the case in spite of Gavin's "confession." The subsequent analysis of her cellphone records turns up the conclusive evidence that she was pushed. Because Warrick is a crime scene investigator, his mindset predisposes him not to be content with husband Gavin's sheepish account of his wife's so-called "suicide." In a court of law, the defendant is presumed innocent and it is up to the prosecution to establish his guilt. In the court of the criminalists' a priori opinions, all deaths are to be treated as homicides unless proven otherwise.

Warrick's work in this episode provides an *explanation* for the events in question. Explanations are multifaceted. They are sparked by an element of surprise. Rebecca's death is surprising. In what manner did she die that so many of her bones were broken, that her flesh was lacerated, and that her brain was knocked completely out of her skull? Accidentally falling off of the cliff could account for that. Or did she purposely seek to end her own life? Explanations commonly seek to establish the intentions of the human agents involved in the case. Her cellphone video records put the lie to her husband's claims that she committed suicide. He intended to weasel out of it by concocting a phony story about Rebecca's suicide. The cellphone record refuted it But how does a cellphone's video function work? There is a sense of explanation that is satisfied by showing how technology does a specific thing. Rebecca's death could only be explained by showing how it was caused, which was her husband stomping on her fingers as she dangled perilously over the cliff. The application of scientific theory to the events surrounding Rebecca McGill's death determined "howdunit," which in turn led straight to whodunit. Without the application of scientific theory to the evidence, there would have been no "how," let alone any "who."

Perplexing Issues About Cartesian Methodology

The only shortcuts the *CSI* series takes with the application of the Cartesian scientific methodology to its cases are those imposed on it by the unavoidable limitations of TV formatting. Each episode only has about 45 minutes of air time, not nearly enough time to show the tedious wrinkles inherent in scientific problem solving. Criminal investigation is a tedious and time-consuming enterprise. TV has to speed up the process to hold the audience's attention. While these foreshortenings of the *CSI* crime scene investigation timeline in no way detract from the validity of the underlying methodology, they do leave the audience with less than a full appreciation of the interesting complexities contained within many *CSI* episodes. Running-time limitations aside, philosophical perplexities about the Cartesian methodological format remain.

Are there really conclusive excluders or conclusive includers? On *Larry King Live*, Mark Geregos claimed that, "Criminal investigation is more a matter of an art than a science" (December 18, 2005). Mark Geregos is a high-profile defense attorney. If crime scene investigations were a matter of connecting the dots by the application of the appropriate algorithms, much like applying mathematical equations, his job as a defense attorney might be much more difficult. Geregos does defend many guilty parties. Evidence processed by these Cartesian algorithms could then decisively determine the guilt of his clients. It would be in Geregos's vested interest to have criminal investigations viewed as artistic enterprises, creative processes in which more than one outcome or interpretation could be correct. Accordingly, from Geregos's perspective, there are no *conclusive* includers or excluders; merely ones that may look that way from certain points of view, points of view which it would be his job as a defense attorney to manipulate for the benefit of his client. If Geregos were Gavin McGill's defense attorney in "Toe Tags," for example, he would argue that the important video records retrieved from Rebecca McGill's phone did not show her struggling to escape the murderous advances of her husband Gavin. Instead they showed the futile, but heroic, efforts of her husband as he vainly sought to prevent her despondently driven suicide attempt. It would then be up to the jury to determine which understanding of the evidence to accept.

The viewpoint that Geregos would apply to the criminal detection enterprise is called *perspectivism* by philosophers. According to this approach, there is no absolutely correct way of understanding the evidence in a criminal justice case. Rather, there are only many equally correct, but contrasting ways of looking at the situation. Perspectivism is an epistemology that compares the scientific understanding of the world to a person's observational viewpoint. When an object is observed by the senses, the observer always sees that object from a specific point of view. Looking straight down at a football field from the famous Goodyear Blimp, for example, the field appears to be a perfect rectangle 120 yards long by 50 yards wide. When the blimp moves its position slightly, the field may still appear to be 120 yards long, but it will no longer look to be 50 yards wide. The perspective of the field's width will be foreshortened by the changing angle of the TV camera. Another commonly experienced example of visual perspectivism is the well-known sighting of the full moon. When first seen in the evening close to the horizon, the moon appears to be much bigger in size than when it is seen later at night while directly overhead. The moon's apparent size (and color) varies with the angle of its observation. Perhaps the size of the moon itself varies, larger when it is nearer to the Earth's horizon, smaller when it is farther from the horizon. Either account fits the visual data equally well.

Perspectivism maintains that visual observations vary with the observer's viewpoint. Similarly, the intellectual understanding of crime scene evidence varies with the judge's viewpoint. From the point of view of the defendant in a criminal trial, the accused was not present to commit the deed in question. The presence of O. J. Simpson's blood at the crime scene and Nicole Simpson's and Ron Brown's blood in the Bronco were due to the police planting the evidence against him. O. J. is black; the cops are white. Therefore the racist cops must have framed him, or at least all that blood evidence did not mean that he slaughtered the victims in question. To seek a completely objective, Cartesian understanding of the crime scene is to seek a will-o'-the-wisp view from "nowhere." But all observations, all understandings, are views from somewhere. Accordingly, the very aim of the crime-fighting methodology espoused by *CSI* is an illusion foisted on the public by the frustrating inability of the criminal justice system to convict the accused whom the public knows damned well to be guilty. Curse those evil-genius defense attorneys! Damn their trial motions! Full Cartesian speed ahead!

Furthermore, it is an axiom in the philosophy of science that data underdetermine theory. No matter how much evidence the *CSI* personnel collect at a crime scene, determining "whodunit" is not and cannot be directly deduced simply from the evidence itself. Howdunit does not entail whodunit. The evidence is always consistent with more than one possible explanation.

Consider the illustration on the next page (Figure 1). This is called the My Wife and My Mother-in-Law illustration for the obvious reason that it can be seen equally well as a young woman or as an old woman, depending on how the viewer looks at it. The data of the illustration can equally well be seen as two separate things. There is no one single right way of seeing it. Similarly, according to perspectivism, there simply is no one single right way of seeing the crime scene.

Sometimes it would seem that *CSI* itself agrees with this issue. In "Anonymous" (Episode 8), Warrick and Nick are assigned to investigate the scene of an accident in which a victim is found buckled into the back seat of a car that crashed over a guardrail after teetering on it following a high-speed crash. Walter Bangler, the Bentley's driver, is temporally sedated and unconscious and to speed up the arrest of a possible carjacker, the *CSI* investigators want to determine whether he is the victim of an assault even before he regains consciousness. Humorously, Warrick and Nick bet $100 (later the bet is raised to $300) on who has the correct explanation of the evidence, Nick's missing phantom driver against Warrick's absentee criminal. Is the unconscious person

FIGURE 1 My Wife and My Mother-in-Law.

a victim of a robbery and failed carjacking, or was there another person driving who wrecked the car and managed to escape it unharmed after the car
finally tottered over the cliff? The episode presents a visual depiction of each
of these scenarios coupled with the evidence that favors each account. Much
to Warrick's and Nick's surprise, after Bangler regains consciousness they discover they are both wrong. It seems Bangler himself was driving drunk. After
crashing his Bentley into the guardrail, the drunken Bangler climbs into its
back seat and fasten his seat belt, only to have his very efforts cause the tot-
tering car to tip over the railing. Without the aid of the eyewitness testimony,
the physical evidence by itself will fail to provide the necessary conclusive
indicators to settle the case.

   "Secrets and Flies" (Episode 123) presents a debate about conflicting
explanations of evidence. Appropriately enough, it occurs in a (rare) courtroom setting during which Grissom is called on to rebut the testimony of
another forensic expert concerning the victim's likely time of death. The
debate turns on the length of time certain blowfly larvae take to mature. It is
found that the presence of a certain preservative on the body of test animals
gave a misleading maturity rate for the blowfly larvae and thus a misleading

time of death for the real victim. Grissom then concludes that the other forensic pathologist has purposely skewed the test results, although the skewed test results just as easily could be due either to accidental contamination or a simple miscalculation. While this episode may show that, contrary to the *CSI* goal, there is always more than one way to understand experimental failure, it fails to show that the pathologist purposely rigged the test. Incorrect test results could be the results of sloppy test procedures or simple oversight.

It is telling to the puzzles presented by evidential epistemology that *CSI*'s criminalists are seldom found in the courtroom. Though real-life criminalists spend a great deal of time presenting the results of their investigations in courts of law, *CSI* chooses to underplay that component of the job. While some episodes do feature courtroom testimony, these episodes only incorporate the courtroom as an excuse to goad the team into further efforts outside of the courtroom. "Invisible Evidence" illustrates this format nicely. Unlike the detective teams and assistant DAs of *Law & Order*, the *CSI* criminalists do not have to play defense against defense attorneys.

Contrary to the exception presented in "Secrets and Flies," rarely do *CSI* episodes find the investigators testifying about their findings in courtroom settings. This allows the show to present their findings as conclusive indicators of guilt or innocence. Defense attorneys, whose jobs turn on providing alternative explanations of the physical evidence, are never given their turn at bat. As was shown earlier in the "My Wife and My Mother-in-Law" illustration, there is always more than one way of seeing the data. Remember Johnnie Cochran's famous quip as O. J. Simpson "struggled" with the famous glove in his murder trial? "If it doesn't fit, you must acquit!" Alternative accounts of evidence can always be supplied. It is up to the jury, not the *CSI* investigator, to determine guilt because guilt is a "legal" claim, not a "scientific" one.

"The Accused Is Entitled" (Episode 48) provides only an apparent exception to this rule. Movie star Tom Haviland is charged with the gruesome murder of party girl Kim Hsu. At his trial, Haviland's defense attorney, Marjorie Wescott, ingeniously employs Grissom's own mentor, Dr. Phillip Gerard, to undermine the forensic evidence against Haviland. Gerard's efforts succeed in casting doubt on the evidence collected by each member of the *CSI* team and Grissom is forced to discover new evidence linking Haviland to Hsu's murder. He succeeds in doing so because he does not allow the teacher/pupil relationship he has with Gerard to undermine his self-confidence. As Nietzsche said, "A student repays his teacher poorly by always remaining a student." Grissom is all grown up now. The thrust of this episode is not the legitimately different perspectives on the physical evidence against Tom Haviland; it is Grissom's struggle to show Gerard that "When last we met, Obi-Wan, you were the master. Now I am the master."

The Cartesian methodological approach to criminal detection is not without a response to the problem of multiple interpretations of evidence as presented by the cases cited above. While Mark Geregos may be right that there are always multiple ways of understanding the evidence, it does not follow that there are multiple *correct* ways of understanding the evidence.

In "Anonymous," it turns out that both Warrick and Nick have incorrect understandings of the evidence, not that they each have equally correct, but incompatible, understandings of the evidence. Both of them work from misconceptions of what really happened, but each has a different misconception. One assumes correctly that there must be someone who was drunk while driving the car, but incorrectly that that person could not be the accident victim who is in a coma. The other assumes incorrectly that the "missing driver" must be a hijacking victim who has not yet turned up, not the accident victim himself.

"Rashomama" (Episode 138), modeled after Akira Kurasowa's famous film, *Rashomon*, cleverly shows the prospects of perspectivism. It concerns the wedding day murder of Dragon-Lady-like Diane Ray, the groom's mother, who is found tied to the wedding getaway car along with the usual array of tin cans. After spending the entire day processing the scene, the team meets for dinner before adjourning to the lab. During dinner, Nick's car, which contains all of the day's newly gathered evidence, is stolen, The team must start all over again. They do so in a series of flashbacks during which each team member gives his or her account of what happened that day. Their waitress sets the tone for the retelling of the day's events, "Weddings are like Rorschach's. Everyone sees what they want to see. My first five were good." Each team member's account begins with that person walking through the bridal bower. Sara has a pessimistic viewpoint on marriage. "Ah tradition," she says of it. "Like being property exchanged between your father and your husband." Nick's view is much more traditionally romantic. "No, that's not what a wedding is. It's a public declaration of love." Greg's view is taken right out of film noir. "I'm with Vince Vaughn [of *The Wedding Crashers*] on this one. Dozens of horny single women with access to an open bar and coupling on their mind." His recap of the day's events is told in black and white with a splash of blood red thrown in for color. Gil stops as he walks through the bower to examine a ladybug on a leaf. Enough said.

Yet each story told by team members, unlike the episode's titular namesake, *Rashomon*, does not contain inconsistent information concerning the crime. Following its namesake, a *Rashomon*-like event is one in which there is no way of determining what really happened. But this perspective would completely undercut the whole point of *CSI*, which is to discover what really happened in spite of conflicting eyewitness accounts. Rather, in *Rashomama*, each team member adds another coherent piece to the crime scene puzzle, and with the help of some further evidence from the lab and good old-fashioned gumshoe work, they discover that all the bridesmaids together have a hand in the accidental death of the groom's "Dragon Lady" mother. In this episode, perspectivism only applies to each team member's attitudes about marriage, not about their attitude toward the evidence they are assigned to collect. For *CSI*, perspectivism does not mean that there are incompatible, but equally true accounts of a crime scene. It means that different perspectives can each add separate ingredients to the evidential stew, which cooks up to the single, correct account of the crime under investigation.

To serve up that meal, *CSI* criminalists employ several investigative principles. Locard's Exchange Principle is one of them. According to this principle, the close proximity of the criminal and his victim provides the occasion for a swap of physical evidence between them. The investigators then have to find the criminal's residual pawmarks left on the victim. Locard's Exchange Principle implies that a close examination of the crime scene will always reveal evidence of the criminal's presence, and the apprehension of the criminal will always lead to evidence of the victim's presence on or about the criminal's body. Maybe; maybe not. Whether the criminal will swap spit with his victim depends on many empirical factors governing the biology, chemistry, and physics of interaction.

Consider DNA, a mainstay of *CSI*. Episode after episode employs trace DNA evidence to track down its criminals. But how long does this trace DNA evidence last before degrading to an unusable condition? Like the lifespan of viruses, many factors affect the longevity of DNA samples. A DNA swap between the criminal and his victim is worthless if a cleaning solution or some other chemical bath destroys the DNA sample, not to mention the problems caused by environmental pollution, rain water, wind, or mere sunlight.

An even worse problem for DNA evidence and other sorts of trace materials is that there usually is too much of it. Locard's Exchange Principle does not merely imply that the criminal and her victim swap samples. It implies that everyone and everything swap with everyone and everything else when they come into close quarters. It is not just that victims exchange with criminals and criminals exchange with victims. Everyone exchanges with everyone else with whom they come into contact. How does the criminalist know which exchanged materials are significant to the case and which ones are only accidentally on site? The team members all have their own fingerprints and DNA on file so that their presence at the crime scene can safely be discounted as irrelevant to the case. But if DNA flies all over the place, irrelevant DNA can jolly well fly into the crime scene too. The criminalist's investigation has to establish that the DNA found at the crime scene was left there by the criminal when she committed the crime, and not left there accidentally, unrelated to any criminal misconduct. That determination requires more than the mere presence of the DNA itself; it requires an account of the crime scene that shows the only way the DNA evidence found at the scene could have gotten there was through the presence of the criminal committing just this crime in just this sort of way.

"Leaving Las Vegas" (Episode 152) made this very point. It opens with Willow's courtroom testimony in Jay Finch's murder case. Finch fatally stabs his mother with a butcher's knife. Traces of Finch's blood are found on the knife's handle, but defense attorney Adam Novak convinces the jury that Finch left his blood on the knife before someone else used it in the commission of the crime. It is, after all, a knife from his own kitchen. Accordingly, the mere presence of Finch's DNA on the murder weapon does not by itself prove that Finch cut himself in the process of carving up his mother. In principle, it is impossible to tell just when his blood got on the knife. Apparently, even "slam-dunk" DNA evidence does not always score the winning basket.

"Invisible Evidence" makes the same point. The bloody towel and knife found in the trunk of Michael Fife's car are indeed linked to Rachel Lyford's murder. But Fife does not put them in his trunk; he doesn't even know they are there in the first place. He is framed by Gary Quinn, who stashes the towel and knife in Fife's car when the latter goes to the carwash where Quinn works. It is not just the existence of the evidence; it is the circumstances surrounding the appearance of the evidence at a particular location at a particular time that the criminalists must take into account. Locard's Exchange Principle, while promising the presence of the evidence, promises equally well the presence of much irrelevant information at the crime scene. What is the wheat? What is the chaff?

Gottfried Wilhelm Leibniz was a German intellectual who is historically renowned for inventing calculus. He also formulated a principle used in determining problems of identity, called the principle of the identity of indiscernibles, or Leibniz's Law. In a nutshell, Leibniz's Law states that if Murderer A is identical to Suspect B, then every attribute of A is also an attribute of B, and vice versa. This may sound like gobbledygook, but it amounts to the invention of the criminal *alibi*. An alibi is the claim that there is at least one thing that is true about the murderer that is *not* true of the suspect. For example, Suspect B was not at the scene of the crime; however, the one true thing we know about Murderer A is that he *was* at the scene of the crime. Therefore by Leibniz's Law, A cannot equal B, or the suspect cannot be the murderer.

"The Unusual Suspect" (Episode 135) deals with a perplexing application of Leibniz's Law. A teenager, Marlon West, is charged with the murder of one of his high-school classmates, Stacy Vollmer. During his trial, Marlon's twelve-year-old sister, Hannah, confesses on the witness stand that she is Stacy's real killer. But Marlon already confessed! He possibly confesses to the murder to throw suspicion off of his sister Hannah. Or Hannah may only appear to know certain details about how the crime was committed in order to provide an alibi for her brother. Hannah's mother claims that Hannah has an I.Q. of 177, well into the genius range. But she is only twelve years old, seemingly too young to be able to carry out such a dreadful crime. Is she fabricating evidence to raise the question of reasonable doubt in the minds of the jury? Or is she the real murder? Sara Sidle worries that "If we can't pin this on Hannah or Marlon, they could both walk." At the end of the episode, Hannah whispers in Sara's ear "I didn't kill Stacy," leaving Sara completely perplexed. So both the original suspect Marlon and his sister Hannah do and do not match the evidence of the murderer. Lab tech David Hodges suggests his own interesting application of Leibniz's Law as a way of settling the issue. "You could flip a coin." So much for conclusive indicators of guilt! Perhaps they both killed Stacy. Maybe Stacy really committed suicide. At the end of this episode neither the *CSI* personnel involved nor the TV audience knows who's who in this murderer's zoo.

To be fair, *Law & Order's* "Gunshow" (Episode 206) also features a case in which executive assistant DA Jack McCoy can't prove Dennis Trope responsible for mass murder. *CSI* could do so using better forensics, but better forensic evidence is simply unavailable. *Law & Order's* "Dissonance" (Episode 232) features a case in which Marian Reger pleads guilty to murdering a member of Carl Reger's orchestra. She makes her plea while she is on the witness stand in order to show reasonable doubt to the jury. In these two episodes, McCoy knows that both Trope and Reger are guilty, but forensic evidence is incapable of determining their guilt. *Without a Trace's* "He Saw, She Saw" (Episode 3) also features a case in which eyewitnesses offer different accounts of the victim's kidnapping and forensic evidence is incapable of establishing which account is correct. While it is alright in principle and in practice for forensic evidence to be insufficient for determining whodunit in a police procedural such as *Law & Order* or *Without a Trace*, such a failure of problem-solving strategies cuts too close to the bone for *CSI*. *CSI* is all about absolute answers, and absolute answers purport to establish conclusively the identity of the villain *du jour*.

Another philosophical perplexity gnaws at the bones of *CSI*. The theories, laws, and paradigms that science uses to solve puzzles are based on a limited sampling from a much larger sample set. Take fingerprinting, for example. It is assumed that no two individuals have identical fingerprints. How do we know this? There are literally billions of individuals, and fingerprints in criminal justice files represent but a tiny fraction of them. The same thing can be said for DNA, ear lobes, retinas, and snowflakes. Philosophers call this concern the problem of induction. Our knowledge of scientific laws and theories comes from experience. That is the mainstay of evidentialism. But our experience is necessarily limited, fragmentary, and incomplete. How can fragmentary evidence about a miniscule sample taken at random from a humongous array of fingerprints, for example, provide proof that no two of the billions of humans who have ever existed or who will ever exist have exactly the same prints? It is sheer hubris to make such a claim. It is like saying that because all of our efforts to determine whether π (pi) has three successive 3s in it have failed to show this, we therefore know that π does not have three successive 3s. We may believe this. Our belief may be correct. But we do not know it. We just act as if we know it.

To complicate things even further, for any set of data there is always more than one theory that correctly describes it. Consider the data set emeralds. Experience shows that they are all green in color. It follows from this that if a new emerald were to be discovered it would be green too. It does not matter whether that new gem has already been discovered and examined. If it is an emerald, it has to be green. But it also has to be *grue*. To be grue means to be green before a certain point in time and to be blue after that point in time. Because that hypothetical point in time has not yet occurred, any emerald in question would currently appear as green. Experience shows that. But after that (imaginary) point in time, all emeralds would immediately turn blue. That turning point in time just has not occurred yet.

This may sound like complete nonsense, but it is not. Liquid water is already known to display this grue-like characteristic. While it is still a liquid, cool a container of water just to its freezing point. Quickly, the entire contents will turn to ice. Scientists call this sort of thing a "tipping point." If ice had never been experienced beforehand because the air temperature had never become cold enough for water to freeze, its post–tipping point appearance and characteristics as ice could never have been predicted. Maybe emeralds also have their own tipping point. Maybe emeralds are like water, green at one "temperature" and blue at another. It is just that the blue tipping point "temperature" has not yet been reached. They have yet to tip.

The same thing can be said of DNA, fingerprints, and snowflakes. Maybe they are all at the green stage now because the blue tipping point "temperature" simply has not arrived. But that does not mean that the blue stage never will, or that they can never tip. We simply know too little about the world to say with any justifiable confidence that DNA, fingerprints, or snowflakes are not "grue" and they never will be "grue." Future experiences may surprise us. Like water as it freezes, DNA, fingerprints, and snowflakes may hold some tipping point surprises for us too. DNA evidence may be the current gold standard for purposes of identification, but like the Aristotelian notion that biological species are fixed forever and the Newtonian notion that there is an absolute space and time, a new Darwin or a new Einstein may arise to show DNA's limitations.

However these fascinating theoretical puzzles work themselves out, the equipment *CSI* uses is real enough. They do not make up the technology just because they need it to do their job. The trouble with the technology in the real world is that most crime labs do not have much of this fancy equipment. It is too expensive. It is akin to every university astronomy department owning its own Hubble telescope. Instead, most criminal investigative units must farm out their tests to private commercial companies, which have long backlogs of tests and poorly paid, minimally trained personnel using equipment that is hardly state of the art. For example, in the United States there are currently more than 350,000 collected DNA samples awaiting tests. Real lab technicians are not the hotshots we see on TV. They are the unsung lab rats, who like Grissom's fire ants, are martyrs for science. To make matters worse, recent accusations have alleged that the FBI's own lab cooked data to suit the prosecution, hardly the image of an impartial investigative body. Whether these accusations are valid or not, lab work is not the impartial application of uninvolved individuals applying magical technology that *CSI* suggests it is. It is the sweaty work of harried individuals who have to make countless judgment calls concerning the identification and classification of the materials submitted to them. The tidal wave of technology certainly allows for the more accurate assessment of data. It also allows for the creation of much more data than our current system can process in a reasonable amount of time. Technological progress is not without its own drawbacks.

Suggested Reading

Cortez, Donn. *Investigating CSI: An Unauthorized Look Inside the Crime Labs of Las Vegas, Miami and New York.* New York: Benbella Books, 2006.

Descartes, René. *Discourse on Method* (1632) and *Meditations on First Philosophy* (1641). [Descartes' views on the philosophy of science are found in these two works.]

Flaherty, Mike. *C.S.I.: Crime Scene Investigation Companion.* New York: Pocket Books, 2004.

Goodman, Nelson. *Fact, Fiction, and Forecast.* Cambridge: Harvard University Press, 1955.

Kuhn, Thomas. *The Logic of Scientific Revolutions.* Chicago: The University of Chicago Press, 1962.

Leibniz, Gottfried Wilhem. *Monadology* (*circa* 1710). [Leibniz's views on epistemology and personal identity are found in this work.]

Marrinan, Corinne and Steve Parker. *Ultimate CSI: Crime Scene Investigation.* London: Dorling Kindersley Ltd, 2006.

Ramsland, Katherine. *The C.S.I. Effect.* New York: Berkeley Boulevard Books, 2006.

———. *The Forensic Science of C.S.I.* New York: Berkeley Boulevard Books, 2001.

CHAPTER 2

COLD CASE: A ROMANCE

There is something about unsolved mysteries that make them especially appealing to many TV viewers. Most episodes of TV detective shows devote themselves to presenting and investigating a single crime problem or a series of related problems. As part of the standard fare for these episodes, the guilty party is identified and apprehended. The questions of who did what to whom, why they did it, and how they did it are presented and answered. Episodes seldom end without specific, identifiable resolutions for all of these problems. Rarely does the audience not know the identity of the bad guy, although the criminal apprehension of the culprit may not actually occur at the conclusion of some episodes.

In the real world crimes often remain unsolved for long periods of time. Many are never solved. Unsolved cases are disconcerting to our picture of the world. We want our world to operate completely in terms of some perceived, if abstract, rules of justice so that the guilty and the innocent alike receive their proper and just desserts. But we also recognize this pipe dream for what it is and thus are willing to settle for a second best world view, one in which "crime does not pay." Bad guys never get away with it (for long). Justice will be served (in the end).

Cold Case launches its weekly format by cleverly combining the traditional fictional TV detective format of the identification and the apprehension of the bad guys with the actual reality of unsolved cases. Detective Lilly Rush and the rest of her crew of investigators step in long after the original investigation of a crime has gone belly up. Instead of showing the audience why the original investigation proved fruitless, *Cold Case* takes that very fruitlessness as its starting point. Each episode begins with a brief reconstruction of aspects of the original crime. The players are put on stage and enough information is presented to whet the audience's appetite for more. After the obligatory commercial break, the case appears as a cardboard box bearing the victim's name, which has been ensconced in an anonymous storage room—the cavern-like basement of the Philadelphia police department building housing the cold case files. The case is in cold storage, so to speak. Unsolved cases are boxed in this room like dusty, unused library books on long-neglected shelves.

While the point of *Cold Case* episodes is to provide closure for the victim of the crime, the dead victim does not by herself initiate the revival of her own case. Her reincarnated self appears at the end of the episode and puts her seal of approval on the identification and apprehension of her murderer before evaporating as a ghostly shade. But her resurrected self will not personally provoke anyone to reexamine her case nor will it stimulate the detective team to take an interest in the case. Nor are there instances of a dead person haunting her killer or badgering her friends or relatives to give her justice. Her ghost does not haunt the dreams of her survivors, goading them into action. Shakespeare this is not.

For a variety of reasons other than the personal intervention of the deceased, interest is reawakened in her case. New evidence comes to light, or a victim's surviving family member or friend provokes renewed interest in the investigation by persuading the detectives not to allow the victim's memory to die along with his body, not to allow the killer to get away with it, not to allow justice to be denied. The reinvestigations of these cold cases never begin with Detective Rush visiting the police storage room and singing "eenie, meenie, minie, mo" before randomly selecting a case. Living memories of the dead always have pride of place in each episode. They are the vehicles that provide the impetus for the case's selection as well as the means by which the story line is resolved and the murderer's true identity uncovered.

Memory

Without the appeal to memories, *Cold Case* would lack its identity. Though the *Cold Case* detective team employs all the standard police procedural methods, these methods merely provide the backdrop for the case's solution. The real logic of each *Cold Case* episode uniquely turns on the completeness and the accuracy of the memories of the crime's survivors. Whether the person being questioned is a peripheral associate, a key eyewitness, or the suspected killer, the appeal to his memories provides the glue that binds together the various plot components. Such memories supply not simply the bulk of the evidence needed to crack the case but crucial data whose absence would leave the cold case squad out in the cold. In this series, objective forensic evidence, *CSI*-style, plays a limited role in uncovering the bad guy's identity. The same can be said for the *Law & Order*-style police work needed to sift tediously through the bulk of unrelated data to separate the relevant from the irrelevant. Forensic evidence and police teamwork are simply taken for granted. The real focus of *Cold Case's* crime-fighting methodology is utilization of the evidence provided by the memories of the surviving witnesses to the crime. The bulk of the programming in each episode is devoted to a flashback parade of eyewitnesses who, in turn, relate what they remember about the case until enough information has been assembled to solve the murder. The memories of the murderer are the capstone of each episode, which always ends with the killer's confession, during which he relates the final moments of the victim's life. These memories are never wrong! The final flashback scene of each episode restages the victim's death, all of it unerringly recalled by the victim's killer.

Cold Case brings into focus a key aspect of the human ability to gain knowledge. Without the faculty of memory, any sort of knowledge would be impossible. This may seem surprising. The human ability to acquire knowledge is sophisticated and multifaceted. It consists of a number of components.

First, there must be some data, evidence, or information to know, hence Sergeant Joe Friday's famous insistence in the old TV series *Dragnet* on "The facts, ma'am; just the facts." But awareness of the "facts" by itself does not equal knowledge. Mere facts are like a child's connect-the-dot picture book. Facts are the dots. Knowledge of the picture requires that the dots be properly connected together. Second, for that to happen, the dots must be seen as something specific. For example, in a typical crime show, the deceased may be seen either as a murder victim, a suicide victim, an accident victim, or a victim of natural causes. These are quite different and mutually exclusive ways of viewing the deceased. How does the detective know which label correctly applies to the victim at hand? Third, in order to make the correct determination, the detective must know the concepts of murder victim, suicide victim, accident victim, heart attack victim, and so forth. These concepts are abstract ideas. They characterize the "victim" in distinctly different and incompatible ways.

Finally, the detective must know how to apply these wide-ranging abstract concepts correctly in practice.

Connecting any of the data dots of evidence presupposes the faculty of memory. Evidence of criminal activity is not all revealed in the same instant, but successively. Information discovered early in the investigation must be correctly correlated and integrated with information discovered at the investigation's midpoint and at its conclusion. Like the card player being dealt a series of cards, each of these evidence cards must be placed in its proper order to form a hand. Unlike a card game, all of the evidence cards do not appear at the same moment, open for a godlike visual inspection. Accounts of events relayed early in an investigation must be successfully integrated with later information to form the card hand called the *crime scene*. The detectives must remember the evidence cards as they flow in and out of play.

The faculty of memory has four characteristics: 1) factual; 2) emotional: 3) habit; and 4) episodic. Without these capacities, crime fighting would be impossible.

Factual memory is the capacity to recall information, whether that information is empirical or conceptual. Unless the detective correctly remembers that she has already interviewed a suspect or called the crime lab about some trace evidence, she will not be able to process her case. She must also remember what the terms "homicide," "suicide," "accident," and "natural causes" mean, or else she will be unable to use these notions properly to understand the evidence before her.

Emotional memories are formed when strong emotions are present at the original experience. When a person cognitively reviews any aspect of these experiences, the attendant emotions are automatically evoked. Music has the ability to evoke emotions. Many couples have a special song such that even snatches of its lyrics or melody can reawaken strong feelings in one person for another.

Habit memory is the ability to act routinely and automatically in a regular manner. Walking, singing, and driving a car require this sort of memory capacity. Unless the detective remembers habitually how to apply the tools of her trade to an investigation, her "book learning" will be useless in practice because it will not translate into being "street smart."

Finally, the detective must collect the witnesses' stories about the case. This presupposes that the detective and the witnesses all have *episodic memory*, that is, they must have the ability to recall what they have experienced. Episodic memory is what we usually think of when we discuss the concepts of memory, although the other three types of memory are equally as important as episodic memory to the investigation of crime.

Memory is closely linked to the faculty of imagination. Memory recalls what the case *was* like; imagination constructs what the case *could be* like. The faculty of imagination is necessary to supply data or connections between data when they are not obvious. This amounts to constructing possible scenarios to explain how a crime might have occurred and who might have committed it. To construct possible crime scenarios, a successful detective must have both a good imagination and a good memory. It takes both faculties to reconstruct an understanding of what happened at the scene of the crime given both the conclusive evidence and the ambiguous evidence the detective always confronts.

But the detective's imagination can result in a misunderstanding of the crime scene just as easily as a real understanding of it. Just because the detective can imagine how a crime might have occurred does not mean it really happened that way. Touché! The detective's faculty of imagination may not always conjure up a correct understanding of a case. Memory, like imagination, can also go on a holiday. When we "remember" something there is generally a feeling of rightness about that memory belief. The potential trouble with this is that just because the detective or the witness thinks she "remembers" something, it does not necessarily follow that she actually remembers it. It may feel right without actually being right. There are such things as "apparent memory beliefs." Apparent memory beliefs seem accurate or authentic to the person doing the recalling, but they actually are not. The problem is that in cases of both accurate memories (called *veridical memories* by the experts) and apparent memory beliefs, the subject's feeling of recognition is the same. Both veridical and apparent memory beliefs "taste the same." They both seem to present an accurate recollection of what a person really experienced.

To make matters even more interesting, the more vivid the recollection, the more likely the person is to believe that the memory in question is veridical, and the less vivid the recollection, the less likely the person is to believe in the recollection's accuracy. The same thing can be said for the importance of the event recollected. The more vividly an event seems to be remembered, the greater the weight given to it when analyzing its importance. But this is fallacious thinking. The vividness of a memory does not necessarily correlate to the memory's accuracy any more than the vividness of an imagination actually correlates to its validity. Inaccurate beliefs can be as firmly held as accurate ones. Vivid recollections are no more likely to be valid than those that are hazy in the mind of the remembering person. They are more likely to be accepted as valid by that person, however, because they seem real to the mind's eye, not because they accurately convey the facts.

Another wrinkle with knowledge claims is that they are multifaceted. Sometimes knowing something only means that the knower does in fact have the relevant information in his memory data bank. This presupposes that at one time the knower had "been there and done that." On the other hand, simply having had a specific experience does not count as knowledge about that experience if a person can no longer accurately remember it. There are two distinct, but related issues here: Did the witness have the specific relevant experiences? And can he now accurately recall those experiences? Another way of putting this is to distinguish between the questions: Does he know x, y, and z? and Does he know that he knows x, y, and z? Having certain experiences in the past is a sufficient condition for knowing these things, but it does not follow from this that a witness can right here and now correctly and adequately recall the events he experienced. He may know of these events, but he may not now know that he knows them.

Cold Case completely ignores this distinction. If an eyewitness confidently relates a set of memory beliefs to the detective team, then, de facto, these belief claims are treated as legitimate evidence that the person knows that she knows. Knowing that she knows is collapsed into being confident that she knows of the events in question. This mistake is depicted in "Fireflies" (Episode 77) when Cherise Pierce seems to remember vividly the death of her best friend, Melanie Campbell. Eight-year-old Cherise is so traumatized by these events that even thirty-one years later in 2006, she is reluctant to tell the cold case squad about them. In fact, her long-held memory beliefs are false. Little Melanie Campbell was not murdered that night even though Cherise "remembers" that she was. It is only later in this episode that the squad discovers that Cherise's memories are indeed incorrect. In Cherise's case, she neither knows that Melanie was murdered, nor knows that she knew that. She is wrong on both counts.

As a TV detective series, *Cold Case* detectives seldom deal with another wrinkle in memory—amnesia. Amnesia means the loss of memory. Temporary amnesia is commonplace. Ordinarily, it concerns the inability to recall factual information. It is usually experienced as the inability to bring into consciousness what a person knows that he knows but cannot currently put his mental fingers on, if you will. Sometimes the irretrievable information can even be "on the tip of his tongue." Failing to recall factual information in this manner can be very frustrating. In *Cold Case* this failure would be more than simply frustrating, it would be fatal to all of the story lines, as the series' logic of detection turns on the squad's ability to integrate memory claims to unravel whodunit.

Even more frustrating for the detective is the phenomenon of total amnesia. This is the incapacity to remember who one is at all. This incapacity may be only temporary or it may be permanent. A victim of total amnesia has his episodic memory wiped completely clean, but he does not lose his factual memories, except as they involve his capacity to recall any information regarding his own personal identity and episodic history. Neither does he usually lose his habit or emotional memories. He cannot recall his name, his family, where he grew up, and who his friends are, but he still knows how to speak his native language in its accustomed dialect, drive a car, and obey the rules of etiquette. When he comes into contact with the legal system, only third-person evidence is relevant in determining who he really is. Does he have fingerprints on file? Are there friends or relatives who can identify him? In this manner, a victim of total amnesia is like a body found in the woods. He cannot speak for himself. He may even come to believe that he is someone other than the person he really is. Others must be found who can speak for him.

Just such a case of total amnesia is presented in the aforementioned "Fire-flies." In 1975, eight-year-old Melanie Campbell disappears. At the time everyone assumes that she was murdered. She committed a grave social indiscretion by befriending her new next door neighbor, Cherise Pierce. Cherise is black; Melanie is white. When the Pierce family moves into the all-white Campbell neighborhood, many of the white homeowners deeply resent the Pierce's presence. Racism is rampant, and the white homeowners are afraid that the presence of a black family will lead to white flight and the subsequent destruction of their property values. Young Melanie is oblivious to these concerns. She is happily caught up with the discovery of a soul mate who shares her magical view of the world. The two children vow to be "friends forever." But all that comes crashing down when the teenage son of one of the white property owners tries to scare the black family out of the neighborhood by threatening to shoot Melanie and Cherise when he discovers them one night in the woods. Cherise runs away, falsely believing that the gun shots she heard signaled Melanie's death. Subsequently she is afraid to talk to the police about this because she fears that she will be next. But Melanie doesn't die that night, although she suffered a serious head injury which resulted in her total amnesia. Thirty-one years later, the cold case squad locates the adult Melanie in West Virginia and reunites her with her childhood friend, Cherise. Though Melanie retains no cognitive memories of the events surrounding her shooting and her previous life as a Campbell, psychologically she seems ready to reconnect to her relationship with her long-lost best friend. While her intellectual recall seems to be completely lost, her emotional attachment to Cherise is largely unimpaired by the trauma of her assault. They are, after all, "friends forever."

Complicating the problem of memory and knowledge, the person who knows what really happened because she remembers it does not have to know that she knows it in order to remember. This means that the person who possesses specific episodic memories does not have to be able to explain to anyone why it is that she in fact remembers these things. She does not even have to be able to explain it to herself. The total amnesia victim may not know that she accurately remembers events in her past. Melanie's faulty memories could not be used to crack the case of her disappearance. If her memories were in fact accurate, however, she really did remember these things, even if she did not know that she remembered them. She may not have been able to distinguish in her own mind between her veridical memories and her fictitious, imaginary beliefs. What counts is only that she really did remember them. What provoked the memory is a separate issue. How licit the memory feels to that person is another separate issue. She may not know why she remembers these events or even whether she remembers them, but that does not matter to the validity of her memory beliefs if she in fact does remember them accurately. If she does, her memories are veridical; if she does not, they are not.

From the point of view of the story line, knowing that memories are accurate makes a big difference. Many detective stories try to explain why someone has the specific memories he has and how he comes to have them. These explanations can be valuable additions to the story line, but they cannot be used to judge the accuracy of the memory claims. The remembering person does not have to explain why he remembers certain events as long as what he remembers actually did happen in the manner his memory depicts.

In "Beautiful Little Fool" (Episode 65), Felix Spyczyk does not need to explain how he can recall in 2005 why he murdered Violet Polley in 1929 as long as his memory of having done so is accurate. Even though the murder transpired seventy-five years ago, perhaps he remembers the murder now because he is filled with remorse or because he had a nightmare. Perhaps he only had indigestion. None of these factors speaks to the accuracy of his recollection, although they may well speak to the storytelling art. The only thing that counts is whether he accurately remembers what he believes he remembers.

The faculties of imagination and memory both allow the knower to (re)construct the evidence. The events that sparked the criminal investigation lie in the past, and detectives cannot simply hop on a time machine to observe them as they happened. Such time-machine experiences are the sole prerogative of TV audiences. Like historians, those who work in the criminal justice system are stuck in the present. They attempt to reconstruct the past using present evidence as their guide. Their problem becomes the following: Given the current state of the evidence, how must these events have occurred? There are many ways the imagination can reconstruct the original crime scene. Detectives must select the correct option from among the possible variations.

Veridical memory testimony provides material for correctly reconstructing the past. But memories do not come labeled as "veridical" or "false." Mere strength of conviction alone cannot divide memory beliefs into the veridical or the fallacious camps. Rather, memory beliefs, like any component of the reconstruction, must be consistent with the available evidence and coherent with the physical laws that govern the real world.

To compound the problem, memories about the distant past are frequently treated with more skepticism than memories about the recent past. Psychologists divide the faculty of memory into two components: short-term memory and long-term memory. Short-term memory is the ability to recall events that occurred within about the last half hour or so. Short-term memory is what provides the answer to the infamous question, "Where are the car keys?" Our short-term memory is one of the capacities that weave our time-laden experiences into relatively smooth tapestries.

Long-term memory takes over after about twenty minutes, as demonstrated by the example of finding one's car after a day spent at the shopping mall. The storage capacity for short-term memories is very limited, so the presence of new experiences forces the mind either to forget the not-too-distant past completely or to shift these experiences into long-term storage, the capacity for which is very large. Long-term memory is the intellectual capacity that allows us to park at our favorite parking spots in the mall, season after season, year after year. Older adults frequently have the reputation for having better long-term memory capacities than short-term ones, but this may only be a diffuse way of acknowledging that our elders have more long-term experiences to remember.

Problems frequently arise for experiences stored in the long-term memory. Because there are so many experiences stored there, it becomes reasonable to ask whether specific long-term memories are in fact veridical or are delusions the mind accepts because they seem to be authentic to it at the time. In "Factory Girls" (Episode 25), Detective Rush asks eighty-year-old Martha Perkins in 2004 whether she can remember accurately events that transpired in 1943 when Alice Miller died at the B-25 assembly plant. Martha replies in a huff, "You get old; you start forgetting things. You don't start making them up."

Martha treats the issue as akin to picking out the correct puzzle piece from among the many laid out before her on the card table of her memory. She does not "make up" the pieces; she simply finds the correct one. But there is more to it than that. Rush's concerns can equally well mean, Why does Martha think that the puzzle piece she selected is a piece of the puzzle in question? Just because Martha firmly believes she accurately remembers the events of sixty years ago does not mean that her memories are in fact veridical. She may have mistaken sincere, deeply entrenched, memory beliefs in her long-term storage for accurate ones. She may have selected a faux puzzle piece, or a piece from the wrong puzzle. She may indeed be "making things up," albeit unwittingly. It is not simply a question of whether Martha can access her long-term memories about Alice's death. It is whether what she does manage to access is a valid memory, the product of her fallacious imagination, or a mixture of the two.

Like those of the amnesiac, memory beliefs of young children and the mentally challenged or disabled can also be especially difficult to evaluate. Viewing or participating in traumatic events such as murders, robberies, rapes, unsuccessful suicide attempts, or auto wrecks can easily distort viewpoints and testimony when attempts are made to recall them. The emotional components of these events can be readily magnified or lessened in the minds of the survivors by the impact they had on their participants. In turn, these emotional components may infect the participant's cognitive beliefs about those experiences. While the adult Cherise will never forget the trauma of being shot at in the woods during the dead of night, for her companion Melanie, the whole event in question remains a total cognitive blank. It was too traumatic even to recall. It was not simply the head injury that scrambled Melanie's recollections; it was also the terror surrounding the assault itself. Happily for the resolution of the episode, Melanie's emotional memories seem not to have been completely erased by her head wound, as she seems to be ready to reconnect with Cherise when the two finally meet again in Melanie's old backyard.

Another wrinkle in memory's fabric is presented in "Churchgoing People" (Episode 4). The cold case squad must question the wife of a church organist who was murdered in 1990. Caroline Baye, the victim's widow, is now suffering from severe Alzheimer's disease. She is also having flashbacks to the night of the murder. Rush wants to solve the case on Caroline's behalf before Caroline's senility completely overtakes her. Caroline's recognition of her surroundings and her memory are tenuous at best. She resembles a total amnesiac at times. The story line, however, allows her to come to her senses completely to relate what actually occurred on the night of Michael Baye's death so that the audience may view the events accurately via the device of the TV flashback. Ironically, it turns out that Caroline herself murdered her husband in a fit of jealous rage after she discovered his affair with a member of the church choir. At the end of the episode a now hopelessly addled Caroline is locked up for her crime. Without the momentary clarity of her flashback, it would not be clear to the viewers that she, not her teenage son Ryan, had committed the murder. The issue of legal incarceration for Caroline, given her fragmented mental state, is never raised in this episode, nor is the accuracy of her memory flashback ever questioned.

Another counterpoint to the problem of amnesia is presented in "Saving Sammy" (Episode 74). This episode concerns the 2003 murder of Brent Harris's parents. Brent is autistic. Newly discovered evidence seems to show that Brent was in the back seat of his family's car when his parents were shot to death in the front seat. Brent therefore knows who killed his family, but his mental condition makes a straightforward interrogation impossible. The affliction of autism is interpreted in this episode as implying that Brent cannot tell a lie and has eidetic recall concerning numbers. Brent's memory of the family car's odometer reading leads the detectives to believe that he was present at the time of his family's murder. His recollection of a cell phone number and the serial number of the gun used to shoot his family implies that his sister's boyfriend killed his parents with their own gun right before she phoned him. The "testimony" that Brent gives regarding these numbers is treated as incomplete, but infallible as far as it goes. The task for the detectives is to understand what each string of numbers that Brent recites by rote means for the case. It is possible, however, that the detectives have misunderstood Brent. He may have eidetic recall of these numbers, which he has seen in a context other than the night of the murder. The fact that he can infallibly recall a sequence of numbers does not mean that he in fact witnessed these numbers in the context understood by the detectives. In this episode, Brent's infallible memory of the dots is interpreted to mean the cold case squad also has an infallible understanding of the connection between the dots.

Many sorts of memory problems make detective work extremely difficult. Investigators must fill in holes left in the understanding of the crime scene owing to various sorts of memory failures of the eyewitnesses or the crime victims. Different memory beliefs also may contradict each other, even those within the same person. In "Baby Blues" (Episode 73), thirty-year old Devon Felice incorrectly "remembers" that when he was six, he accidentally drowned his baby sister, Iris, in the bathtub while attempting to baptize her. Because of the trauma of Iris' death, the adult Devon even refuses to hold his own infant daughter. The course of the investigation shows that Devon's mother Molly killed Iris in a fit of postpartum psychosis while a helpless Devon could only stand by and watch. At the end of the episode, the adult Devon is seen holding his own infant daughter at Iris's graveside. His correct memories of the events surrounding Iris's death have been restored by the success of the investigation.

One of the curious facets of *Cold Case's* story lines is the nearly complete unwillingness to acknowledge the problematic nature of memory beliefs. While different participants in a crime may have different memories about what occurred, each episode takes for granted the accuracy and compatibility of each witness's memory. Differences between memory beliefs are usually omitted entirely from the scripts. Acknowledging them would only wreck the show's story lines. They are not explained by assuming that someone is lying, or is seeing things from different experiences or different points of view. It is generally assumed that the person remembering accurately recalls his past experiences. It is also assumed that individuals' memory reports, like those of different eyewitnesses, will dovetail with each other. Additional memory reports are simply seen as additional information, different puzzle pieces, which when compiled complete the picture.

The 2006 season opener "Rampage" (Episode 70) presented a good example of the series' general rules about the reliability of memory. Detective Kat Miller remarks at the start of the show about the inaccuracy and incompleteness of the memories of a mall massacre's traumatized survivors. Rush recognizes the complexity of this problem when remarking that the witnesses cannot even agree on whether one of the gunmen wore a hat. But the unfolding story line ignores these problems and treats memory claims as business as usual because the episode again unfolds largely through the memories of the massacre survivors.

Television viewers certainly have the edge over real-life detectives. The TV format provides viewers with a time-machine-quality flashback that the real-world detective lacks, although the flashback format affords the *Cold Case* squad the same observational viewpoint enjoyed by the TV audience. Episode producers can rerun past events as flashbacks as often as they like. These flashbacks are designed to show everyone "what really happened." *Cold Case* does this to a tee. Indeed, the bulk of its story lines are contained within these flashbacks. It also cleverly portrays the former and current appearances of certain characters by the their quick juxtaposition within a scene. In this manner the audience can see how a character has aged during the years separating the traumatic criminal events from the present. The audience can see that the detective is in a sense talking to "two people" at once. This is a terrific storytelling device. The audience can more easily form a judgment about who was originally involved in the crime and how that person's perspective or limited experiences when the crime was originally committed may affect her memory of that crime now. Although the detective team is not the audience for the show, it gets the same chance as the audience to witness and rewitness the original crime, as if to check its opinions against the actual facts.

Memories, the eye of the soul on the past, may be accurate, jaded, biased, or incomplete, but the pride of place they have for the show's story lines means that they represent for this series the best possible method for gathering the evidence needed to solve these cold cases. *CSI*-type forensic analysis plays a distinctly secondary role in *Cold Case*. For example, in "Sandhogs" (Episode 72), the 1947 death of Hank Bishop remains unsolved until one day in 2006 when Bishop's cigarette lighter is found in the possession of his former workmate, Mateo Zaccardo. The case is solved when Zaccardo, who was confronted with the lighter, confesses and tells the detectives and the audience in a flashback how he murdered Bishop because he coveted Bishop's job slot. The forensic evidence of the lighter is reduced to a device for inducing the suspect's confession and retelling of the murder, without which no guilt can be established. Without complete, accurate, and consistent memories, there can be no closure in this series.

Closure

Cold Case is all about closure. While this series sets a criminal detection task before the investigative team in each episode, unmasking the villain's identity is only one of the episode's central issues. The activities surrounding the identification and arrest of the culprit also serve the purpose of providing closure, not only to the surviving friends and family members, but to the deceased as well. The show is all about doing right by the victim. Real closure lies in the mind's eye of the victim and the victim only. Secondarily, it lies in the eyes of the victim's friends and family, the detective team, and the TV audience.

Closure interweaves legal, psychological, and philosophical strands. Legally, closure refers to the identification, apprehension, and successful prosecution of the culprit. This component is standard detective show fare. Other than the key role played by memory in identifying the perpetrator of the crime, *Cold Case* pays little specific attention to standard criminal investigation techniques. They are simply taken for granted and applied in a straightforward manner. What distinguishes *Cold Case* from other fictional detective series is its focus on cases that have literally been put on the shelf because initial efforts to solve them using standard techniques have failed. Viewers are often left to wonder about the reasons for these failures. In *Cold Case*, this issue is, surprisingly, a moot point. Story lines pay brief attention to the reasons for the original investigation's failure. This issue is dealt with mostly through the introduction of new evidence unavailable to the original investigators.

Such was the case in "Rampage," when the case of a shopping mall massacre is reopened because of the discovery of new evidence. The two teenage gunmen responsible for the rampage use a video camera to tape themselves before opening fire in the mall, but the video footage continues even after the shooting begins, leading the cold case team to assume that there was a third shooter involved—namely the person holding the video camera. The video camera, originally hidden in an air duct, is only discovered during renovations to the mall. The case is initially thought to be solved because the two shooters commit suicide in the mall itself.

"Static" (Episode 75) concerns the apparent suicide of a radio deejay in 1958. A tape playing at the time of his death catches the sound of the gunshot that killed him. Newer electronic equipment now allows the squad to hear the sound of footsteps and a door opening and closing after the gunshot. This indicates that "The Hawk" was not alone at the time of his death, as was originally believed. It is assumed that the person with him in the studio must be his murderer, and so the hunt is on to establish his identity.

Most *Cold Case* episodes provide only cursory explanations for the failures of the initial investigations. In "Fireflies," the initial investigation floundered because the original investigators wrongly focused on Cherise's older brother, Terrell. When they could not pin Melanie's disappearance on Terrell, the case went dry.

Sometimes the failure of the initial investigation is laid at the feet of the victim and not at those of the criminal justice system. In "It's Raining Men" (Episode 30), the 1983 death of Jeff Kern was poorly investigated at that time because he was HIV positive. His body remains in the pouring rain for more than three hours before the emergency medical responders will even touch it.

At that time, being HIV positive was not only a physical death sentence for many gay men, it was a social death sentences as well. The police did not care to put much effort into an investigation of the deaths of those marked by these cultural stigmas. "Good riddance to bad rubbish" seems to have been their perspective. Even given the renewed interest in the case in 2004, cold case squad detective Nick Vera is obviously repulsed by the lifestyle of gay men. Even "liberal" detectives Rush and Valens exchange meaningful looks of discomfort when Kern's former lover, Artie Russo, reawakens interest in the case by demanding justice for Kern as a "wedding gift" for Russo and his current gay lover.

"Churchgoing People" proves an interesting exception to this "don't ask, don't tell" policy regarding the failure of the initial homicide investigation. Uncharacteristically, this episode offers a detailed explanation about the initial investigation's failure. The detective responsible for the original 1990 investigation still works for the police, and Rush asks him directly why it had failed. After some initial defensiveness and embarrassment, the detective admitts that from 1988 to 1993 he was an alcoholic and "overlooked some things." The original failed investigation was the result of liquor ruling the detective and not the detective ruling the case. As it turned out, the detective's point that he had "overlooked some things" meant that he failed to search the bedroom at the murder victim's house, which would have revealed the murder scene as the blood bath that it became when the victim's wife bludgeoned him fourteen times with a fireplace poker. The application of a little Luminol would have popped this case in a heartbeat. The multiple locks on the husband's bedroom door should have provided the original investigators some clues. Rush's team would never have overlooked such "subtleties."

Some episodes open with the discovery of the previously unknown victim herself. In "Best Friends" (Episode 45), the case opens with the discovery of human bones in an old truck found in the Delaware River. The bones belong to a girl who disappeared in 1932. In "Boy in the Box" (Episode 14), the 1958 case of a murdered child found in a cardboard box is reopened when a suitcase containing the child's picture is discovered in front of a church. In "The House" (Episode 27), the case opens with the discovery of a prisoner's body found in a newly discovered escape tunnel outside of a closed state prison.

Occasionally, episodes focus on reopening "solved" cases to discover who really committed the crime because the initial criminal investigation misidentified the culprit. In "Death Penalty: Final Appeal" (Episode 66), the team is called upon to discover the real killer of a sixteen-year-old rape victim. A person wrongfully convicted for the crime is about to be executed. Interestingly enough, the team only discovers the real killer's identity after the execution of the innocent person wrongly convicted for the crime. Closure in this episode primarily involves the redemption of the person wrongly accused and executed by the state and only secondarily the original rape victim.

No matter how cases are introduced to the team, once the real culprit has been uncovered and an arrest has been made, the series makes no attempt to follow the criminal trial proceedings of the accused. Viewers are left with the impression that the apprehended person is in fact guilty of the crime and that a court of law would find that this person did commit the crime exactly as the show depicts. What would constitute a fitting punishment for the person who committed the crime is another issue that is never addressed. Considering the dire nature of some of the crimes committed, the failure to address the guilty party's legal punishment is a curious omission, especially given its importance for judicial closure. The answer to this puzzle lies in the fact that *Cold Case* does not focus on closure for the social system. Legal punishment is viewed by *Cold Case* as more of a social issue than an issue for the crime's victims. The original *Dragnet* series covered the social dimension of punishment by parading the convicted criminal, in all his sweaty, guilty glory, before the audience while a voice-over narrator read off the results of his criminal trial and punishment. *Cold Case* makes no attempt to give the audience this sort of satisfaction. Whether the audience thinks legal justice was really served in a given case is beside the point.

Most *Cold Case* villains don't even make it as far as jail at the end of the episode. In "The Hen House" (Episode 67), a former Nazi concentration camp guard assumes the identity of a real person named Noah Pool in order to escape from Nazi Germany. In America, "Noah" meets and falls in love with newswoman Lo Kinney. When she unmasks the truth about him, he kills her by pushing her in front of a train. He is reidentified and arrested in 2005. At the end of the episode he is paraded in a fanfare before the family of the real Noah Pool as each of them appeared in 1945 and as each appears in the present. Though he was headed for jail, he was not yet incarcerated at the episode's conclusion. His real "punishment" was to be unmasked for the charlatan that he was. In marked contrast to the ending of "The Hen House," "Death Penalty: Final Appeal" found the innocent Andre Tibbs already in jail and about to be executed in 2005 for a murder committed in 1994. Only after Tibbs's execution is the real culprit arrested.

Psychologically, *Cold Case* is primarily concerned with the relief of personal burdens. The surviving friends and family of the deceased are burdened by the knowledge that the victim's murder remains unresolved. "It's Raining Men" presents Artie Russo, murder victim Jeff Kern's surviving lover. He is nagged not simply by Jeff's death but by the *injustice* of Jeff's unsolved murder. He wants Jeff's killer uncovered as a sort of wedding present for himself and his current lover. Helena Bradley in "The Key" (Episode 76) never forgets the 1979 death of her mother, Libby Bradley. Coincidently, this is also Detective Jefferies' first case as a detective. Jefferies promises Helena Bradley that he will solve this case, and his failure to do so bothers him. But it does not haunt him. Helena may call him every week to keep in touch with the case, but she does not ride him about it. No one, including the deceased Libby, was driven to seek revenge. While graphically brutal in some ways, *Cold Case* is too polite for juicy blood vendettas. Unmasking the identity of the murderer is a nagging issue, not a burning issue.

Solving these cases nags at the detectives who make up the cold case squad in the "City of Brotherly Love." The resolution of these cases is not simply a job for them, from which they could hang up their hats at the end of their shifts and head home to their real lives. For all intents and purposes, they have little in the line of real lives outside of work. It is not simply that the show pays little attention to the home lives of the detectives. They have virtually no existence outside of their avocation, although TV ratings wars mandate that more attention be paid to the personal lives of show characters as the seasons roll on. "Rampage," for example, shows that Lilly Rush keeps pictures of the victims of the closed cases on her nightstand. Important as they may be to the viewers, these tidbits are inconsequential to the format of the show. Lilly may have troubles with her mother's wacky indifference to her, her sister's flightiness, and which of her two boyfriends to favor, but information about these events in Lilly's life are doled out piecemeal and do nothing to further the story lines. The same can be said for Scotty Valens' sexually victimized childhood, Nick Vera's divorce, and Will Jefferies' ghetto youth. Besides the fact that he fought in Vietnam and is currently divorced, squad leader Lieutenant John Stillman seems not to have any significant background. The detectives' very essence is to "speak for the dead." They are what they do. Everything else is secondary to their goal. While the detectives are neither neurotically driven nor obsessive/compulsive, their jobs are their missions. These are dedicated people, but they are not fanatics. Their task is to right terrible wrongs done to victims by uncovering the identity of their murderers. They don't simply collect their paychecks, nor do they tilt at windmills. Because their focus is on solving the heretofore unsolved mystery, their personal lives simply do not factor importantly into the equation. Details about their personal lives slowly emerge as this series matures only because, following Hume's rule, TV audiences are not content to allow these issues to forever remain silent.

In the real world, many murder victims' relatives never find psychological relief from the burden of hurt and loss that carry around with them. In *Cold Case*, the murder victims themselves seem not to have this problem. They may be dead, but they are not traumatized! They do not become vengeful harpies. Their afterlife apparitions seem satisfied at the end of the show by the results of the team's investigations. The apparitions of the dead usually make eye contact at the end of the story with the squad's detective, and give a nod of approval to signify a job well done. Whether surviving friends and family are equally satisfied by the successful outcomes is usually not shown. There is no question of some abstract philosophical issue of justice at stake here and there is never a payback time. The victims' mindset is best categorized by the concept of satisfaction. Ironically, the deceased "get a life" after their deaths.

Philosophically, there are a number of questions raised by the format of *Cold Case* plot lines. Concerning closure, how can a dead person find psychological closure in any outcome? The dead party is, after all, *dead*. Dead people do not have any psychological desires, let alone ones for justice or personal vindication. Because they don't exist anymore, they cannot take personal satisfaction in having their murders solved. The deceased do not need to "get a life" after death. They only exist in the mind's eye of the cold case detectives, who imagine what the victim would have said if she could. But this viewpoint pays insufficient attention to the plight of the dead. It also ignores the conclusions of episodes such as "Daniela" (Episode 26) and "Forever Blue" (Episode 79), in which the shades of the dead cavort with their living lovers unobserved by the cold case squad. The dead have been wronged by having their lives cut short. It is up to the detectives—fairy godpersons, one and all—to right these terrible wrongs from the victims' viewpoint.

The proper response to the tiresome truth that the dead cannot be truly compensated for what has been taken from them is that *Cold Case* is an exercise in fictional storytelling, and a romantic one at that. In the world view of the series, mere facts cannot trump hope. Contrary to reality, our culture's set of hopes does not simply view a dead person as dead, if death is understood to be total annihilation. Phrases like "rest in peace," "rot in hell," "his blood cried out from the ground," and "he rolled over in his grave" give at least metaphorical credence to a postmortem existence. Some religions also view humans as having an afterlife. These phrases are common currency in our culture, even if it is a bit unclear what such an afterlife actually entails. But whatever it is, this afterlife cannot include an ordinary body, unless it is (re)obtained via some sort of reincarnation. Death destroys the body. That much is obvious. After all, that is what murder is all about. But does death completely destroy the person? This is not so, the argument goes, if living persons consist of more than their material bodies. Perhaps, as Plato insists, death is the separation of the body from the immortal spirit or soul. Death is then seen as a mere flesh wound.

Regardless of the metaphysical complications, a way must be found to depict the existence of this postmortem existence in a manner that living TV viewers can comprehend. Mere disembodied voices or creepy cold chills will not do it. *Cold Case* fills this need by having the deceased reappear exactly as he looked prior to his murder, only to fade away as a sort of ghostly shade once the case is solved. The deceased reappears as a normal-sized person who is seen facing the audience. He wears the very clothing he had on at the time of his death. He bears no signs of physical damage or trauma resulting from his murder. Even his clothing appears to be freshly laundered. His only limitation, aside from being dead, is that he does not speak. But he can clearly see and listen to what has just occurred, namely, the identification and arrest of his murderer. The arrest is acknowledged by the deceased's approval. The deceased does not express excitement or glee, nor is he sad. His facial expression indicates approval, but he does not jump for joy. His is more the satisfaction from a job well done. Then, turning to go, he simply fades away.

What happens next to the deceased? That is left unclear; it does not matter to the show. The deceased has expressed satisfaction that the murderer has been caught. That is enough. Whether the murderer will be legally convicted at trial does not matter to the victim. The further existence and desires of the victim are not subject for speculation, except that again, somewhat ironically, her file goes back into the same box bearing her name. It goes back on another shelf, only now on the closed case shelf. Ashes to ashes, shelf to shelf, box in, box out. Does the victim remain herself? Fairy tales end with "And they lived happily ever after." Looney Tune cartoons end with Porky Pig saying "Thhhhat's all, folks!" *Cold Case* episodes end with a fade back to the storage box. Well, all stories have to end somewhere. It may be true that death is but a journey in another, hidden country seen through a glass darkly, but the *Cold Case* audience is not going with the victim on that trip.

Romance

A romantic world view in the narrowest sense of the term is one that involves a love affair at its core. More broadly speaking, it is one that involves a picturesque exaggeration or embellishment of its core story line to suggest that wonderfully interesting things have occurred or are going to occur to its participants. The search for true happiness is the motor that drives the vehicle of romance. Happiness as the fulfillment of one's essence is the goal of the romantic journey.

In his *Symposium*, Plato depicts perfectly the romantic world view. It seems that originally humans had four arms and legs, two sets of genitals, and two sets of faces on the opposite sides of their head. Unfortunately, the original humans got too big for their britches, and in a fit of hubris they decided to storm the heavens and evict the gods. To prevent this, Apollo sliced them in half lengthwise, leaving them with only two arms and two legs. He then moved the remaining face around to the "front" so that the disfigured could see the terrible dismemberment for themselves. Alas, this left each surviving "person" with a desperate longing for its missing other half. Thus human life consists of the quest for our missing "other half," the presence of which is necessary to restore us to our properly completed self. Without our other half we humans remain incomplete. Apollo then relocated our genitals around to the front so that with all the hugging and kissing going on, humans could at least reproduce the species.

The romantic world view sees the present human condition as incomplete. We are currently divided from ourselves. Happiness is understood to be the fulfillment of a deep personal longing for the completion of one's being, achievable only by the reunification with one's missing other half. Key to the romantic journey is the insistence that personal completion, while possible, is fraught with difficulty. Life is a struggle. Impediments to the fulfillment of one's self present a serious stumbling block to its successful completion, though strenuous efforts can overcome these impediments. The stumbling blocks preventing romantic fulfillment are usually external to the protagonist, such as a jail cell, or a rival for the affections of one's missing other half, or a life cut short. They can also be internal as in the case of conflicts between heartfelt desires and perceived social responsibilities. The protagonist's sincere desire for complete fulfillment must always be involved, not merely the achievement of some trivial concerns. The protagonist's very essence is at stake, the complete blossoming of which can only be obtained after the removal of these internal or external impediments. This perspective is perfectly captured by Jerry Stone in "Yo, Adrian" (Episode 35), who can best be imagined as echoing Marlon Brando's famous lament to Lee J. Cobb in *On the Waterfront*, "I could have been a contender. I could have been somebody."

"Discretion" (Episode 33) presents the character of Greg Vizcaino who, like Brando's famous character, could have been someone. He could have been a candidate for local public office in New Haven, or statewide office in Connecticut, but his life is tragically cut short when he is viciously stabbed twelve times in the streets of north Philadelphia. As an assistant DA, Vizcaino incurs the wrath of his own detective, who arrested the wrong man and framed him for murder. In his quest for justice, Vizcaino traces an eyewitness to that murder to Philadelphia. Rather than allow Vizcaino's noble efforts to pay off, Detective Salvador Martin viciously ends Vizcaino's life. The cold case squad, Cupid's little minions, labor throughout the episode to show that Vizcaino is neither a drug addict nor a sexual exploiter of young boys, but a true and just and noble public servant who dies in the pursuit of the real killer in the case he was prosecuting. At the end of the episode justice triumphs. Vizcaino's real character and reputation are rightfully restored to him, the innocent victim of Detective Martin's railroading is released from prison into the loving arms of his mother, and the true rapists and killers of the dead girl are arrested. Eros indeed conquers all.

Romance stories commonly involve sexual attraction between the main characters. In "The House," Hank Dempsey lands in jail after stealing a pair of boots for his true love, Bobbi Olsen. Rather than serve out his light sentence, he attempts escape time and again in order to be with her. He cannot live without her. In the end, he kills his prison friend, Johnny McCoin, in an escape tunnel when Johnny tries to steal Bobbi away from him. After successfully escaping, Hank and Bobbi lead a perfect married life together until the cold case squad uncover the truth about them. Undaunted, Hank escapes to a foreign country to await his reunion with Bobbi at the conclusion of the episode.

"Forever Blue" also illustrates the theme of the sexual attraction between its protagonists, though with a twist—the protagonists are two men struggling with their sexual attraction to each other. Set in 1968, and shown in black, white, and red flashbacks, cowboy street cop Sean Cooper and his partner Jimmy Bruno share more than just a patrol car. Their blossoming sexual attraction is socially forbidden, however, and they suffer the harassment commonly inflicted on gay men during that time period. They were cops and cops are "real men." Real men cannot be gay, so Cooper's partner Jimmy has a difficult time accepting his affection for his partner. Shortly before Cooper's violent shotgun slaying, a conflicted Jimmy rejects Cooper's advances and vows to get a new partner. Cooper's dying words were, "Jimmy, we're the lucky ones. Don't forget that." These words will haunt Jimmy for the rest of his life. Detective Rush prods Jimmy to accept and embrace that fact. "Coop was right. That kind of love comes around once in a lifetime. You've got to hold on to it or you'll lose it. We're the lucky ones." Rush's point is quintessentially romantic. In this episode's poignant dénouement, sixty-year-old Jimmy is able to share one last hand touch with the shade of the slain Cooper, a notable break from *Cold Case's* usual ending. . . .

Romance story lines do not require a sexual component to be truly romantic. While sexual desires, especially those between male and female lovers, are common in romantic story lines, they are not essential. It's not all Bogart to Bergman, "Here's looking at you, kid," of *Casablanca* fame. What is essential to romance is the protagonist's recognition that he is an incomplete person and that he will never be a complete person until he reunites with his missing other half. One can be romantically attracted to a political or religious ideology, a career, or an arduous and difficult task. Think of Don Quixote, for example. Also, because the romantic world view need not include sexual attraction, there is no age limit imposed on romantic pairing. Eight-year-olds Melanie and Cherise are friends forever in "The Fireflies," although our culture would be troubled by a romantic sexual attachment between them because their age does not make them fit subjects for the expression of sexual interests.

The key thing is that the completion of one's true essence can only be found in the struggle for personal fulfillment. The romantic's goal is to be true to one's self. Misery is the recognition of our incomplete nature; happiness is found only in the overcoming of the impediments to our goal. We are restored to our essential self only by overcoming these obstacles, only by being "friends forever."

In "Who's Your Daddy?" (Episode 28), we see another example of a fairy tale romance that did not involve sexuality as it is commonly understood. Channary Dhiet, its lead character, is a member of the Cambodian royal family who flees Cambodia after its fall to communism. In America she and her husband assume the Dhiet identity to escape deportation and certain death at the hands of the Khmer Rouge. All that remains of their royal heritage is a solitary gold bracelet, which is stolen when they are both murdered in their home in 1991. In 2006, their daughter, Kara, who was six at the time of their deaths, sees that very same bracelet for sale on eBay and gets the cold case team to reexamine her parents' unsolved murder. The squad discovers Channary's royal heritage, a heritage she never relinquished even when she was reduced to working as a seamstress. Channary never forgot her special attachment to her lost royal heritage, and her daughter Kara is robbed of that heritage when her parents are murdered just as surely as Channary was robbed of her royal bracelet. Indeed, Kara is unaware of her own royalty until Detective Rush uncovers it for her. At the end of the episode, the murderer is discovered and the bracelet is returned to Kara, thus restoring her heritage and partially fulfilling her dead mother's royal wishes for her daughter.

Romantic sexual relations may be between males and females, as in "The House," or between members of the same sex, as in "Forever Blue" and "It's Raining Men," but romance also may concern desires shared by groups of individuals, as in "Red Glare" (Episode 31). In this episode, a primary school teacher, Elliot Garvey, is murdered on the same day that Julius and Ethel Rosenberg are executed for alleged spying for the Soviet Union. Like the Rosenbergs, Garvey is suspected of being a communist. He is active in the early civil rights movement and this activity leads to his death, although in fact he is murdered by a friend who believes that Garvey is a rival for the hand of an Eastern Block refugee, Reina Kraus. But Garvey is only in love with justice; he was not in love with Reina Kraus.

Romantic love would still be romantic without a sexual component. The important thing for romance is not sex but a deeply felt yearning for fulfillment. The persons involved must experience their situation as a longing, even a desperate longing, for the desired object. Religious or political passions serve this function equally as well as sexuality. A longing for one's proper place can be romantic. A longing for one's homeland, hometown, or old house, or for "the good old days," also can be properly classified as romantic, provided it is sincere and experienced as the fulfillment of one's basic identity.

Romantic tales such as this can focus on restoring the past or building a new and brighter future. In another example of this theme, "Factory Girls," Alice, a housewife, is tempted by the country's need for war workers in 1943 and takes a job building B-25s while her husband serves overseas in the armed forces. After working for six months, Alice Miller refuses to return to her traditional role as a housewife when her husband returns home disabled from the war. Like Channary in "Who's Your Daddy?" Alice wants to "be all she can be." She too wants to be a contender. She is accidentally killed by her own husband, however. In his fumbling attempts to "shake some sense into her," he unwittingly knocks her off the catwalk where they are standing and she falls to her death on the factory floor precisely at the spot where she had sought her own self-fulfillment.

In "The River" (Episode 68), emergency room physician Grant Bowen dies in 1984. A gambling addict, he has a poker-playing friend, Cyrus Tisdale, kill him so that Grant's son, Jason, can get the money to go to medical school. Grant believes his death will somehow send him into the great gambling house in the sky where he can fulfill his poker-playing dreams. Being a terrific ER doctor wasn't enough for him. "I'm just a glorified electrician," he says of his medical skills after saving someone's life.

"The Lost Soul of Herman Lester" (Episode 17) presents another example of nonsexual romantic fulfillment. When the son of a murdered high-school basketball star receives a death threat, Rush and Valens reopen the 1987 case of Herman Lester, who was stabbed to death only hours after leading his team to winning the state championship. Herman's essence was to be a great basketball player. Which college he should attend to achieve that goal was unclear. His son was also a great basketball player who, courted by colleges and the pros alike just like his father, also may lead his team to a state championship. Will fate also deny him the romantic fulfillment his father inspired to achieve?

"Debut" (Episode 59) offers both sexual and nonsexual romance. Its heroine, eighteen-year-old Emma Vine, dies in 1968, apparently by accident, the night of her debutante ball. In 2005 her mother comes forth with new evidence when a local art dealer, Travis Steinholz, is accused of murdering his wife in the same manner that Emma died. He was present at Emma's death in 1968. Did Emma accidentally fall down a flight of stairs, breaking every bone in her body, or did Travis push her? Emma wanted to go to college at Harvard and study physics. She wanted to achieve fulfillment by working for NASA like her father when she met and lost her heart to rich society scion Travis, who himself had to fight being ostracized to achieve his dreams because he was Jewish in a WASP culture. The music, Henry Mancini's *Moon River*, provides a perfect accompaniment for the romantic mood of the cotillion at which Emma meets her death.

In "The Hen House," the cold case squad reopens the 1945 case of a murdered newspaper reporter when new evidence suggests that the victim was thrown in front of a passing train by someone she knew. Noah Pool and Lo Kinney were in love, but neither could escape Noah's criminal Nazi past once Lo uncovers it. After Lo's death, Noah becomes a reclusive romantic painter who forever mourns her. He tells Rush, "Lo was my second chance after so much darkness. I came here to start over and there she was [my] light. When she died, though, that light went out for good." His paintings always depict her loss so that as an artist at least he achieved a secondary sort of happiness.

In "Beautiful Little Fool," the case of Violet Polley, killed in 1929, is reopened by her great-granddaughter. A working class girl and aspiring song writer, Violet falls in love with rich ne'er-do-well Nick Bartleby, who is attracted by her looks, her song writing talent, and her lively personality. After impregnating her, he renounces paternity of their daughter and throws them both out of his life. Violet's torch song, "Three Hundred Flowers," plays a key role in setting the romantic mood of this case as well as in helping to resolve it. Violet first sings it from atop a piano. She dies reaching for her daughter, whose granddaughter believed she had abandoned. That infant daughter is then raised by washed-up actress Carmela La Fleur, who achieves her own personal fulfillment not in the theater, but as the surrogate mother of Violet's child. In the end, Grand Dame Muriel Bartleby "restores" Violet's place within the Bartleby family by writing the names of Violet and her descendents into the family tree book.

"Daniela" offers another interesting wrinkle on pure romance. It concerns a 1979 case of what was thought to be a murdered prostitute. It turns out that Jane Doe (Daniela Ruis) is really a transvestite with whom Chris Taylor falls in love before realizing that "she" is really a "he." The discovery of Daniela's true identity does not present an impediment for Chris, although Daniela tragically commits suicide when she incorrectly believes that Chris has rejected her. At the end of the episode, Chris is seen dancing with Daniela, his one true love, to their love song as they both would have wished had she lived.

All *Cold Case* episodes are really versions of the same thing. No crimes are ever portrayed merely as sordid events. They, are all tragedies. Their victims all have their lives cut short by their deaths, but happily, that is not the end for the victims. Real happiness is somehow obtainable for the dead person. This happiness might be obtained via a love affair in the traditional sense of that term or by the recognition of the nobility of the dead person's lifelong goals. In the end, real happiness comes to the victim when her murderer is caught or uncovered. Like Cupid's little helpers, the cold case squad is there to snatch victory from the jaws of apparent defeat. The victim's reincarnated self appears at the end of the story to put her seal of approval on its outcome, to bask in her delayed, but not finally denied, restored essence.

In the *Cold Case* series, closure is found through the reawakening of bittersweet memories for the living and the dead alike. The detective work involved in unraveling these mysteries exists primarily to reawaken these memories so that the final chapters in the victims' stories can be told at last.

Suggested Reading

Plato's views on personal dualism and romantic love are found in his *Phaedo* and *Symposium* (*circa* 380 BCE).

CHAPTER 3

WITHOUT A TRACE: WHERE'S WALDO?

"Don't make a federal case out of it!" is an angry retort often heard in school-yards between squabbling children trying to neutralize their opponents' taunts. *Without a Trace* does just that, it makes a federal case out of it. Unlike the other police procedurals discussed in this book, *Without a Trace* is a TV series devoted to federal law enforcement.

Television has traveled the federal law enforcement route before. Shows ranging from NBC's *Gang Busters* (1952), to ABC's *The Untouchables* (1959–1963) and *The FBI* (1965–1974), to CBS's current *Criminal Minds* have devoted themselves to crime fighting from the federal point of view. Police procedurals devoted to federal law enforcement, however, represent a distinct minority in the extended family of TV cops and robbers. Changing social attitudes toward the law enforcement powers of the federal government can either float or sink the ship of federal crime-fighting dramas. In our post-9/11 era, federal law enforcement is again popular, and *Without a Trace* is steaming along full speed.

Although there are many crimes that rank as federal offenses, *Without a Trace* devotes itself to the narrow issue of missing persons—persons who may have been kidnapped. The U.S. Congress made kidnapping a federal crime in response to the infamous Lindbergh kidnapping case of 1932. That "crime of the century" became a media circus that so galvanized public opinion that state laws against kidnapping were no longer considered to be a sufficient deterrent to such abhorrent activity. In response to the public outcry sur-rounding the kidnapping of the Lindbergh baby, Congress passed the Federal Kidnapping Act, which originally was intended to allow federal authorities to pursue kidnappers after they had crossed state lines with their victims. Although the Lindbergh legislation placed severe restrictions on conditions that must be satisfied to make kidnapping a federal case, the producers of *Without a Trace*, for dramatic purposes, choose to let their fictitious federal agents pursue any and all sorts of missing persons cases.

Missing person cases are always handled by local police authorities first, followed by state authorities. In New York City, the nominal location for most of this series' episodes, that means the NYPD and then the New York State

Bureau of Investigations. But *Without a Trace* shows so little interest in the local authorities that they are seldom ever mentioned in any of the episodes. For the sake of its story lines, *Without a Trace's* missing persons cases are reported only to the FBI. The show makes no attempt to depict the FBI's interface with local law enforcement officials, who seem to hold the same status as the Bureau's clean-up personnel. The place is clean, so they must have been there at some time or other. In a like manner, the TV viewer occasionally sees an NYPD cop car involved in a scene, so the police must have been on site somewhere, but darned if we ever see them in action.

In Season One, "Fall Out" (Episodes 22 and 23) illustrates perfectly the invisibility of local police in this series. In the first part (Episode 22), Barry Mashburn kidnaps Sidney Harrison because Sidney made Barry's wife come to work on time on 9/11, when she was killed in the World Trade Center attack. The death of his wife so unhinges Barry that he never recovers. An increasingly despondent Barry is fired from his job and Sidney Harrison, an employment consultant, cannot find him a new one. FBI Special Agent Samantha "Sam" Spade shows up in a local bookstore to exchange the ransom money for Sidney. In the bookstore things go terribly wrong and Barry takes everyone hostage. At the end of Episode 22, Sam is accidentally shot with her own gun. What is noteworthy here is that the NYPD SWAT team and hostage negotiation officer never appear in these episodes. It was entirely a federal affair, handled by the fictitious New York FBI Missing Persons Squad. In Episode 23, FBI squad chief Special Agent Jack Malone exchanges himself for the wounded Sam and talks Barry into releasing all of the hostages and surrendering. Sidney is then found alive and uninjured in a storage rental space where Barry has stashed her.

"Our Sons and Daughters" (Episode 29) features missing suburban teenager Ethan Sawyer. Phil Damore is the chief of police of this pseudo-suburb of New York City. Chief Damore takes an active roll in the investigation of Sawyer's disappearance; as well he should, since he is the very person who has accidentally strangled Ethan to death. At the end of the episode, our team of stalwart investigators brings to light Damore's role in Sawyer's death and discovers Sawyer's body. Viewers of this series would be right to assume that whenever local police characters are specifically depicted they are up to no good. Not inevitably, however. Sometimes the missing person himself is a cop, and a good cop at that.

In "Lone Star" (Episode 64), Lance Norwood is a sheriff from Nassau County, Long Island, who goes undercover posing as realtor "Lance Hamilton" in order to infiltrate a gang of criminals led by Leo Pelosi. This gang has enticed young women from Romania to "work" in New York City, work that amounts to enforced prostitution, so-called white slavery. Pelosi brutally murders one of the girls, fifteen-year-old Nadia Cosesque, when it appears to him that she has attempted to escape. In reality, Nadia was actually trying to help Sheriff Norwood identify the mysterious Mr. Big, a shadowy leader of the

Pelosi mob. Norwood is so upset by the evil deeds of Pelosi's gang that he single-handedly rescues six of the girls from Pelosi's grasp and makes a run for it with them. After it becomes clear that "Lance Hamilton" is really one of the good guys, Malone reneges on his vow to "kick his ass." At the episode's conclusion, the team arrests Pelosi and tracks down Hamilton to reunite him with his frightened wife Beth. The episode never identifies Mr. Big, but suggests that the Norwoods need to go into hiding to avoid retribution for the damage inflicted on the Pelosi mob of sex slave traders.

As *Without a Trace* unfolds, Paula Van Doran, the boss of Special Agent Jack Malone, offers little help in solving the missing person cases being investigated in each episode. Either she never appears in an episode, which is most common, or if she does, her function is to interfere in the investigation or to chastise someone on the team for somehow messing up. Like the character of Conrad Eckley in *CSI*, Van Doran's role primarily is to get in the way. This is well illustrated in "White Balance" (Episode 93). In this episode, two teenagers are missing, a white girl, Emily Grant, and a black boy, Darnell Williams. Van Doran forces Jack Malone to devote more resources to finding the girl, which results in lots of leads for her case and few for Darnell's case. Jack admits to Darnell's mother Audrey that "We now have more leads than we know how to deal with." To which Audrey replies, "My black son's life isn't worth as much as that white girl's." That seems to be true as far as the investigation went, but it is not Jack's doing. It was a procedure Paula Van Doran forces on Jack against his better judgment. As the episode unfolds, no good reasons are ever presented for focusing the team's resources on finding Emily Grant. The issue was handled simply as the boss's decision and it was up to Jack to deal with it and especially to deal with Darnell's mother Audrey, who had every reason to complain.

The same thing can be said for federal officials working for other organizations. One way or another they are up to no damned good. "Midnight Sun" (Episode 10) depicts this perspective. In it Greg Pritchard, who is really Peter Raymond, witnesses a mob hit. After testifying at the trial of the mobster responsible for the murder, he enters the federal witness protection program where he is hidden for twelve years. Now the very people who were handling him want him to retestify at the new trial of the mobster, thus blowing his cover and putting his life at risk again. To frighten him, they make it seem as if the mobster is on to him. As a result, Pritchard takes his young daughter and runs. After the usual intrepid investigation, the team discovers that he was in the witness protection program, a discovery not aided by the people running the program.

Interdepartmental cooperation among various branches of law enforcement is a misnomer in this series, where officials often work at cross-purposes. In "In Extremis" (Episode 9), Dr. Anwar Samir, a Saudi medical doctor, is suspected of being a terrorist. Dr. Samir actually is one of the good guys who tries to evacuate a hospital in which Kamal el Dudai, the real terrorist, has planted a bomb. At the end of the episode Special Agent Martin Fitzgerald confronts Dr. Samir on the ground floor of Lord's Hospital, which by then is surrounded by the NYPD, the FBI, and members of the Joint Terrorism Task Force (JTTF). Abner Harrington, the leader of the JTTF, sees Samir, who is telling Fitzgerald, "I was just trying to get everyone out of the building." Harrington thinks Samir has a gun in his hand, and encourages Jack Malone to order the FBI's sniper to take out Samir. "You know the practice. We don't have a choice." Hearing this, Malone orders the shooting of Samir, who dies in vain in front of his girlfriend and Fitzgerald. Even these "good guys" of the JTTF are not on the side of the good guys.

Every police procedural needs a hook, an identifying mark that distinguishes it from other police procedurals and makes it unique. Interagency cooperation is not the hook in this series, though to be fair, neither is it the hook in any other series. In *Without a Trace*, the hook is the time line. As FBI team leader Jack Malone says in commercials for this series, "It's all about the time line."

But is it really? The notion of a time line appeals to the American imagination. We are an impatient nation, a nation always in a hurry. When problems arise, we want immediate results; when major problems arise, we want them solved yesterday. In British versions of police procedurals, the detectives have a saying: "Early days." This means the criminal investigation is in its beginning stages and no real progress should be expected yet. Answering the who-dunit question is going to be quite an effort, and as the saying goes, "Rome wasn't built in a day." In World War II during the D-Day landing in Normandy, American soldiers embedded as liaisons with British infantry and tank forces were astonished when, in the absence of appreciable German resistance, British soldiers stopped in their tracks around four o'clock to brew up cups of tea. When impatient American commanders asked why the English forces had stopped short of the day's objective of Caen, the British troops gave the nonchalant reply, "It's tea time." Their mindset cautioned patience and perseverance, whether in the war against fascists on French soil or in the war against criminals on British soil. Piece by careful piece, like his soldier counterpart, the British detective will systematically gather evidence, put it together, and discover whose picture emerges from the ensemble. The only component a British detective series and *Without a Trace* have in common is the final ensemble. How they arrive at the solution is a whole other cup of tea.

Why is the symbolic ticking clock so important for *Without a Trace*? Unlike the standard murder case, there is no dead body with which to begin the investigation. Instead there is a missing body, a missing person, a person who may still be alive whose very life is of ultimate importance. Every tick of the clock puts that missing body further at risk or so it would seem.

Indeed, *Without a Trace* has an episode that fits this pattern. In "Party Girl" (Episode 62), spoiled heiress Chelsea Prince is a poor-little-rich-girl caught up in a life of endless, mindless good times. As Special Agent Vivian Johnson says of her, "She's famous simply for being rich and beautiful." Just when she is showing signs of growing up by volunteering to read to underprivileged children at a grade school in the Bronx, just when she is burned out on the party scene, she is kidnapped by an evil "Snidely Whiplash"-like character, Garrett Palmer, who ties her down before a live video feed, and threatens to murder her depending on the results of an Internet vote on her fate. And the vote is oh, so close! Chelsea becomes a damsel in distress, and the "Dudley Do-Rights" of the Mounties, our intrepid missing persons' team, sets off to rescue the fair "Nell" from Snidely's evil grip. A thrilling rescue it is too. They just did *Beat the Clock*!

In "Win Today" (Episode 102), Special Agent Jack Malone himself is drugged, tied up, kidnapped, and gruesomely tortured by Cynthia Neuwirth, who charmingly styles herself as "a crazy bitch with a nail gun." Cynthia's twenty-something-year-old son, Alex Stark, is missing at the start of the episode and there is a hole in the bedroom wall where his safe had been and blood on his apartment floor. He is a budding con man who has teamed up with Cynthia, who (unknown to Alex) is really his mother. She taught him the con game and Alex fakes his own kidnapping to con her, a "kidnapping" that Cynthia mistakenly believes was committed by Brendon Dillon, a person Cynthia once conned out of $80,000 in Boston. To find the "missing" Alex, Malone goes undercover at a gambling den frequented by Alex and Cynthia. Malone's undercover assignment at the gambling den is treated with much light-hearted amusement by the rest of the team, which sets up an office pool to bet on exactly how much of the government's money Malone will lose at poker. The team does not discover Malone's kidnapping until late in the episode, so there is scant running time left to depict the rush to find him. Ironically, even after being tortured by Cynthia, Jack is able to reconstruct Alex's actions for her, so sympathetically that she realizes she too has been conned, and by her own son. She fills with pride, knowing that her boy has "done good." At the end of the episode, Cynthia is shot dead by an out-of-sight NYPD rescue team, Alex is arrested, and a very bloodied but unbowed Jack Malone staggers off to celebrate victory of a sorts—*24* this is not.

Alas, a couple of swallows do not a summer make. It is not the breathlessness of "Party Girl," but the indolence of "Win Today," that carries over to the rest of the series' episodes. "Party Girl" is a complete anomaly. "Win Today" is closer to the psychological norm for this series. In "Pilot" (Episode 1), missing persons team leader, Special Agent Jack Malone, tells new team member Martin Fitzgerald, "In most cases after 48 hours, they're gone [for good]." But this remark should not be interpreted to mean "going, going, gone."

Each episode opens with a scene that introduces the case. In this scene the soon-to-be missing person is seen in his or her normal haunts, and then in a kind of reverse *Cold Case* manner, that character vanishes "without a trace." Subsequent scenes carry tagged temporal markers—"4 hours missing," "6 hours missing," "31 hours missing"—all coupled with nicely ominous music, marking the time elapsed between the missing person's initial disappearance and the eventual recovery. The ominous musical effects and the mazelike aerial shots of a teeming metropolis, would seem to build tension as they convey to the viewer a sense of the awesome difficulties the team faces in finding the missing person.

But as "Win Today" illustrates, tension does not build this way. This TV series is not about breathlessness. If that was the main focus, the show's "ticking clock" should tick *down* to zero from that fabled forty-eight-hour parameter that FBI Special Agent Jack Malone established in "Pilot." But the clock does not tick down in this manner.

There is a symbol even more important to the gestalt of this series than the vaunted time line. It is that aerial view of the teeming metropolis. When *Without a Trace* displays the passage of time from the onset of the missing person's disappearance, the captions "17 hours missing," "22 hours missing," and so forth, are superimposed on aerial shots of New York City or one of its suburbs. Each shot lasts mere seconds as it is used to introduce a new scene in the episode. Other than the aerial view of the actual federal office building in New York City that houses the New York branch of the FBI, there are two kinds of reoccurring aerial shots, those that look straight down at the ground and those that look off in a distance. Shots aimed straight down display New York's sky-scrapers as they are seen by a bird of prey as it slowly wheels overhead. They are meant to portray the Grand-Canyon-like nature of Manhattan. Distance shots are similarly designed to show the breadth of the territory from the bird of prey's vantage point. Both wonderfully convey the sheer dimensions, the sheer complexities of the search for a missing person, and they convey this far more effectively than the time line can ever do. "Where, oh where, is Waldo?"

These birds-of-prey aerial shots are a superb metaphor for the search for a missing person. Simultaneously, they convey two opposing viewpoints. The first is one of omniscience. Seeing things from the bird's point of view as it circles the city seeking its intended target puts the viewer in the lap of God. The viewer now knows what it is like to see things from on high, peering down on people who look so tiny and insignificant in their strivings. Nothing escapes one's view. Being above it all, the bird of prey sees into earthbound lives at will. There is nothing you can do to escape his all-seeing eye, which peers through petty mortals to the depths of their souls.

On the other hand, the sheer amount of detail thrown into the vision of the circling bird of prey shows just how daunting his task really is. Who could possibly find a single specific person in all that confusion? Like searching for a needle in a haystack, it is an impossible dream, a hopeless task, an unreachable goal. Even the mighty Hercules would throw up his hands at this impossible labor of finding our single missing person in such an urban jungle.

Essentialism

If *Without a Trace* is not really about the ticking clock but about the circling bird of prey seeking its target in the modern American urban jungle, how is it ever possible to find those who have gone missing "without a trace?" The answer given by this police procedural is that the missing person can be located only by discovering what makes that person really tick, discovering the hidden essence of that missing person, his essential self, as manifested by his dynamic emotional tensions and their satisfaction and release. In a nutshell, that is the problem-solving strategy of *Without a Trace.*

Since the days of classical Greek philosophy, thinkers such as Plato and Aristotle have defended a specific metaphysical doctrine for understanding the ultimate nature of reality. This doctrine is the *substance/attribute view of reality.* *Substances* are the basic building blocks of reality. They are the things that are most real. Thinkers such as Democritus held that all substances were material atoms. Thinkers such as Plato held that there are also immaterial, psychological substances—minds and souls. Aristotle and others held that substances are just specific individuals, such as the old dog "Cinder" or a brand new tennis shoe or the pizza someone ate for lunch yesterday. Regardless of their views about the ultimate nature of all substances, these philosophers distinguished the substance itself from the characteristics that applied to it, which are its *attributes.* "Cinder," for example, is a dog (substance), but he also has the attributes of being black and having short hair and barking at the moon. A shoe is a shoe (substance) but it is also a white running shoe, size eleven. A pizza is a meal (substance), but it is also thin-crusted, round, and piping hot. Black, short haired, white, size eleven, round, piping hot, etc., are the attributes of specific substances. They modify the substances to which they are attached. The attributes depend on the substances for their existence. Attributes cannot exist by themselves. They exist only insofar as they are modifications of substances.

Some of these attributes are essential to the substances they modify and others are only accidental. Essential attributes make a substance what it is, and they make a specific kind of substance the specific individual it is. Essential attributes make the dog "Cinder" a *dog* and not a cat or an aardvark. They also make the dog "Cinder" the specific dog whose name is "Cinder," and not "Fido," "Rover," or "Rex." Accidental attributes only provide additional information about the subjects they modify. "Cinder" the dog must have the attributes that make him the *dog Cinder,* but the dog "Cinder" does not have to be prone to barking at the moon. He could jolly well shut up at night and let all of us sleep in peace.

What is the point of this substance/attribute distinction? Its point is that *Without a Trace* is a whodunit that turns on the efforts of a detective team of FBI special agents—Herculean birds of prey—to locate a specific missing person. From the show's point of view, the subject they seek is essentially a *missing* person, a *Waldo.* Right in front of the viewers' eyes, the missing person turns into the very person whose essence it is to be missing. Whoosh! Viewers literally see the drama of it. She is not simply a person whose spouse or friends don't know her accidental location at a specific moment. Everyone is a "missing person" in that trivial sense of the word. The team of FBI special agents has no interest in locating people who simply happen to be momentarily out of sight. They are only interested in locating persons whose essence is to be missing, those who have essentially vanished "without a trace."

Furthermore, from the perspective of this TV police procedural, a missing person is missing because of a specific essential characteristic that uniquely shapes his identity. Each missing person disappearance is linked to secret emotional factors, deeply felt emotional desires, which are either completely hidden from that person's friends, family, or co-workers, or are at most known to a very few. These secret emotional desires give that person his identity. In "Pilot," Maggie Cartwright may appear to be a different person to each person who knew her. As Jack says of her, "Everyone we talk to, we see a different Maggie." But in her heart of hearts, she was essentially that person who emotionally longed to be the free-spirited lass who once roamed Nepal. It was only in Nepal where she could be her true self. And it was only by uncovering this significant, essential (but secret), emotional attribute about her identity as the specific missing person Maggie Cartwright, an emotional attribute that drove her actions, an emotional attribute that made her "tick," that the FBI missing persons' team could discover her location.

In "Pilot," team leader Jack Malone establishes the central problem-solving procedure that reappears in each subsequent episode of *Without a Trace*. It is this: "We gotta work [this case] from the inside out. If we find out who she is, the odds are that we'll find out where she is." Only by finding out *who* Maggie Cartwright really is in her secret heart can the team locate her after she goes missing. To find out who she is the team must uncover the essential emotional components that made Maggie Cartwright the kind of person she was, that moved her soul. To accomplish this, the team has to uncover a great deal of information about what emotionally made her the kind of person she was. The team interviews the people who knew Maggie best: her parents, her siblings, her friends, and her co-workers. Only they possessed, albeit unknowingly, the key informational pieces necessary to unlocking the secret life of Maggie Cartwright.

There are two kinds of missing persons in *Without a Trace*: the voluntarily missing and the involuntarily missing. If a person is missing voluntarily, the team's job is to discover the hidden emotional factors that caused the missing person to do a runner. If a person is not missing voluntarily, if he was a kidnapping victim for example, then the detective team must determine the secret essential attributes of the victim that motivated, occasioned, or allowed his kidnapper to kidnap him. The key to finding the kidnap victim is not primarily to find out about the emotional life of the kidnapper. The emotional life of the kidnapper is usually a secondary issue. It is the emotional life of the kidnapped victim that makes him vulnerable to being kidnapped.

The ancient Greeks dramatists had a saying, "Character is destiny." *Without a Trace* adopts this perspective as its mantra. The emotional nature of the missing person is the prime factor in turning her into a *missing* person, a

Waldo. Everything else is secondary. One upshot of this viewpoint is that the normal range of factors that collide haphazardly around her on a daily basis are inconsequential in establishing her true identity. Those manifold collisions are only accidental issues that don't affect her real identity.

"All the Sinners, Saints" (Episode 101) presents a great case for *essentialism*. In it Katie Duncan goes missing after an exorcism. Katie is mentally ill. She is afflicted with an unspecified illness such as schizophrenia or paranoia. If "character" is destiny, then Katie is doubly cursed. She is a *missing person* in many senses of the term. She is well enough at times to know that she is ill, and her inability to control her illness torments her even more than the illness itself. Katie's loving mom and brother are at their own wit's end emotionally over her. When Special Agents Vivian Johnson and Martin Fitzgerald react skeptically to Father Robert McGuinness's claim that "Only God can cast the evil out [of Katie]," her mom responds in desperation, "What harm can it do?"

Unfortunately, Katie's delusions drive her to believe that her boss, Chris Buchanan, is attracted to her. Knowing that Chris is engaged to marry Tracy Harrison, and seeing Tracy as a rival for Chris's "affections," Katie confronts Tracy in the parking garage of the building where Tracy works and kills her. In exasperation, Agent Johnson asks of her actions, "What? The devil made her do it?" Tragically, the exorcism allows Katie to recognize the very evil that her illness drove her to commit. At the end of the episode, believing that her case is hopeless, Katie commits suicide by slashing her wrists in her bathtub. In a scene straight out of *Cold Case*, Agent Fitzgerald sees Katie's ghost recede from his presence. How sad was this whole situation.

Of course, all of this "essentialistic" moping about may be complete hogwash. This perspective is one of many possible in the nature or nurture debate. Do individuals really have unique identities that are constant and unchanging throughout long periods of their lifetimes? Essentialism says they do. But the opposite position, known as *existentialism*, argues that individuals craft their identities by the choices they make and the goals they affirm. To existentialists, individuals always have the capacity to reinvent themselves at any time, to remake their identity from scratch. Existentialism sees human nature as highly plastic, not subject to the rigid strictures of necessary attributes claimed by essentialists, and certainly not subject to the deep-seated emotional baggage that *Without a Trace* brings into focus. Missing persons have simply chosen to go missing for any number of reasons, good or bad. They can choose to go "unmissing" just as easily. Kidnappers kidnap their victims for many reasons that have nothing to do with the dark, emotional issues lying deep within their victims' psyches. If he chose to, even Graham Spaulding, a recurring villain in *Without a Trace*, could get off of his torture and murder kick; even *he* could "get a life." Nor must it be the case that an "essentialist" analysis of human nature commits anyone to viewing human essence as being primarily emotional. While Sigmund Freud famously saw humans as driven by the power of the irrational id and David Hume thought reason should be the slave to passion, philosophers such as Aristotle, Rene Descartes, and Immanuel Kant argued that humans are primarily rational creatures. Maybe humans are essentially rational animals, as the ancient Greeks believed. Maybe as Plato thought, humans can use their power of reason to control their often unruly emotions.

Even if humans are primarily emotional animals, there is no need to adopt a quasi-Lamarckian view on personality. The French biologist Jean-Baptiste Lamarck believed in a non-Darwinian evolutionary theory that supposes that parents can acquire characteristics during their lifetimes which they then pass on to their children. In *Without a Trace*, the focus is not on the acquired characteristics passed from parent to child, but on the acquired characteristics that a person passes on to her future self. Key to the quasi-Lamarckian perspective is the view that allows a person's essence to be determined by events that happen in that person's lifetime. In *Without a Trace*, emotionally dramatic situations are believed to determine the nature of an individual's psyche for the duration of that person's lifetime. These environmental events affect the personality of the person experiencing them and make that person "essentially" the kind of person he is. They determine that person's actions, which spring from specific, hidden, emotional drives. Psychoanalysis, here we come!

Perhaps Queer Theorists have it right. "Queer Theory" is a brand-spanking-new take on an old, old issue. According to Queer Theory, *essentialism* is an ideology that imposes a rigid set of categories and distinctions on a reality that is far more diversified and fluid than essentialists would like to acknowledge. Consider "Gung Ho" (Episode 40), which featured Kevin Grant, an Army soldier wounded in Iraq. Shortly before he is wounded, he receives a "Dear John" letter from his girlfriend Sara Powers. He is also about to lose the house he inherited from his mother because he can't meet the mortgage payments. There is no Dudley Do-Right to come to his rescue. After receiving the Dear John letter he tries to get himself killed by the insurgents, but he only succeeds in getting himself wounded. Things are really rough when he is "only" wounded! At home he goes missing because he is mentally messed up by his ill luck. To raise the mortgage money, he and his buddy, Chuck Whiting, foolishly decide to rob a bank in Tyrone, Pennsylvania. During the robbery he kills a female detective. When Special Agent Danny Taylor is interviewing Sara back at Kevin's house, Kevin comes home and gets the drop on Danny.

When the FBI SWAT team surrounds the house, Kevin takes the clip out of his handgun and rushes outside to commit suicide by cop, even though Danny and Sara desperately try to talk him out of it. This emotional episode ends tragically with Kevin's death.

Did Kevin have to die? Did he have to choose suicide as the only way out of his desperate situation? The existentialist and the Queer Theorist would both reject the inevitability of Kevin's choice. To them, Kevin simply had a string of bad luck. He was not an inherently cursed individual whose essence doomed him to be miserable. Rather, Kevin was a victim of both a run of bad luck and his own stupid choices. He could have changed his luck by making different, more intelligent choices. Sara was not the only possible girlfriend for him. There were other homes to live in. He could have had a good career in the Army. Instead, he chose to commit suicide, the final and stupidest choice he ever made.

"The Calm Before" (Episode 100) presents another hard luck case, although one with a happier ending. Aaron Gibbs loses his home to Hurricane Katrina. In the process of rescuing his sons, he encounters a man whose own desperation almost causes the boat holding Aaron's sons to capsize, potentially drowning them. To save his sons, Aaron clubs the man with an oar, killing him. Later in the story, as a refugee in New Jersey, Aaron loses his job and finds his pickup truck burned out by men to whom he owes money. As Special Agent Jack Malone says of him, "Man, first flood, now fire. If it wasn't for bad luck, this guy would have no luck at all." In desperation, Aaron steals $2,000 from members of a fight club he joined to raise money. He drops out of sight, taking the money with him back to New Orleans to find the son of the man he killed while escaping Hurricane Katrina. In New Orleans he finds Jesse Lewis surviving by salvaging stuff from homes wrecked by the hurricane. Jesse Lewis is not at all happy to see Aaron, especially after Aaron tells him what happened to his father. He takes the $2,000 from Aaron, but he is not happy about that either. "I got nothing left. I got nothing," Jesse says of himself. Jesse then causes the wrecked building he is working in to collapse, pinning Aaron in the wreckage. Eventually Jack Malone rescues Aaron, although his *sub voce* utterance, "I'm too old for this crap," perfectly captures Jack's self-assessment of his Dudley Do-Right heroics.

Existentialism's point is made with a great deal of humor in "Check Your Head" (Episode 87). Danny Taylor worries that, "We're morbid, Jack." Jack Malone asks, "Why is that?" To which Danny replies, "Well, unless something really bad is happening to somebody, it just doesn't feel like a day at the office." Fortunately for the team's "day at the office," Rachel Gibson, an agoraphobic advice columnist, vanishes. After ferreting out a possible kidnapping and connections to a mob boss in Boston (who happens to be Rachel's father) Rachel is found alive and "well" lying within a pinsetting machine in a bowling alley. To Rachel's lament that "I'm an agoraphobic," Jack Malone responds ironically, "You live fifteen miles from here. You've got to be the world's worst agoraphobic." In the end, Rachel decides she can live with being a lesbian backsliding agoraphobic, and she, the cops, and the robbers all go bowling. *That's amore!*

No matter which metaphysical viewpoint about human nature is correct, many people unreflectively believe they possess a specific emotional essence that determines the kind of person they are. People believe they have a "heart of hearts" that makes up their persona. While *CSI* depicts humans as physical nuts and bolts and *Cold Case* portrays humans as romantic souls seeking their missing halves, *Without a Trace* sits squarely in the quasi-Lamarckian essentialist camp, which posits that the essential attribute of the missing person involves hidden emotions. These hidden emotional components make the missing person who he is. These attributes, and only these attributes, explain why the voluntarily missing person is missing or why the kidnapper had the occasion to kidnap the person. Only by extracting these hidden emotional components from the victim's or runaway's psyche and revealing them publicly can the team learn why the missing person is missing. This insight enables the team to locate the missing person. So goes the essential premise of this series.

The story line of "Legacy" (Episode 41) exemplifies the role played by the quasi-Lamarckian view of the missing person. Following an argument with his wife Martha, George Stanley goes missing on his way to the bank to deposit the week's receipts from Martha's beauty salon. Thirty-nine hours into his disappearance, the *Without a Trace* team is called into the investigation. Initial inspection of the rear of the beauty shop uncovers a human tooth with part of its gum attached, yet no member of the Stanley household, nor any employee of the salon, shows signs of any dental injury. Further investigation of Stanley's family members show that they are emotionally distant from one another. As Martin Fitzgerald says of them, "There's something about this family. It sure isn't love that keeps them together." Perhaps George is having an affair with a woman he has been meeting for some time at a local bar. Maybe he just ran off with her. But this proves to be a red herring. The reality behind George's disappearance is much uglier.

It turns out that Martha was raped and savagely beaten eight years ago in her bedroom by Ray Logan, who tied up a helpless George and forced him to witness these awful events. George's inability to do anything about the terrible things that happened to his wife causes him to withdraw into himself. To live with the psychological trauma, Martha herself practices a complex form of denial. Their eleven-year-old son, Sean, is also psychologically wrecked by his parents' ordeal. Unknown to George and Martha, Sean had witnessed the whole thing. So each member of the family is psychologically scarred by this traumatic event, and these scars make them the persons they are. Each is living in an abject state of denial. By age nineteen, Sean has become a drug user because of the pain he carries with him. When his supplier, Daryl Wyeth, follows Sean home to collect the thousand dollars Sean owes him, Wyeth makes the mistake of sexually assaulting Martha. In a blind rage fueled by her pent-up misery and helplessness, Martha picks up a statue and viciously clubs Wyeth to death. Upon arriving home to another scene of domestic tragedy involving his abused wife, husband George rises to the occasion this time and disposes of Wyeth's body by incinerating it in a dumpster. Subsequently, George meets his friend Layla King at the bar, where he spots Ray Logan, his wife's rapist. Moved by a newfound sense of empowerment, George later confronts Logan at his apartment and kills him in a knife fight in which George is seriously injured. After being missing for fifty-three hours, George is discovered in Logan's apartment.

Purged of the trauma from past events, the Stanly family hopefully can emerge as though each has been born again. The fact that Martha is guilty of a brutal murder, Sean is a drug addict, and George has hidden a murder, desecrated a corpse, killed another man, and himself been grievously injured in a brutal knife fight completely falls away from the scene. At the episode's end, no one is arrested. Why? Perhaps because they are now healed, an essence-changing event, and being restored to their wholeness trumps mere picky details like murder, manslaughter, and drug addiction.

Like *Cold Case*, but unlike *CSI*, the tale of a missing person like George Stanley is portrayed as a tragedy. Only an essentialist's world view can allow for tragedy. Existentialist's world views are comic. As those condemned to crucifixion in *Monty Python's Life of Brian*, sing "Always look on the bright side of life!" Is there anything more tragic than a missing person, especially when that person is vulnerable? In our culture it is terrible when an adult male goes missing, but it is worse when the missing person is an adult female. Worse still are missing teenagers and worst of all are missing children. In general, the more socially vulnerable the missing person, the greater is the tragedy of that person's disappearance. Even for those who go missing voluntarily, who run away (as is true with most missing people), it is sad that they should want to drop out of their current circumstances and seek escape from themselves, an impossible goal. It is unfortunate that they cannot handle the internal turmoil produced by circumstances beyond their control.

Without a Trace is all about the emotional turmoil that occasions the missing to run away or that puts the vulnerable in the position to be kidnapped. It is significant for a proper understanding of this series to notice the amount of attention *Without a Trace* pays to the melodramatic lives of its FBI team members. This attention is not accidental. Each team member's life is more or less an ongoing train wreck. This is not a result of bad writing, nor is it what any viewer would expect from a successful television series. *Law & Order* and *Cold Case* also pay attention to the personal lives of their series characters. Even a casual viewer of *Law & Order* knows that Detective Lennie Briscoe was an alcoholic who had a difficult relationship with his drug-addled daughter. Detective Rey Curtis had an affair that nearly wrecked his marriage and had to quit the force to take care of his ill wife, while executive assistant district attorney Jack McCoy carried a torch for assistant district attorney Claire Kincaid. *Cold Case's* Detective Lilly Rush has ongoing problems with her two gentlemen friends, her mother, and her sister; and Detective Scotty Valens was molested as a child. Even *CSI* characters have personal issues, though to be fair, they are minimally portrayed in the show. Sara Sidle's "love affair" with Gil Grissom and Catherine Willow's problems with her dad, Sam Braun, are not exactly the stuff of legends.

But the personal entanglements of the FBI team of *Without a Trace* are essential to this show's format because they are an outgrowth of its focus on emotion-laden secrets. Samantha "Sam" Spade had affairs with both Jack Malone and Martin Fitzgerald, affairs that entangled her emotional life with her professional responsibilities. Danny Taylor's brother, Rafael, is an ex-con and drug addict who threatens to drag Danny back down into his problems. Martin Fitzgerald's father not only abused him as a child but is a big-wig in the federal system who has little respect for Martin's talents and abilities. Vivian Johnson has serious heart problems. Elena Delgado, an addition to the cast midway through the fourth season, has a dirty cop husband Carlos. In the middle of a bruising custody battle with Elena, Carlos kidnaps their daughter Sophia. Then there is the leader of the pack, Special Agent Jack Malone. Jack has more personal troubles than the proverbial barrel of monkeys. His dad has Alzheimer's and eventually dies from it. His wife Maria takes a position with a Chicago law office, causing Jack to ask for a transfer to the Chicago FBI office. In the midst of all of that Maria coldly demands a divorce and threatens Jack's relationship with his two daughters. He has an affair with Sam Spade, complicating their work relationship. He is kidnapped and brutally tortured. Then he falls in love with his colleague, Ann Cassidy, gets her pregnant, rescues her from a kidnapper threatening to kill her, and watches her lose the baby. Jack Malone's life has more melodrama than most soap operas.

Perhaps that is why Special Agent Vivian Johnson says about her boss, Jack Malone, in "He Saw, She Saw (Episode 3), "I love the way your brain works, always going to the dark side." Yet in "Between the Cracks" (Episode 4), she also recognizes of him, "You're a hope junky." With that personal life, who would not be a hope junky with a taste for the dark side?

Like the personal lives of the FBI special agents, the missing person cases featured in this series are not mere case studies. These are not dead bodies ripe for the autopsy skills of a Dr. Albert Robbins or the forensic analysis of Greg Sanders. They are (or were) living, breathing people with lives of their own. Each missing person presented in *Without a Trace* has secrets, which are not simply missing puzzle pieces awaiting assembly. No, these secrets mask deep emotional turmoil that prompts many of the missing to "do a walk about," or, if they have not disappeared on their own, to be vulnerable to kidnapping. Each episode is a search for the missing person's hidden secrets, which when brought to light, are essential for locating the missing person.

Unlike the use of *CSI*-style technology, these searches are decidedly low tech. At most, they occasionally uses video camera images, as in "Gung Ho," when missing Kevin Grant and his buddy Chuck Whiting are caught on tape as they rob a bank in Pennsylvania. The most frequently used crime-fighting "technology" in this series are the phone records, credit card records, and artfully drawn and accurate composite drawings of suspects that pop up in most of the episodes. Where would these legal beagles of federal justice be without phone records, computer files, and sketch pads? Finding phone logs is a snap for the team and computer passwords never present much of a challenge to our legal ferrets. Special Agent Sam Spade can gin up computer passwords faster than the owners of the computer files themselves, thank you. Each episode features a nice grade school quality color picture of the missing person tacked on the office's white board. Apparently every missing person goes to Wal-Mart to have his picture taken before he decides to turn up missing. Perhaps for Sam Spade's sake they also post their computer passwords on their monitors using sticky notes, complete with little smiley faces.

Technology is pretty much fluff in this series. As team leader Jack Malone earlier describes the show's problem-solving methodology in its inaugural missing person case, "We gotta work from the inside out. If we find out who she is, the odds are that we'll find out where she is." If the team discovers Maggie Cartwright's emotion-laden secrets, it will be in a position to discover her present whereabouts. If they don't discover her secrets, they won't be able to find her. White boards, class pictures, composite drawings, and phone records are minimal means to the greater end of discovering the missing person's secrets. *Without a Trace* is all about secrets, the secrets of the self unfamiliar to others, even their most intimate partners, the secrets that lie beneath the pretty bulletin board picture.

Once the agents arrive at the missing person's locale, they immediately bring into play the show's main problem-solving heuristic: uncovering the missing person's secret life. Nominal attention is paid to the tedious routine of gathering forensic evidence, checking police arrest reports, checking with hospitals, or checking with the morgue to determine if any recently deceased persons match the missing person's description. In the series, there has never been a single on-camera instance of such investigative activity being pursued. They might as well stick their heads out of the back door and shout "Dinnertime!" to see if the day's missing person is still around. Instead, negative results of these "backdoor searches" are generally reported as mere afterthoughts. Rather, the search really begins by questioning, for example, the spouse of a missing married person. Was she having an affair? Was she being abused by her lover or her spouse? Was she unhappy at work? Has she stopped beating the family dog? This is what it means to cut to the chase.

The Voluntarily Missing

As mentioned previously, two kinds of missing persons populate *Without a Trace*: the voluntarily missing and the involuntarily missing. Since it is not a federal crime to be voluntarily missing (frequently it is not any kind of crime at all), in order to "make a federal case out of it" the show's FBI team must assume that every missing person case involves a kidnapping victim. By the end of many episodes it becomes clear to the TV audience that the missing person has not been kidnapped at all, but has usually chosen to drop out of sight temporarily for a variety of reasons. What has happened "without a trace" is that the missing person has a hidden life, and it is the job of the team to reveal it, whether the missing person is a kidnapping victim or not. If the team discovers that the missing person is missing voluntarily and has not been kidnapped, legally they no longer have a vested interest in pursuing the case. From the viewers' perspective, however, if the team drops the case there is no satisfactory resolution of the story. Viewers want to know whether the missing person is going to be found, whether she will live "happily ever after." They aren't interested in the legal nit-picking over whether or not the case involved a federal crime.

Often a person voluntarily goes missing because he is running away from something. In "Silent Partner" (Episode 6), Patrick Kent, the vice president of an investment banking firm, disappears from San Diego airport, leaving behind only two empty suitcases. After pounding the shoe leather on both coasts, the team discovers that Kent actually had two wives, one on each coast. His life is split between them, two weeks on one coast, two weeks on the other. On the East coast he is married to Katherine, the daughter of the owner of the firm Kent works for. On the West coast he is married to Amalia, who has a son, Luis, from a previous marriage. Of course, neither wife knows about the other.

Juggling a bifurcated existence is not what drives Patrick Kent. That is the easy part! What weighs Kent down is his knowledge that the company he works for, the one run by his East coast father-in-law, is guilty of shady business practices that illegally and unfairly deprive many people of their life's savings. Patrick Kent is morally disturbed by these practices, and especially by the knowledge that Katherine's own father is guilty of them. Following his conscience, Kent decides to blow the whistle. But to rip the lid off of the company's corrupt business practices Kent must go underground. Indeed, his father-in-law becomes so worried about Kent's capacity to blow the whistle on his company that he hires a private investigator to birddog Kent's actions. Kent spots the tail on him and drops out of the picture, occasioning the involvement of the missing persons' team to investigate his "disappearance."

When the team discovers all of this, Kent stages his own death by apparently driving his jeep off a bridge and into a river in San Diego, ostensibly drowning himself. A person who has been defrauded by Kent's company vouches that he saw Kent drive into the river and drown. But when the jeep is pulled out of the river it is empty. The absence of Kent's body is "explained" by saying that it was swept away by the current. But Kent is alive at the end of the episode. Interestingly, Jack Malone and his team know that Kent is alive out there, but they don't care. They actually root for Kent because they believe he is doing the morally right thing. The upshot of this episode is that the "missing person" of Patrick Kent stays a missing person with the blessings of the very people whose job it is to find him. Patrick Kent's bigamy aside, doing the right thing trumps doing the legal thing.

Nor was this the only episode where moral right trumps legal right. "Requiem" (Episode 92) opens with the disappearance of Ted Jordano and his children, Dylan and Nichole, from their home, leaving behind evidence of a bloodbath in their living room. At first glance, it seems the Jordano family has been massacred. Given the crime-ridden neighborhood in which they live, their deaths appear to be more of the same. Things are more complicated than that. They are on the run from a murderous Mafia-style gang of Albanians who want to kill Dylan because he witnessed one of the gang members, Costas Velo, kill someone in cold blood. Sadik Marku, the gang's leader, sends a henchman to murder the entire Jordano family but the hitman is fatally wounded in the Jordano living room, leaving the blood-splattered evidence found at the beginning of the episode. Following the assassination attempt, the Jordano family takes off for parts unknown. The FBI team successfully pieces the puzzle together and finds the Jordano family on a highway in Connecticut, stuck by the side of the road with car trouble. Like the Dudley Do-Rights that they are, the team arrives just in time to prevent another assassination attempt by the Marku mob. Jack later confronts Sadik Marku himself and warns him to stay away from the Jordano family. Following a tense exchange between them, Marku spits on Jack. In response, Jack beats Marku to a pulp, pressing Marku's own gun to his head and threatening personally to blow him away if he ever bothers the Jordano family again. Like other famous celluloid detectives before him, Jack was entirely willing to take the law into his own hands for the sake of achieving a morally satisfactory goal. As he warns Marku, "You think because there are rules that I have to follow, that you don't have to fear me. I don't care about the rules." What he cares about is successfully protecting the innocent Jordano family from the likes of the evil Marku Mafia.

"Connections" (Episode 112) presents another case of a voluntarily missing person in which moral right conflicts with legal right. Fifteen-year-old Rebecca Howard goes missing from an Internet café. Given all the sexual innuendos lacing the beginning of this episode, it seems Rebecca is the victim of a sexual predator she met online. Indeed, she met Craig Dalton online—a 35-year-old security guard who has sex with Rebecca. After Sam quickly runs through a list of 6,000 known sexual predators, Dalton is identified. The team raids his home, only to find him handcuffed to his own bed. After hearing his story, Jack Malone confronts the sheepish Dalton. "Clean up this douche bag and bring him downtown." Dalton's fellow security officers ask Malone, "Can we have a few minutes alone (with him)?" To which Malone replies, "Take as much time as you want." It is clear that Malone's colleagues are going to beat the snot out of Dalton for his actions with an underage Rebecca. Malone agreed with them. Dalton deserves his punishment. Sometimes justice is best served off of the books.

In the meantime, Rebecca remains missing. It turns out that she drops out of sight to search for her father, Darren. She has just found out that he is alive, after her grandfather George had told her long ago that he had died in a car accident. George took baby Rebecca away from Darren when a rattled Darren worried that he might end up abusing her. At the end of the episode father and daughter are reunited and Darren realizes that he can indeed successfully parent Rebecca.

Morality does not have to conflict with legality. In "911" (Episode 97), Jessica Lawson, an emergency call operator, is missing. In a good example of its basic philosophy, the team works through a series of red herrings and other false leads to discover what is really bothering Jessica Lawson. Fish by red fish, they discover that although she held an emotionally draining job for more than six years, she was not a 9-1-1 operator burn-out case. Nor was she running from a husband whose wife died from anaphylactic shock when a system overload delayed a 9-1-1 response to his call. She was not worried about the break-in at her apartment that resulted in the death of her pet dog, nor was she afraid of gang banger Trey, who was actually her friend.

After unpeeling all of the layers of Jessica's life, the team finally discovers her hidden essence. Six years ago, Jessica Lawson was a promising nursing student. One fateful day she attends a party for her unit's doctors and nurses, at which she meets a doctor who kidnaps and rapes her. This trauma causes her to call off her impending marriage to Frank Gallo, drop out of medical school, and take a job with the 9-1-1 emergency services. While on the job she fields a call from Dr. Ben Burton, a physician, who supplied emergency medical attention to a gunshot victim. Dr. Burton's voice sounds exactly like the voice of the doctor who had raped her. Reliving the trauma of the rape, Jessica disappears, launching the FBI's search for her. While missing, Jessica finds a surveillance video made while Dr. Burton called 9-1-1. She then locates and kidnaps Dr. Burton and brings him to the very place at the docks where he allegedly raped her. She threaten to kill the stunned and bewildered doctor. Fortunately for both Jessica and Dr. Burton, Jack Malone showed up just as she points a gun at the doctor's head. Jack explains that she has mistaken Dr. Burton for her real rapist, who was in fact in prison for another rape. Malone talks the totally distraught Jessica into doing the right thing by putting down the gun, releasing Dr. Burton, and surrendering herself to him. At the episode's conclusion it is unclear whether Jessica was relieved of the emotional burden her rape had inflicted on her. In this case knowing the truth may not have set her free.

"Kam Li" (Episode 17) explores another case where knowing the truth did not set its victim free. In this episode, John "Bull" Carver, a retired army sergeant, is missing following a reunion of the surviving members of his Vietnam War squad. Dark things occurred to this group in Vietnam. Congressman Robert Whitehurst was a young officer in the group who called in an air strike on a Vietnamese village, which allowed Carver to get away with the fact that he had raped villager Kam Li and murdered squad member Tommy Lewis when Lewis had tried to stop him. Wallace Sykes, another squad member, is aware of Carver's crimes, but is too scared to blow the whistle on Carter. When squad member Manny Aybar starts to put together the pieces of these awful past events, Sykes gets even more freaked out. When Special Agent Sam Spade visits Sykes at his home in South Carolina, Sykes blows his brains out. Sykes is never a missing person in the eyes of the episode, but he clearly exhibits the characteristics of a person who has a hidden emotional agenda driving his identity. Sykes was traumatized by his inability to interfere with Carver's actions in Vietnam, so traumatized that Carver's horrible deeds were imprinted on his soul. When Aybar and Spade threaten to reveal Carver's crimes, Sykes cannot bear to bring his hidden pain into the light of day. Death was preferable for Sykes and for Carver, as well. Carver's penchant for young Asian girls led him to rape other young Asian women. When it became clear that Aybar was about to expose Carver's horrible deeds, Carver commits suicide rather than face the truth. Reunions can be hell.

"Clare de Lune" (Episode 16) also deals with the issue of the psychological pain and suffering of its featured missing person, Clare Metcalf. In a scene right out of *Cold Case*, Clare is plagued by a false memory syndrome. At the beginning of the episode Clare is a patient in a mental hospital. With the help of one of the attendants, she escapes from a locked room. Clare's problems began at a young age when she supposedly remembers finding her mother's body right after her mother had committed suicide by jumping off of the balcony of their home. Clare slowly "realizes," however, that her mother did not really jump to her death. Rather, her father threw her mother off the balcony. Worse yet, Clare then accurately remembers that it was she herself who accidentally pushed her mother over the railing after her mother chastised Clare for having a hissy-fit over something completely inconsequential. As a result of this accident, Clare suffers from a form of posttraumatic stress syndrome. But now, all of Clare's past is revealed. A despondent Clare understands that she was the one truly responsible for her mother's death. Special Agent Danny Taylor finds Clare on the shore of a lake holding a knife in her hand. She intends not just to spike her eyes out, but to kill herself to put an end to her wretched existence. Danny talks her out of killing herself by confessing to her that he also was the occasion for his parents' death. They died in an auto wreck caused when Danny's father turned around while driving to discipline a disruptive Danny in the back seat.

Will Clare ever forgive herself? The episode suggests a negative answer to this unhappy question. The trauma Clare experienced by accidentally killing her mother has become so much a part of her essential being that she would literally have to reinvent herself to be rid of it. Sadly, such a complete reordering of her personal identity seems to be far beyond Clare's capacities.

"Expectations" (Episode 89) portrays another case of a woman with deep-seated problems, although in this case the problems are physical, not psychological. Megan Sullivan is almost nine months pregnant at the time of her disappearance. She recently was diagnosed with non-Hodgkin's lymphoma, but Megan's problems really began when she contracted HIV from her boyfriend, Justin Pomeroy. Enraged, Megan bashes in his van windshield, giving back to Pomeroy a bit of what he deserved. Initially, it seems Megan is simply and understandably running away from her own death sentence. She says "I want my baby to know who I am, what I was like."

But Megan was not really running away from anything. She was running towards something, namely, her own father. Her mother told her that her father was dead, but Megan's father ran off with his secretary, a fact that Megan's mother could not face. Recently Megan's sister told her the truth about her father. In her search she discovers that he is in a nursing home after recently suffering a stroke. After visiting her dad, she drives off, only to go into labor, and gets lost on the road. The team locates her car in a dark and deserted section of the city in time to get her baby delivered. Though Megan may be doomed because of AIDS and cancer, her child does not contract HIV.

"Risen" (Episode 39) also focuses on a missing woman's deep-seated emotional needs. Four years ago, eighteen-year-old Jessica Rabb went missing and Special Agent Vivian Johnson still could not turn her case loose. As Special Agent Jack Malone describes her, "Somebody messed with this kid somewhere down the line." Jessica had become a self-destructive sex addict who wanted to unburden herself of her awful affliction. "I want to stop hurting myself. I want to change." But change is not going to come easily for Jessica. Her mother gives up on her. Even her therapist, Dr. Remy Polk, had sexually abused her. Special Agent Johnson says to the good doctor, "You are a disgusting pig. I am personally going to see to it that you never see the light of day."

Jessica's wanderings lead her to upstate New York, where she falls in with a religious cult led by a Jim Jones-like figure, "Father" Cavanaugh. Trapped in a sexually abusive situation, Jessica escapes with the help of another cult victim, Kristen Walters. "Bad things have happened to people who have tried [to escape]." Miraculously, she does escape not just from the evil cult but from herself. When Special Agent Johnson finally traces her to her home in Connecticut, Jessica seems to be living a complete and happy life, which includes a loving boyfriend and an equally loving dog. So all's well that ends well.

"Second Sight" (Episode 66) ends well in a different sense. It features another story of a damsel in distress, Agnes Deschamps, a self-styled "psychic." Young Agnes knows she is not a real psychic. She belongs to a gypsy clan that makes its dubious living by pulling insurance scams. Several years ago in an attempt to recreate herself, Agnes absconds with $50,000 of the clan's money. But she cannot escape her heritage, and not just her gypsy origins. Agnes comes from a family that carries the gene for Huntington's disease, and the deformity that promises her a wretched, protracted death before she turns forty. Agnes returns to her father and her family, which then uses her to fake another abduction scam to recover the rest of the money that Agnes stole from the family. The story ends on a sort of happy note, which is not "do not steal from your family," but "even after you have stolen from your family, they are still your family." Unlike Jessica in the miracle of "Risen," Agnes stays true to the series story line. She cannot escape her own pain-filled destiny, but at least she is back in the bosom of her family, a family that will indeed stick with her past her bitter end.

Finally, "Watch Over Me" (Episode 103) gives us the story of idealistic, dedicated social worker Eric Hayes, another person who tries to escape his destiny. Eric is not trying to reinvent himself, but to refashion the inept system he works for. Amy Jensen, a pregnant woman at full term, has already lost one child due to the ineptitude of the social welfare system. Now she is threatened by her abusive boyfriend, Damon Winters. Eric goes missing while trying to help Amy deliver her child off of the books. He arranges for her to deliver her baby in a motel room. If she does not give birth at a hospital, the social system will have no way of knowing about her and thus cannot interfere with the custody of her child. Unfortunately, Damon Winters catches up to Amy and Eric. He pulls a gun on Eric to get him to hand over the money Eric had withdrawn from his own savings to help Amy and her newborn daughter. Damon then decides to sell his infant daughter to a baby broker, who wants the child for a profitable underground adoption market. In the end, Winters is wounded in a shootout at Eric's office. Eric is unharmed and reunited with his wife, while Amy gets her newborn back. But the inept social work system still spins merrily on its way, unchanging and unchangeable.

The Involuntarily Missing

Not every missing person in *Without a Trace* has gone missing voluntarily; nor has each missing person committed suicide or otherwise died. Some missing persons are genuine kidnap victims and some of these kidnap victims are found alive. To find kidnapping victims, the team must focus on the essential attributes of the kidnapped victim herself, attributes that make the victim vulnerable to being kidnapped in the first place.

Of the episodes that feature kidnapping victims, many focus on the victim's sexuality as the locus of the kidnapper's fatal attraction. "There Goes the Bride" (Episode 15) features just such a case. In this episode, newlywed Audrey Rose Beckworth is kidnapped in the middle of her wedding reception. Following the early death of her parents, young Audrey is welcomed into the Beckworth household. Though she knows Charlie Beckworth her whole life, familiarity in this case does not lead to indifference or contempt. Instead the two young people fall in love and are about to consummate their fairytale life in a fairytale wedding and a fairytale honeymoon in Italy, after which they will "live happily ever after." Or not. Unfortunately, reality is not so rosy. Charlie's father is not the personal friend of Audrey's father who graciously "adopts" the orphaned Audrey into his family circle. The grubby Beckworth senior is far more interested in Audrey as a nubile young thing. He sexually molests the young and vulnerable Audrey for years until she is old enough to refuse to cooperate with him. Following the wedding ceremony, she tells the senior Beckworth, "There are some things that I need to tell Charlie. You will never see us again."

Threatened with the exposure of his shameful deeds and the loss of his only son, Beckworth senior hastily arranges for Audrey's kidnapping. While being held hostage, Audrey manages to wrestle a gun away from her kidnappers and shoot them both dead. In a scene straight out of Sophocles' *Antigone*, Charlie

and the FBI team arrive on the spot where Audrey also threatens to shoot her
no-good father-in-law. Shocked to discover his father's crimes against his wife,
Charlie takes the gun and shoots his father himself. At the conclusion of the
episode, a wounded Beckworth senior is led away in disgrace, and the junior
Beckworth and his bride are left to concoct whatever they can make out of
"happily ever after."

"In the Dark" (Episode 48) presents another victim of sexual violence,
another damsel in distress. Kelly Corcoran sees herself as a hard luck girl. She
suffers from degenerating retinas, which recently left her completely without
sight, and is having a difficult time adjusting to her blindness. To help her
adjust to her condition, her personal trainer and companion, Louisa Cruz,
takes her camping in the wilderness, where they are attacked, kidnapped, and
raped by two teenagers, Trent Barker and Lott Mardell. Kelly escapes when
the teenagers get themselves wasted on drugs. Found by a sympathetic motor-
ist while she is wandering alone and discombobulated, Kelly has to accept the
responsibility of showing the team where she has been held hostage. In the
end Louisa is rescued, Barker surrenders, and Mardell is shot, though it is
unclear if he is killed. Though Kelly survives her ordeal, she still cannot reconcile herself with her blindness.

Not every kidnapping victim fits the "revenge is best served piping hot"
mold of "There Goes the Bride." Some episodes focus directly on the kidnapper and only secondarily on the victim. "Suspect" (Episode 5) does this and is
also noteworthy for introducing the super villain of the *Without a Trace* series.
That villain is none other than Graham Spaulding, who runs an upscale
boarding school for privileged high school students. The boarding school,
however, is really Spaulding's day job. His "night job" is that of a sexually
twisted serial killer of young men. At the school Spaulding kidnaps Andy
Deaver and holds him in a cave while practicing unspeakably evil things on
him. Spaulding is not just a pedophile, but a sick, twisted degenerate masquerading as a concerned head of a prestigious academy.

Because Spaulding oozes perversion from his very pores, Malone correctly
deduces that he is responsible for Deaver's disappearance. The episode turns
on evidence obtained illegally by Martin Fitzgerald when he breaks into
Spaulding's home in search of Deaver. Martin uncovers plenty of evidence
linking Spaulding to disappearances of other teenage boys throughout the
region. Regarding Spaulding's connection to the missing Deaver, however,
Judge Roger Adderly rejects an arrest warrant based on the illegally obtained
photo evidence. Malone acknowledges that "It's too early to tell if any of the
leads are real." Spaulding is then arrested for lewd acts with minors, not for
kidnapping Deaver. After arresting Spaulding, Jack gets him to confess where
he stashed Deaver by offering Spaulding fifteen minutes alone with Deaver, no
questions asked. The perverted Spaulding cannot resist this ridiculous offer,
and as they drive away to prison, Spaulding leads Malone to the location
where he is holding Deaver. To make for the necessary plot twist that would

eventually free Spaulding so that he can continue to menace others in future episodes, Malone makes the legal mistake of continuing to question him even after he asks for his lawyer. Judge Adderly has no choice but to throw the case against Spaulding out of court because it is based completely on the illegally obtained evidence. Deaver is found alive, but much traumatized. Tough guy Jack Malone throws up when Spaulding's sick countenance becomes too much for him to bear. Spaulding returns in future episodes to haunt Special Agent Jack Malone's nightmares.

And none too soon, "Are You Now or Have You Ever Been?" (Episode 21) concerns the investigation of Jack Malone's handling of Spaulding in the "Suspect" case. In this unusual episode, Jack Malone is grilled about the legal methods he employed handling some of his past cases, particularly that of Graham Spaulding. The issue at stake here centers on the ongoing dispute between two rules that govern the investigation of criminal cases. The rules are "find the bad guy" and "play by the legal rules of the game." The problem is that in some situations the rules contradict each other. In order to find the bad guy, the investigator sometimes must violate the rules of the game. This occurs in "Suspect." To get Spaulding to tell him where he has imprisoned young Andy Deaver, Jack is forced to ignore one of the key rules of criminal investigations, namely, that once a suspect has asked for an attorney, the police may no longer continue their questioning of that suspect. Absent his attorney, any information divulged by a suspect cannot be used to prosecute him. But had Malone not tricked Spaulding into leading them to the cave where Deaver was hidden, Deaver might have died from exposure. Martin says "You just can't make up the rules as you go along, Jack." Had Jack not "made up the rules as he went along," however, young Deaver would have died and his body never would have been found. The message is that when the rules of "fair play" get in the way of protecting the innocent, the rules have to give way. Rescuing children from a gruesome death trumps so-called fair play.

What's in a name? "Stolen" (Episode 95) deals with another case of a kidnapped child, although Malone need not break any legal rules to crack this case. Young Bryan Parker is found wandering down a road one night; apparently, he is a runaway. But the truth is that Bryan Parker is really Max McNeil. When Max was on a vacation with his mother seven years ago, he was kidnapped by Robert Pratt, who subsequently changed his own name to Randall Parker. Pratt attempts to change Max's very identity, his person, by changing his name, but fails. More recently, Pratt had kidnapped five-year-old Todd, who was really Daniel Ellison. Max escapes Pratt's clutches after failing to liberate Daniel. After tracking down Pratt's phony Parker identity, the team locates property he owns in the country. When they surround the trailer in which he is hiding, Pratt kills himself. It seems that Pratt could not live up to the identity he tried to manufacture for himself.

Episodes that feature attacks on young children are especially difficult to watch. They present hard-sell test cases for Hume's dictum. They also present huge problems for Aristotle's analysis. What can possibly be *entertaining* about the reality that young children are sometimes kidnapped, sexually abused, and murdered? Even for aficionados of cinematic mayhem, there is something deeply disturbing about such tales.

Evil often lurks just out of sight. Medieval mapmakers sometimes depicted the unknown regions that bordered their maps with the legend "Here there be Monsters." Taking its lead from the classic 1960 *Twilight Zone* episode, "The Monsters Are Due on Maple Street," *Without a Trace's* "Maple Street" (Episode 11) introduces Barry Mitchum, an all-too-human monster. Laughed at by two young girls, Annie Miller and Siobhan Arintero, for being "creepy," Mitchum responds by kidnapping Annie. Twelve hours later he abducts Siobhan. True to format, the episode focuses its attention on the innocent "secrets" of its two twelve-year-old victims, Annie and Siobhan, and not on the secrets of their kidnapper, Barry Mitchum. Much like the aliens in the *Twilight Zone* original, Mitchum maintains an elusive, lurking, off-screen presence throughout most of this episode. Stunned by the disappearance of his young daughter, Annie's father ponders, "I never thought it could happen here." As Special Agent Danny Taylor comments about the whole community, "This town . . . it seems so innocent." To which Special Agent Vivian Johnson responds, "Wait till we're done with them." Hidden secrets will not remain hidden for long.

After Siobhan disappears, her father draws the team's attention to an adult friend of the girls, Derrick Trainer. "It's unnatural for a man his age to spend so much time with two teenage girls." But field work shows that Trainer is innocent. He really is just a friend of the two girls. Viewing the video archive "secrets" made by the girls, Special Agent Sam Spade discovers their reference to the creepy Barry Mitchum. After Annie is found dead, the team visits Mitchum's house and rescues Siobhan, who is still alive in his car trunk at the episode's conclusion. In the end, the team slew the monster, though for young Annie Miller, there was no fairytale rescue.

"Hang On to Me" (Episode 13) has a fairytale ending, but one not achieved until its protagonist has gone through sheer hell. In this highly emotional episode, Chet Collins is searching for his son Sean, missing for the past six years. Three-year-old Sean was kidnapped during a camping trip with his father. Sean's disappearance literally brings Chet's life to a standstill. Chet Collins can do nothing, think of nothing, enjoy nothing, until he finds his young son. Collin's search becomes a crusade, a crusade that costs him his friends, his job, the relationship with his teenage daughter, Kelly, and his very marriage itself. His wife, Helen, was driven into an affair because she wanted to move on with their lives, which Chet simply couldn't do. Chet periodically shows up at Malone's office with another lead that turns out to be worthless. Jack Malone is so moved by Chet's plight that he urges Chet to "hang on to me,"

Now Chet himself is missing. To find him, Malone visits Chet's apartment, which has become a combination of a shrine and a search headquarters. Malone literally put himself in Chet's shoes. Sam suggests that perhaps Chet developed a problem with drugs or alcohol. Vivian suggests suicide. But Jack rejects each of these suggestions out of hand. He will not give up on Chet, though he feels that he has given up on Sean.

Field work leads the team to the apartment of Tyson Dibbs, where they find Dibbs's body. Did Chet Collins kill him? No, he did not. Dibbs was working for Gene Clarkson, an attorney who had used Dibbs to kidnap half-Asian, half-African American children to fill a specialty adoption market. Years ago Dibbs kidnapped the young Sean for that market. When Collins threatens to close in on Dibbs, Clarkson kills Dibbs. Malone arrests Clarkson for Dibbs's murder. Tracing through Clarkson's business leads to a charity foster home in Detroit, where at long last Chet is reunited with his nine-year-old son, a son who no longer remembers him. The end of this episode suggests that the Collins family will indeed be reunited and live happily ever after.

"Crossroads" (Episode 94) has a mixed outcome for its two main characters. The episode opens with the disappearance of former assistant district attorney Jennifer Nichols. Now in private legal practice, she has discovered Mr. Right in the form of Allen Davis, the owner of a travel agency. But a chance encounter at dinner one night with a mysterious woman who knows Davis leads the suspicious Nichols to do a background check. As Nichols nicely puts it, "Just because you're paranoid does not mean that they are not out to get you." Touché! In that background check she discovers to her horror that the straight-arrow Davis is really a former bank robber who killed two people in his getaway from his last job. The loot from that heist enabled him to set up his travel agency and "go straight."

Suspicious about Nichols's relationship with Davis, Malone seeks to interview Davis. At the FBI's office, things go very wrong. As Martin and Danny run down Davis's story, they also interview Davis's ex-partner, whose wife was the woman at the dinner that blew Davis's cover for Nichols. Confronted with his real identity, Davis slugs Jack, steals his gun, shoots up the office, and kidnaps Special Agent Ann Cassidy in his getaway. To complicate this mess even further, Ann is pregnant with Jack's child. In the race to track down Davis and rescue Cassidy, Malone discovers poor Jennifer Nichols's body at Davis's apartment. She went there to confront him, and Davis put a bullet in her head. So much for Mr. Right. So much for true love.

In the end, Malone tracks Davis and his hostage to a private airport. When challenged to free Ann and give up, Davis, who tried to go straight, acknowledges the essentialist's argument that "People don't change." Once a bank-robbing murderer, always a bank-robbing murderer. Failing to outrun his past, Davis dies by the very sword he lived by. Happily, Ann is rescued unhurt, but viewers have not seen the last of her and her pregnancy.

Some missing persons are neither missing voluntarily, nor are they kidnapping victims. Some missing persons drop off of the radar scope primarily because they are dead. "More Than This" (Episode 90) is just such an unfortunate case. Breck Mulligan was born with the proverbial silver spoon in his mouth. He found himself among the down and out when he was sentenced to community service following a drug bust. That service amounts to helping out at a family shelter in the Bronx. The desperate problems of the families housed in that shelter and the dilapidated status of the shelter itself refocus Breck's energies. At the beginning of the episode, he is apparently kidnapped, but that turns out to be his friends who try to reconnect him to their former party-hearty lifestyle. Breck refuses to be sucked back into the hedonistic swamp he just climbed out of. Maybe not. In order to raise the money needed to fix up the homeless shelter, Breck does what he knows best; he hits up all of his rich friends and acquaintances. When that money pit dries up, Breck starts sleeping with rich older women—for charity. As Special Agent Danny Taylor says, "Breck was pimping himself out for charity." It was a tough job, but someone had to do it. The leopard Breck had not really changed his spots after all.

Usually, all's well that ends well, but Breck's fate does not end well. He dies in a car crash caused by his girlfriend Heidi, who at the end of the episode fesses up and leads the team to the location of Breck's body. The women's shelter needs a new knight in shinning armor. But all is not lost, as the ending suggests that Breck's father will continue with his son's mission.

"The Damage Done" (Episode 99) also features a dead son, only this poor soul is merely five years old. He is the son of the infamous Sadik Marku, the villainous gang leader first featured in "Requiem." In that episode, Special Agent Jack Malone develops a terrible animosity toward Marku when the latter tries to murder the Jordano family. This time the shoe is on the other foot, as Sadik's son, Petros, and the boy's mother, Julia, both go missing and it becomes Jack's job to find them. Julia wants to flee the mob scene. She makes plans to take young Petros to Europe, beyond Sadik's clutches. But alas, for human destiny, as Aeschylus says, is but a picture written in shadows. Young Petros is so enamored by the guns he continually sees around him that he makes the fatal mistake of playing with one that proves to be loaded and deadly. Petros accidentally shoots himself and dies. Julia buries him in Harrington Park. After Julia resurfaces, Jack catches up with her and drags the tragic tale of Petros into the light. Jack then has the unenviable task of informing Sadik, who is headed to prison for beating up an undercover cop, that he will be making the rest of his life's journey without his only son. Sadik's essential gangster essence had doomed a young and innocent child, the only child that Sadik would ever have.

"Between the Cracks" also features a missing person who dies by the end of the episode. It begins with the disappearance of nineteen-year-old Eve Cleary, a budding actress on the New York club scene. Eve poses a difficult challenge for the team because each photo of her seems to show a different person. As Special Agent Jack Malone puts it, "We don't know what she looks like. We don't know where she is. We don't know when she disappeared."

Standard field work by the team uncovers the fact that "Eve Cleary" was just a stage name. "Eve" is actually Becky Radowski from Indiana. Abused by her father at home, Becky fled to the big city to attempt to reinvent herself, a goal she was crashingly incapable of accomplishing. Followed to New York by her hometown boyfriend Alex Livingston, she seems ready to give up on her golden dreams and settle down back home in Indiana with someone who genuinely cares for her as herself, not with scum bags like druggie Goran Davitz who ran the local dance hall. Alas, this is not to be. After arguing with Alex late one night she gets out of his car and disappears. The team eventually finds her in the morgue lying under a sheet and an assumed name. Hit by a taxicab, the living "Eve Cleary" finally had to settle for just being plain old dead Becky Radowski.

Suggested Reading

Essentialism is defended in Aristotle's *Categories* and *Metaphysics* (*circa* 340 BCE); René Descartes' *Discourse on Method* and *Meditations* (1640); Sigmund Freud's *The Ego and the Id* (1930); Immanuel Kant's *Critique of Pure Reason* (1781) and *Critique of Practical Reason* (1790); and Plato's *Phaedrus, Phaedo,* and *Republic* (*circa* 380 BCE).

Butler, Judith. *Gender Trouble: Feminism and the Subversion of Identity.* New York: Routledge, 1990. [Butler defends queer theory and develops a philosophical attack on essentialism found in Michel Foucault's, *The History of Sexuality* (1976) and *Politics, Philosophy, and Culture: Interviews and Other Writings, 1977–1984.*]

Hume, David. *A Treatise of Human Nature,* 1740. [Introduces method of reasoning and attacks on essentialism.]

Lamarck, Jean-Baptiste. *Philosophie zoologique* (1809). [Lamarck's version of evolutionary theory is found in this work.]

Sartre, Jean Paul. *Being and Nothingness.* Paris: Gallimard, 1943. [This philosophical treatise is considered to be the beginning of the existentialist movement.]

———. *Existentialism Is a Humanism.* Paris: Editions Nagel, 1946.

CHAPTER 4

BOOMTOWN: THE LOST AND FOUND DEPARTMENT

It is the job of epistemology to explain the nature of knowledge, to delineate the proper sources of knowledge (as opposed to mere beliefs or opinions), and to discover the limitations of knowledge. Many things currently are unknowable in practice because the empirical conditions set by the work-a-day world are too difficult to meet. Cures for cancer (or even the common cold) fall into this camp. They are works in progress. Other things are simply unknowable in principle, such as the ultimate nature of the universe, whether there really is life after death, and how they get 1,000 clowns into those tiny circus cars. The human soul may also be something that is unknowable in principle.

Perspectivism is an approach in epistemology that is designed to answer empirical questions. Perspectivism has its roots in painting, drawing, photography, and architecture. Practitioners in these artistic fields commonly produce images of objects or scenes that purport to be accurate portrayals of what they represent. But pictures or images are always produced from specific viewpoints. Like a cosmic Lost and Found Department, perspectives show the onlooker how to see things from a specific point of view or perspective. The viewpoint of the artist is the perspective of the picture. It encompasses two things at the same time: the place from which the artist views her subject and the way the subject looks from that viewing point. Changing the location of the viewing point changes the way an object appears from the new perspective or viewing point. Similarly, changing aspects about the artist will change the way the subject matter appears to that artist. People who are colorblind see a different world than those who are not colorblind. Perspectivism thus includes two forms of relativism, standpoint relativism and viewer relativism. This idea is exemplified by the well-known saying that the glass is either half full or half empty, depending on the viewer's perspective.

Reflecting the strictly visual application of the artist's viewpoint, epistemic perspectivism applies the two aspects of viewing to all cases of knowing. Accordingly, knowledge about any subject matter originates from the specific standpoint adopted by the knower. Change aspects about the knower (standpoint relativism) or the way the knower understands his subject matter (viewer relativism) and a different knowledge results. Is the aforementioned glass half full (or empty) of fine wine or swill? To most people it would make a difference, but not to the wino.

Perspectivism has a kissing cousin, *contextualism*. Contextualism shares with its cousin, epistemology, the position that knowledge is relative in a significant sense; only contextualism ignores the identity of the knower and focuses on the fact that the objects of knowledge are embedded in a framework of relationships that make those things what they are. Whether an activity such as shouting is unduly loud and boisterous or subdued and controlled depends on the context of the shouting. Was it done in the library or at a basketball game? Factor in the context to make knowledge possible. Proper descriptions of human and animal activities are then a function of the conditions that surround those activities. Absent an understanding of the context, no correct understanding of an activity can occur. Different contexts will make the same set of physical motions involved in producing a vocal noise either inappropriate *shouting* or entirely appropriate *cheering*. The same noise embodies entirely different activities, depending on the context.

According to the *correspondence theory of truth*, a belief about the world is true if, and only if, that belief corresponds to specific facts about the world. The belief that the cat is on the mat is true if and only if the cat is indeed on the mat. If the cat is off the mat or if the animal on the mat is a dog, then the belief is incorrect.

While this may seem straightforward, perspectivism and contextualism posit that it is not quite that easy. In their view, what constitutes a matted cat depends entirely on the perspective from which the cat/mat combo is viewed, or the context of the cat/mat setting. The correspondence theory of truth appears a bit simple-minded if the viewer's perspective and the viewed object's context are ignored.

Perspectivism and contextualism can be better understood if each of these epistemologies is seen as embodying a *coherence theory of truth*. According to the coherence theory of truth, true beliefs about cats on mats are true not because they correspond to bematted cats, but because they form a logically consistent set. The belief that the cat is on the mat is true if and only if that belief is consistent with other beliefs about said Tabby and her sleeping quarters, including empirical data perceived in a given context. If the kitty in question does not appear to be resting on the mat in question, if she blinks out of existence, if her owner grasps at thin air when he goes to pick her up, if she fails to set off her owner's allergies, and so forth, then the belief that she is on the mat is not true. For that belief to be true, it must be internally consistent with an open-ended range of other issues. It is only the whole internally consistent set of claims that is true. A specific item in that range is true only because its denial is not consistent with the other items in that belief set. In short, all of the coherent beliefs in that set must tell a story, a story that makes sense only because its components all fit properly together. Like a

Rubik's cube, the proper solution is not satisfied if only one side has squares all of the same color. All sides must have squares with all the same colors. Partial consistency is not enough, although it is a start.

Cold Case and *Without a Trace* are police procedurals which are both firmly cemented to the perspectivist/contextualist camp. In these series, discovering the correspondence of who did what to whom presupposes that the criminals, the victims, and the detectives experience their worlds from different perspectives. Discovering "whodunit" requires the detectives to uncover the viewpoints of both the victims and the villains. Solving the case demands that the detectives discover the right—the coherent—contexts that allowed the villains to perpetrate their evil on their victims. Perspectives and context are everything. Correspondence requires coherence.

Boomtown is a TV police procedural that also employs perspectivism, an approach that gave rise to a specific storytelling style in two important ways. First, character name cards were inserted at the beginning of each segment, indicating to the audience that events portrayed in the segment were meant to be seen from that character's point of view. The early episodes of *Boomtown*'s first season depicted each segment from the viewpoint of each of the seven main characters, as well as from the viewpoint of the episode's chief antagonist. Later episodes in the first season did not provide equal time for the perspectives of each of the main characters, but concentrated instead on a specific character's experiences of the crime *du jour*. Second, the same sequence of events was repeated several times in each episode, and with each repetition the camera angle changed, telling the viewer that a different character's perspective was providing the viewpoint for that specific segment.

Different lighting techniques were also used in segments that repeated the episode's central events, indicating to the audience that the perspective had shifted. In filming each of the episodes, producer Jon Avnet captured the same action simultaneously using different cameras and different camera angles to achieve this multiperspective effect. An interesting side effect of this filming technique was that the production team had fewer events to film since the same scenes were repeated but from different perspectives.

The epistemological use of perspectivism dovetailed with the show's heavy reliance on soliloquies, especially those of the show's lead character, assistant DA David McNorris. Many of the episodes feature this theatrical technique. Because he talked out loud to himself, the TV audience had a direct pipeline to this character's worldview. If this series was classical Greek drama, then the character of David McNorris was Oedipus Rex, or perhaps more aptly, "Oedipus Wrecks."

Perspectivism also allows this series to present the character of Bobby "Fearless" Smith as a storyteller. In many of the episodes, Fearless related an independent vignette to the main story line. In telling these fables, Fearless embodied a Yoda-like character whose insights were full of pithy bits of wisdom that shed light on how he saw the unfolding events and how the audience could be encouraged to imitate his wise example. Smith's stories were primarily designed to educate their listeners about important and proper reactions to the events in the stories.

Bobby "Fearless" Smith put his storytelling art to an unusual test in "Possession" (Episode 2). This story opens with a scam telemarketer's random morning phone call, answered by a desperate Chris Griggs, who is about to be shot to death. Hearing the sounds of a struggle, the resulting gunshots, and the promise to kill "Laura" at noon, the telemarketer calls the police, who send Detectives Bobby "Fearless" Smith and Joel Stevens to investigate. Fearless and Joel then set off in high-speed pursuit of a person later identified as Wilson Miner.

It turns out that "Laura" is the party name of Vanessa Griggs, the wife of the murdered Chris Griggs. Vanessa has an unusual job. She performs the role of a sexy stay-at-home "wife" and exotic dancer working at a club operated by Ivan Vronski, who is in the business of staging play-therapy parties for wealthy frustrated men who like "the appearance of sex" in their fantasies. Wilson Minor is a regular visitor to this play-therapy group, but he forgets that it is all just playtime. He loses his heart to the sexy "Laura," and wishing to change the context, proposes to marry her. But Vanessa is already married to Chris, who is a bouncer at the club. When Wilson becomes so involved in his fantasy that he tries to touch Vanessa, she literally blows the whistle on him. After the crestfallen Wilson accuses Chris of being Vanessa's pimp, Chris beats him and throws him out of the club.

Not discouraged by being expelled from paradise, Wilson tracks down Chris and Vanessa to their house, where he voyeuristically spies on their lovemaking. The next morning, after Vanessa leaves for her doctor's appointment, Wilson invades the house and shoots Chris to death. Following a series of misadventures, Joel and Fearless at last succeed in locating Vanessa's doctor, where they arrive just as Wilson has made the shocked Vanessa his love prisoner.

Using a clever ploy to distract Wilson so that he can grab Wilson's gun, Fearless tells Wilson a story to the effect that while growing up, Fearless and his brother had played cops and robbers with each other using popgun .22s just like the weapon Wilson is holding. Ignoring the fact that Wilson already used that "popgun" to kill Chris, Fearless claims that his brother shot him in the rear with a .22, leaving a still-visible scar. Dropping his trousers, Fearless backs toward Wilson, apparently to allow Wilson to get a better look at his scar. The sight of Smith's buttocks edging toward him so befuddles and distracts Wilson that he completely forgets he is holding a gun on Detective Smith. Finally getting close enough to reach the bewildered Wilson and hysterical Vanessa, Fearless grabs the gun and disarms Wilson.

The perspectivism found in "Possession" served as *Boomtown*'s main storytelling format, placing it at the opposite end of the spectrum from a series like *CSI*. While a police series such as *CSI* focused on examining the evidence at the crime scene, *Boomtown* focused on the doings of the crime fighters. That the police personnel of *Boomtown* are crime scene investigators is secondary to the focus of this series. They just as easily could have been cast as military personnel. As the show's chief writer Graham Yost originally envisioned it, the "Boom" of Boomtown represented the sound of a bomb going off, not the spectacular sprawl of Southern California real estate development. In this series the crime fighting simply provides the context for the main characters to live out their lives.

One way to understand perspectivism and contextualism as epistemologies is to see what they reject, a position known as *absolutism*. An absolutist position in epistemology was defended by Plato and later by French philosopher René Descartes and German intellectual Gottfried Wilhelm Leibniz. Plato famously distinguished between information about the changing world of the senses and insights into the unchanging world of the "Forms." The world of the senses is constantly changing—aging and falling apart or growing and evolving into something else. Either way, whether growing or degenerating, the world of the senses can never be properly known. That world is ever in a state of flux, ever on its way to becoming something else.

But the Forms are constant and unchanging. Forms never change. They are immutable and eternal. They are the subjects of true knowledge. Knowledge of them requires no perspective; they have no context. For Plato, true knowledge is context free.

Euclid's geometry exemplifies a Platonic position in epistemology. Euclidean circles, squares, and triangles, unlike real-life lions, tigers, and bears (oh, my!), are complete and unchanging. That is why perfect knowledge of these perfect geometrical figures is possible. This knowledge resides in a system that starts with definitions, axioms, and postulates and then uses the simple rules of deductive logic to prove immutable and eternal theorems that govern the relationship between these purely abstract geometrical figures.

The abstract geometrical figures of pure Euclidean geometry should not be equated with mere empirical examples. It is a staple of pure Euclidean geometry that every point on the circumference of a circle is equally distant from that circle's center. But circles drawn on the ground, like lines drawn in the sand, fail to measure up to the ideal standard of the perfect Form Circle. Empirical circles are wobbly, imperfect, squashed, and foreshortened, even if they are perspectively and contextually "close enough for government work." Empirical examples of circles are deficient when compared in the mind's eye with the ideal circle. In one way or another they are all deformed from the ideal, although even these deformations have their uses, for example, in teaching students about real circles. Circles drawn on chalkboards or created in a PowerPoint slide are highly useful in teaching the student about real circles, but these empirical instances should not be confused with the real thing, namely the absolute Platonic Form Circle in itself.

It is no accident that many of the great thinkers who defended versions of absolutism in epistemology were also great mathematicians. One hand washed the other. Truth is truth is truth, immutably. If they are to be true, all subject matters must therefore share the same format, which is that of deductive logic.

Contemporary science mirrors this Platonic perspective in all ways but one, its dismissal of empirical examples. Instead, science adopts the Aristotelian perspective, which integrates the perfect Forms with empirical examples, only now the Forms are called "laws of nature." From the Aristotelian perspective, empirical examples—lions and tigers and bears—can be proper objects of knowledge because they are real-world manifestations of the laws of nature. The laws of natures are the ultimate facts with which beliefs must correspond to be true. Understanding them as true beliefs, as knowledge, requires not just the actual empirical examples themselves; it requires the marriage of these examples with the immutable laws of nature. Empirical, real-world examples are understood to be instances of natural law in action. Knowledge about them integrates the specific object with universal law. How abstract theoretical Euclidean circles integrate with wobbly empirical wheels and hula hoops remains an issue under analysis. It is another "work in progress."

What is the point of this analysis? Murder, most foul. Actual homicide cases can be understood best as instances of the immutable laws of nature. Like lions and tigers and bears, murder victims and their assailants can only be understood if each of them is seen as an instance of the application of the laws of nature to the crime. In the series *CSI* the laws of nature provide the Euclidean point that serves as the basis for all understanding. Science is everything; character and context are nothing.

Boomtown did not depict absolutism; far from it. At the opposite end of the spectrum from Euclidean abstract ideas and scientific crime-fighting techniques, *Boomtown's* Lost and Found Department was a messy, wobbly TV series depicting messy, wobbly events in the lives of messy, wobbly people. Character and context were everything in this series; forensic science was nothing. Yet for its total lack of attention to forensic science and other systematic methods of criminal investigation, *Boomtown* was still a uniquely interesting TV police procedural, a series that came close to the theatrical.

Debuting in the 2002 fall season, *Boomtown* was unique in many ways, the most inglorious of which is that it was cancelled by NBC after only twenty-four episodes, the last four of which were never aired. It is the only TV series discussed in this book that is not currently producing new episodes. Reruns are now available on HDNET and all twenty-four of the first season's episodes are also available on DVD. True to its messy format, however, the DVD version is available only in French and cannot be played on DVD players in the United States. Like the homegrown prophet, *Boomtown* is without honor in its own hometown. *Boomtown* went bust on TV. Theatrical lost out to theatrics.

Why did NBC pull the plug on this terrific series? Although *Boomtown* was a clear hit with TV critics and has many loyal fans to this day, it did not receive favorable ratings. The reason for this is easy to see. The very format that gave this series its identity also doomed it as the *"Boomtown* Shuffle."

The *Boomtown* Shuffle

Boomtown was unique in its storytelling arc. Its initial episodes refused to unfold in a straightforward time line. The coherence theory of truth ruled. As with a pile of shuffled cards, each episode required the viewer to insert each card into its proper place in order to form a coherent hand. The repetition of the same sequence of events seen from multiple perspectives presented the TV viewing audience with a bunch of cards from which to reconstruct the time line of the crime *de jour.*

Boomtown also used the standard storytelling technique of flashbacks in its story lines, but more than mere flashbacks were involved in each episode. Flashbacks are nothing new in the art of storytelling. Homer's *Odyssey* brilliantly incorporates flashbacks as it tells the story of Odysseus's trials and tribulations. But flashbacks usually deal out the story contents in chronological order, starting with the earliest event in time and ending with the most recent event in time.

Without a Trace fits this format. In a typical episode, a person goes missing and some time later the FBI's missing persons' team is called to the scene of the person's disappearance. The team then uses a white board to pencil in supposedly significant details surrounding the missing person's activities. The white board is a chart, with the time of disappearance and the time the team is called in serving as the bookends of the missing person's life. The arc connecting each end is filled in piece by piece, card by card, with the evidence discovered in the course of the team's investigation. Details about the missing person's life are always filled in from back to front, or left to right, both in the order in which they are discovered and the order in which they occurred in the missing person's life, *which always happen to be the same order. Cold Case* repeats the same procedure albeit without the white board. So does *CSI* when it uses flashbacks, although it is so focused on the details of forensic science that flashbacks play a lesser role in it.

Viewing audiences have seen the flashback technique so often they may take it for granted. It is a kind of "law of nature," a Platonic Form: Flashbacks always depict events in the actual order in which they occurred. The coherence of the events is always the same coherence as the discovery of the events.

The real world doesn't work like that, however; neither does an actual police investigation and neither does the storytelling art. *Boomtown* completely rejected this storytelling paradigm in its earliest episodes. In *Boomtown* the order of the discovery of the evidence never fit into the time line in which that event actually occurred. The order of discovery was always randomly "shuffled," hence, the *"Boomtown* Shuffle."

Imagine watching a game of cards. As each card is dealt, a player must pick up that card and incorporate it into a coherent unit called a hand. In making a hand, the order in which the cards were actually dealt is unimportant. The cardplayer will have to rearrange the cards in his possession to discover their logical order, which is what it means to have a hand. A card hand consists of cards as they are organized according to their proper relationship to each other, into a coherent whole. Organization makes the cards a hand. A card hand that cannot be so coherently ordered is worthless: "Who dealt this mess?"

What counts is the internally coherent structure that relates the cards to each other. The order in which the cards were dealt is irrelevant. Accordingly, in the "*Boomtown* Shuffle," the order in which the segments of the episode were dealt to the viewer was irrelevant. They could have been presented in any sequence as long as all of the pieces were included. What *was* relevant was the fact that after all of the "cards" had been dealt, the internal coherent relationship between the segments of the episode should have been apparent. They should all properly interlock to form the hand.

In a similar analogy, five individuals do not make a basketball team. They must be organized into a coherent group in which each person has a distinct role to fill, a role that complements the others. That is what is meant by teamwork. A team whose members are each All Star players does not thereby constitute an All Star team.

Like *Cold Case* and *Without a Trace*, but unlike *CSI*, *Boomtown* reflected the epistemology of perspectivism and contextualism. Given its shuffled format, how could it be otherwise? But perspectivism and contextualism are messy. They are prone to be three french fries short of a Happy Meal.

The *Boomtown* series was all about the organization of that Happy Meal. It was all about teamwork. It was all about forming its main characters into a team. More fundamentally, it was all about *making the viewer a part of that team*. *Boomtown* was the *Rocky Horror Picture Show* of TV police procedurals. Doing the "Time Warp" is doing the *Boomtown* Shuffle.

Like *Third Watch*, NBC's more successful and popular attempt at a show featuring teamwork between police investigators, emergency medical responders, and firefighters, *Boomtown* was all about the relationship between various members involved in police work: uniformed cops, plain clothes detectives, the DA's office, and the press. But unlike *Third Watch*, which tells its stories in chronological order, *Boomtown* told its stories in its first episodes in a manner befitting a card game. Each card had the name of one of the characters on its back. As each "card" was dealt, it was up to the viewer to assess that character's place in the story line. This took a lot of work, and like *The Rocky Horror Picture Show*, is an acquired taste. Clearly many TV viewers were not interested enough in the series to make that effort and *Boomtown's* hand went bust because of it. To most viewers, the order in which the cards are dealt makes all the difference in the world concerning their willingness to play the game.

The shuffled storytelling arc meant that what was told first did not in fact happen first. Graham Yost, *Boomtown's* creator, put it this way: "[We had] to let go of all of the rules [of] being a network show: The bad guys come in

Act One. In Act Two the crime occurs. In Act Three the police chase the bad guys. In Act Four the bad guys are arrested. In Act Five there is the court trial. It required us to let go of what we knew [of that format]."

Anne McGrail, one of the show's writers, put it this way: "We like to think of it as a sort of Rubik's cube." But Mr. Rubik only got his cube assembled in the final frame of the early episodes, a frame during which everything clicked into its proper place.

Boomtown's original shuffle format went bust quickly and only appeared in the early episodes. By the time "Home Invasion" (Episode 13) was produced, *Boomtown* abandoned its original antiformat format. From "Home Invasion" on, *Boomtown* generally moved in the direction of becoming a series like *Cold Case* or *Without a Trace* in that what happened first was told first, and what happened was largely told from a specific character's perspective.

There were two unique components to the *Boomtown* Shuffle: the storytelling arc and multiple character perspectives. These perspectives were retained throughout the brief life of this series, although the storytelling arc was not. In *Boomtown* there are seven main characters: Teresa Ortiz, a paramedic first responder; Andrea Little, a news reporter and David McNorris's mistress; David McNorris, an assistant district attorney and Little's lover; Joel Stevens and Bobby "Fearless" Smith, both plainclothes detectives and partners; and Tom Turcotte and Ray Hechler, street cops and partners.

Teresa Ortiz was a unique character in this series. She was not only the sole medical responder who was also a main character, but she was also the only main character without a designated partner. A healer to her very core, she became a paramedic after years spent caring for her mother as she slowly succumbed to cancer. As she says to Joel in "Reelin' in the Years" (Episode 4), "Somewhere in my brain I knew that I was going to be the parent of my parents. I just didn't think it was going to happen so soon." She was accompanied in the ambulance by Randy Palmer, another paramedic, whose character was too underdeveloped to be seen as Teresa's partner. Each of the other characters in this series had a real partner, someone who not only worked steadily and with him but who was, in a sense, a la Aristophanes, his missing half. After its first season, the producers and writers of *Boomtown* decided to transfer Teresa Ortiz to the police academy. In the only two episodes of *Boomtown* aired by NBC in the fall of 2003, she became the focus of interest, though still without a work partner. To make up for this, the show had her character focus on a potential romantic entanglement with Detective Joel Stevens, but their relationship never developed into a real partnership.

In *Boomtown's* first season, Teresa Ortiz's only role in crime fighting was to clean up the mess caused by the blood and guts inevitably spilled by the cops and the robbers. "All Hallow's Eve" (Episode 5) affords Teresa pride of place when her ambulance is hijacked on Halloween by Holden McKay, who threatens to kill her if she doesn't save his brother, who has been shot in the heart during a bungled burglary. A desperate McKay tells Teresa: "That's my brother. If he dies, you die." Given that McKay's brother does promptly die, Teresa tries to convince Holden that his brother is "simply unconscious" when in reality he had already bought the farm.

Detective Joel Stevens is summoned to find the kidnapped Teresa when the kidnappers release Teresa's fellow paramedic Randy, who promptly blows the whistle on the kidnapping. Interrupted while trick-or-treating with his wife Kelly and his son Willy, Joel is ambivalent about being called into the case. Making his excuses to Willy, Joel says, "Something bad has happened to a friend and I have to go." Joel is unwilling to share the context of his attraction to Teresa with Kelly and Willy. He was more than just Teresa's friend or acquaintance. She was someone to whom he was deeply attracted. For Joel, this assignment is not just business as usual; it's personal.

Teresa is able to communicate with Joel from her ambulance using Randy's cellphone. Using information from the cellphone, Joel tracks Holden and Teresa to a movie studio lot where Holden works. Holden McKay and his brother had come to Hollywood from Oklahoma to break into the movie business, but they quickly discovered that working in the movies turns on who you know, and they know no one. Reaching for the stars as stuntmen, Holden and his brother fall to earth as lowly janitors, and they plung into hell as failed jewelry store robbers.

Holden meets the end of his line when Teresa strangles him from the back seat of a movie studio police cruiser where he is hiding from the real cops. After subduing Holden, Teresa administers first aid to him. Joel's concerns for Teresa's well-being prompt him to tell her that she does not have to provide emergency medical aid to a person who has kidnapped her and threatened to kill her, a person that she just strangled into unconsciousness. Teresa replies that she did have to attend to the fallen McKay. Doing so is simply a manifes-tation of who she is as a person, a caretaker.

"Reelin' in the Years" presents a beautiful example of this series use of per-spectivism and contextualism. It begins with the arrest of a middle-aged suburban housewife who is jogging down the street. But so-called "Nora Jean Flannery" is anything but innocent. Watching her through binoculars, Fearless says of her, "Hide in plain sight." The "innocent" Nora Jean Flannery is really the notorious Sharon Rene Loftin., a.k.a. 1970s radical "Chimera." While she may be ensconced now in a conventional marriage, with a lovely young daughter Louisa, "Nora Jean" was part of a 1960s group of anti-war radicals who funded "the revolution" by robbing banks and using the ill-gotten booty to support their drug habits. On July 3, 1976, Sharon and her cohorts, Billy Togert and Che Jeter, stole $60,000 from the Citizen's Bank, killing a guard during their getaway. They also killed Victor Alfandre, the partner of Tom Turcotte's father, Paul. Victor had innocently stopped at the bank to withdraw some money and schmooze with one of the tellers. Victor's death was to have a profound impact not only on Paul Turcotte ("Worst damn day in my life"), but on Paul's son, Tom, the partner of Ray Heckler. It also significantly affected Andrea Little and her lover, David McNorris.

Brought into the squad room, Sharon Rene will only admit to Joel and Fearless, "My name is Nora Jean Flannery." Stymied by her intransigence, the detectives hit upon the idea of bringing Kevin Van Horn out of prison to confront "Nora Jean." Kevin was a young musician back in 1976. He was in love with Sharon and he innocently let her borrow his car, which she used to rob the bank. Falsely believed to have participated in the bank robbery, Kevin was unjustly convicted of murdering both the security guard and Victor Alfandre and was sentenced to life in prison.

Confronted by the puppy-dog countenance of the now middle-age Kevin, who says "I forgive you, Sharon," "Nora Jean" breaks down in tears and admits that she is Sharon Rene Loftin. But when she tells Fearless and Joel about the holdup, she denies that she personally shot anyone. Sharon claims she was in the bank vault and "By the time I got [out] there, the officer was already dead. I did not kill the officer at the bank. I don't want for my family, for my daughter, to [think that I did]."

Sharon was only arrested on a fluke. Earlier Fearless chased down a purse snatcher, a grubby bum, Dwayne Shover, who nonetheless led Fearless on a merry chase. Confronted with the three-strike provision and the threat of life in prison for such a petty crime, Dwayne rolled over on Sharon to make his third strike go away. Dwayne got his wish–he walked; arrested at last, Sharon finally stopped running. Or did she?

Paul Turcotte never recovers from the murder of his friend and partner, Victor Alfandre. Though the evidence from Sharon's testimony shows that Kevin Van Horn was innocent of any involvement with the bank robbery, Paul is unwilling to accept it. When Tom volunteers to drive Kevin home after his release from prison, Paul can't accept the fact that his own son would betray the memories and world view of his own father by helping out a man whom Paul still held to be guilty of his partner's death.

Ironically, Kevin Van Horn has issues with his own father, who also believed his son was guilty of the bank robbery. After Kevin was sentenced to life in prison, his father ceased to visit him in jail. Kevin says about his father during his ride home in Tom's patrol car, "He gave up on me. I never gave up on him. Maybe he's not ready to see me yet." But Tom's partner Ray will not allow Kevin to cop out on his relationship with his father. "Whatever happened all those years ago, he's still your father." Adding to the irony, Kevin's father now suffers from dementia. When Kevin nervously approaches him for the first time in more than twenty-five years, his father asks "Where have you been? You were supposed to take me to the dry cleaners this afternoon," as if Kevin had simply stepped out for a minute and had not been gone for most of his adult life. But Kevin is more than up to the task of reconstituting his relationship with his father. "I'm here to take care of you from now on."

The Kevin Van Horn murder case primarily explores the bonds between fathers and sons. Kevin's release causes Paul to relive the "worst damn day" of his life. In a complicated double flashback to the night of Victor's death, Paul remembers awakening from a drunken stupor to the sound of gunfire emanating from young Tom's bedroom. In a premature celebration of the fourth of July, eight-year-old Tom has innocently set off firecrackers in his bedroom, and Paul thought it was gunfire. A dazed Paul opens the door to Tom's room and points his gun at Tom, completely scaring Tom and forever estranging him from his father. When Tom offers to drive Kevin Van Horn home from prison, a beleaguered Paul asks him, "Are you trying to get back at me?" Tom, still resentful about having his own father pull a gun on him, responds "When a cop gets murdered, the first question you ask is 'Where was his partner?'" Tom admits to his partner Ray, "He pointed his gun at my head. I never fully trusted him again." By the end of the episode, Tom and Paul nevertheless achieve somewhat of a reconciliation. Tom knows how important his relationship is with his partner Ray, and he can easily imagine how devastated he would be if anything happened to him.

This case involves more than just father and son relationships. It also makes Andrea Little's career and is the occasion for her liaison with David McNorris. Five years prior to Sharon's arrest, Andrea was an unknown reporter working for the *Daily-Weekly*, an alternative free press. In a fruitless attempt to establish his innocence, Kevin writes letters to every newspaper on the planet, but Andrea is the only reporter who sees a story waiting to be told about Kevin Van Horn, innocent or no. That story makes her career. After first interviewing Kevin in jail, Little brings her story to David McNorris, already known as a legal hotshot working for the DA's office. During their first meeting, McNorris agrees to look into Kevin's file, not because McNorris is in any way convinced about Van Horn's innocence, but because he is more interested in getting into Little's britches. Four years later, McNorris and Little have an ongoing affair and Little moves up to a job with the *Los Angeles Tribune*. To McNorris' dismay, Little chooses Van Horn's coming-out party to break off their sleeping arrangements. At the end of this emotionally tense episode, Sharon's husband visits her in jail and pleadingly asks of her, "Tell me one thing. Did you kill that cop?" Sharon replies "No. I am not a killer. I can take anything as long as Louisa doesn't think that her mommy is a killer." But she is. In the final scene of this magnificent episode, the viewer watches her blow Victor's head off with a shotgun after he gets the drop on Billy and Che in the bank. In a gut-wrenching scene, the camera deals the last card of the hand as we see Victor's mangled body on the floor of the bank lobby. Sharon Rene Loftin, a.k.a. "Chimera," was indeed a cold-blooded killer.

"Insured by Smith & Wesson" (Episode 7) tells the tale of a different sort of killer altogether, a former "TV detective." Its logic opens when bad guys Reggie Flood and Spath Monroe invade Moe's sporting goods store, whose manager, Les Van Buren, is a washed-up actor who once played the action hero role in the fictitious TV series *Insured by Smith & Wesson*. The real star of this episode, however, is patrolman Ray Heckler, Tom Turcotte's partner.

The first to arrive at the scene of the failed robbery cum hostage situation, Ray fires his service revolver and accidentally shoots the inflatable giant turkey anchored atop the store as a promotional tool. One down. Indeed, the turkey is the only thing Officer Heckler shoots that fine day. Since one of the store employees was shot during the hostage situation, paramedic Teresa Ortiz volunteers to go into the store and give the woman first aid. Ray Heckler volunteers to take the place of Teresa's usual partner Randy Palmer. Earlier, mistaking Ray's honesty for a lack of self-confidence, Division Captain Ron Hicks had refused Ray's request for an upgrade because, from Hicks' perspective, Ray had not "stepped up" enough as a senior uniformed officer. "They look at a psych report and they see a guy who questions his own fitness." After being denied the promotion, Ray lies to his partner Tom by making himself sound like a hero for turning down the promotion. "I had to turn it down. It meant that I would have to leave the Division. I'd leave you without a partner." But Ray was not done with being a hero just yet.

Another factor motivating Ray to help the hostages in Moe's is the fact that Ray had watched Les Van Buren as an actor in his old TV series. The role Les played in that series motivated Ray to become a police officer. "He inspired me to be a cop." Ironically prefiguring *Boomtown's* own demise, the fictitious *Insured by Smith and Wesson* series was cancelled quickly, though reruns were still on the air. "Cancelled after only thirteen episodes. Kind of broke my heart," Ray says of that series.

But Ray's attempts to step up and change his context by taking on the role of a paramedic backfires when Flood instantly recognized Ray as a cop. "He's a cop," he tells Spath. "I can smell 'em." Ray quickly becomes another one of Flood's hostages, one that Flood will personally enjoy tormenting because he still blames the police for permanently crippling his brother Neil years ago. Neil had been shot in the spine by a police officer during Neil's own failed attempt to rob a woman, which left the victim seriously injured. Holding his cellphone to Ray's ear, Flood instructs Ray to "Call your wife. I want her to get the same call that I got when you cops broke my brother's back."

The perspective of Les Van Buren's failed TV cop career plays an important role in the outcome of this *Boomtown* drama. After Flood handcuffs him to a support beam, Ray tries to talk Les into playing the hero again and helping him out. "You were a hero to millions of people. You don't believe me? Look [at the TV coverage]." Les sees his own countenance on the news and he sees that it is good. As the out-of-control Flood threatens to shoot the helpless Ray, the sound of a gunshot provokes Ray to fantasize about his own funeral in which all of his police station buddies acknowledge what a great man he was. "Ray was a hero. He was the finest man I ever knew," yadda yadda, while his widow, Cherie, complains that he died "before he got around to fixing the toilet!"

The gunshot that provokes Ray's fantasies is not aimed at Ray, however, but at Flood. Using a gun he had hidden in the store, Les shoots Flood in the back just as Flood is about to shoot Ray in the face. Ray says, "What do you know Les? You're a hero after all." It seems Ray will now have time to fix that pesky toilet, while Les can act out his fantasies of being a hero himself and using his newfound fame to host a reality cop show. Or not.

While Les tells Ray, "I saw my face on all of those TVs. God, it was beautiful. You're Jack Wesson," Ray sees Les's face on TV too, only it is the store's video surveillance system, which has captured images of Les conspiring with Flood to rob Moe's, images Les was less than eager to have shown on TV. Playing the final card in this episode's hand, Ray arrests Les for his part in the robbery, telling him that he is no Jack Wesson. "No, I'm Ray Heckler." Busted toilet and all, it is still a good thing to be Ray Heckler.

Flood had his brother's back and failed to protect it, crippling him. Les Van Buren had Flood's back and shot him to death, and Ray had Les' back and arrested him. Watch your back!

Boomtown's "Pilot" (Episode 1) started the card game shuffle. This episode opens and closes with the perspective of Grandpa Cecil La Fontaine's commenting to Tom Turcotte and Ray Heckler that, while London, Paris, and Vienna are all built on great rivers,"LA's got a concrete drainage system. It's all we got." It is not until the context changes at the episode's conclusion that the viewing audience sees Grandpa La Fontaine scattering the ashes of his grandson, Cantrel La Fontaine, into that very same drainage system. The circumstances surrounding the murder of teenager Audrey Darnell and the wounding of Grace Adams in a drive-by shooting lead in a convoluted way to the accidental death of young Cantrel, who dies falling from a window ledge while attempting to avoid arrest for the shootings. Though he is not the killer, Cantrel's fate was sealed when he went for a ride friend, Taylor Gates.

The shooting occurs at a community center where assistant DA David McNorris's wife Marion volunteers. Andrea Little, a news reporter for the *Los Angeles Tribune*, interviews the distraught and blood-splattered Marion as she cleans herself up in the bathroom. Little is at the community center to cover the press conference about the shooting that McNorris convenes on the site. Little asks McNorris "Why are we here? Why a news conference at this particular shooting?" To which McNorris replies, "We are basking in the warm blood of honesty. I know that me being here would get you here." Little's question to David was trying to get at what made this shooting so special when shootings like these are a dime a dozen in LA. The delicious irony of this exchange is the fact that in addition to Andrea's and David's professional responsibilities, they are sleeping together. The rest of the assembled crowd is oblivious to the "warm blood of honesty" in which Andrea and David are basking. Context is everything.

Many characters in this series have serious issues with the warm blood of honesty. Andrea and David cannot publicly admit that they are sleeping together, let alone acknowledge that to David's wife, Marion. Joel Stevens and Teresa Ortiz cannot admit their serious attraction for one another, nor can Joel admit to Teresa that his wife Kelly did not accidentally cut her wrists on the shower door. Joel cannot admit this even to his best friend and partner

Fearless Smith. Fearless in turn cannot admit to Joel that he was molested as a child and still carries those emotional scars around with him. Fearless cannot even admit to the prostitute he visits that his friend "Freaktown" was killed in Iraq in Operation Desert Storm. After that visit Joel asks, "How did the story end this time?" and Fearless replies, "I said he lived. No sense ruining the moment."

Opening up to one another about the truth would ruin many moments. As the episode ends, however, Grandpa La Fontaine opens up the truth and empties out the jar containing his grandson's ashes, pouring them into the waters of the LA drainage basin. "Okay river, take my grandson home."

Bad Faith and the Look

Most people have difficulty "basking in the warm blood of honesty." This knowledge forms the basis of French philosopher Jean-Paul Sartre's existentialist philosophy. *Existentialism* is a philosophical outlook that focuses on the nature of what it means to be a person, what it means to be a specific individual with a personal identity all one's own. Written in the midst of the trauma occasioned by World War II, Sartre's *Being and Nothingness* and *Existentialism as Humanism* laid out far-reaching claims about the basic human condition: Humans are self-conscious agents thrown into a world fraught with perils, a world in which humans are "forced to be free." Humans are *self*-conscious. Unlike other animals, we are beings who are aware of ourselves as "selves," agents who must act in a variety of circumstances and conditions not of our own choosing. Our actions and choices make us the persons we are. To exist as a person is to be an agent fully in charge of one's own character, fully in charge of one's own destiny.

But individuals are not alone. No man is an island. Humans live in communities. This means that the choices we make inevitably affect others, just as we are affected by the choices of others. One individual's freedom is conditioned by the freedom of every other individual. Individuals live public lives, not simply private ones. This is quite dreadful and not simply because our actions affect both ourselves and others, often dramatically, often negatively. Nor is it is dreadful because others are watching us. It is dreadful because others are judging us as they observe us, constantly measuring us. We are all permanent contestants on a lifelong version of *American Idol* and it is not going to be pretty.

Being on stage is the natural human condition. Even Chuck Noland, the character Tom Hanks played in the movie *Cast Away,* invents a pseudo-human companion, "Wilson," from a volleyball that bears a "human" face formed by a muddy hand print. A volleyball is just a volleyball, but slap a face on it and voilà, it becomes a human being. Wilson not only offered Noland the opportunity for soliloquies, he allowed Noland to stay sane in solitary circumstances that otherwise would have driven Noland completely mad. Wilson provided the "human" judgment so necessary for Noland to maintain his grip on reality,

and yet Noland's inability to measure up to Wilson's watchful eye, his imagined expectations, drove Noland at last to find a way to flee from the dreaded
loneliness, an overwhelming loneliness that threatened to turn "No-land" into
no-man.

The inherent public nature of human existence fills each person with dread,
with anxiety, with what the Danish philosopher Søren Kierkegaard rightfully
called "fear and trembling." Each individual's actions are on public display for
the whole world to see. It is not just St. Nick who "sees us when we're sleepin'
and knows when we're awake," or God who is aware of the flight of each little
sparrow. Does the individual have the resources, the courage, or the audacity of
hope to act on stage with the whole world judging his performance?

The public nature of human activity and its resulting anxiety is a product
of what Sartre calls "the Look" or "the Stare." Others are always looking at
us, they are staring at our activities, they are judging us. All the world's a
stage, and we are but players on it. Being stared at, even by a face painted on
a volleyball, is inherently unnerving because it forces us to measure up to the
judgments implied by the viewer's stare. It produces the dismay, the dread,
the anxiety that ever accompanies each of our actions, the fear that we cannot
measure up, that we are too big for our britches, that others—even volley-
balls—are laughing at us.

To avoid the Stare, to avoid the measuring Look, to make ourselves literally
more comfortable in our own skins, we employ a variety of subterfuges to
shake off the heavy hand of the public's judgment. The chief subterfuge is the
insistence that in acting as we did in a given situation, we had no choice. We
lie to ourselves and insist that we could not help it. We practice *bad faith*. Bad
faith is more than the intentional lie to others in order to fool them. Bad faith
involves something much more intimate than merely wearing the public mask
we all wear before each other. That strategy is trivial. Bad faith goes to the
core of our own existence. It is the puzzle of the lies we tell ourselves to fool
ourselves, to hide our "self" from ourselves.

How can we possibly fool ourselves? That is a real puzzle. Freedom is the
human condition. But freedom is too painful, too nerve racking; it is too much
for us to handle. It makes us feel guilty, a surefire sign that our deeds are too
big for their doer. To "escape" from our freedom, to escape from our very
selves, from our human condition, from the "stare" of others, we pretend that
we were never really free in the first place. We had to do it. But that is a lie, a
big, fat lie, the ultimate lie. We are not free not to be free. Freedom is the
human condition. There is no such thing as a victimless crime. Even when a
person's actions affect only herself, she becomes both the doer of her deed and
the recipient of her own action. In lying to herself, she attempts to treat herself only as the victim of her actions and not also as the agent of her actions.
But she is always both.

Boomtown is about the human condition: the Stare and the bad faith we fall
into as a result of it. It abounds with characters who are on stage for each

other, characters who suffer from the Look, the Stare of others who are indeed judging them. Most of the main characters have an intimate association with a partner, another person who is in a unique position to see through their public masks and private subterfuges. But each character also is "on stage" before each other. The context of each character's perspective about the crime is a subject for each episode. Each character's perspective about another's character provides the energy that powers each episode. Each character is the subject of each other's Look, each other's Stare. It is their human condition.

Vanessa and Chris Griggs fall victim to the "Stare" of Wilson Minor in "Possession." Working for Ivan Vronski, who earns his living by peddling bad faith, Vanessa allows others to stare at her body and to fantasize about having sex with her. Wilson's fantasy stare turns deadly when he cannot accept the reality that while he can look, he cannot touch. He can't possess her. Wilson deludes himself into being married to the fair Vanessa, a delusion that provokes him into murdering Vanessa's real husband, Chris. In turn, Wilson becomes the victim of his own "Stare" when he can't look away from the sight of Detective Bobby Smith's naked buttocks when Smith drops his trousers to distract Wilson. A Stare is a double-sided affair.

Sharon Rene Loftin in "Reelin' in the Years" practices bad faith in a spectacular manner when she refuses to confess that she murdered Victor Alfandre. Indeed, it is her bad faith that makes this episode such terrific drama. It is not simply that she lies to the detectives, or to her husband, or indirectly through him to her young daughter. Essentially she lies to herself. She can't admit to herself that she is the kind of person who could murder someone in cold blood in such a brutal, bloody, and senseless manner. In a sure sign that her deed is indeed too much for her, she reinvents her own memories to match what she wants to believe about herself, that she is an innocent bystander, a victim, not a brutal murderer. But the viewing audience is aware of the lie. The viewer sees Victor Alfandre kneeling on the floor of the bank after getting the drop on Sharon's partners and turning to give Sharon the Look. That is why she shoots him. She cannot abide his Stare. Innocent looking though she may be, she is not the innocent bystander. Her husband must come to terms with the fact that the woman he loves is a murderer. Her daughter will have to grow up in a world in which "Mommy Dearest" is a cold-blooded killer.

Les Van Buren fell lock, stock, and barrel for the Look in Insured by Smith & Wesson, only in his case he initially liked what he saw. In his old TV series he portrayed a "Lone Ranger" type hero riding to the rescue of the good and innocent. In the siege at Moe's, he talks himself into becoming a real-life action hero by freeing the imprisoned Ray Heckler. But the Look gets him after all, when the store's video surveillance tape shows his bad faith for all to see, exposing him as one of the bad guy robbers and not one of the good guy cops. A little less TV exposure would have meant a lot more to Les. From his perspective, the warm blood of honesty was not the best policy.

The Look also applies to detective Joel Stevens. In "Pilot," he is introduced as a troubled man. Patrolman Tom Turcotte attended police academy training with Joel and thinks that "Everything comes easy for him. Even in the academy, he sailed through, and he made detective." But Tom had mistaken one of Joel's public masks for Joel's true essence. The underlying reality is that Joel lives a deeply troubled life. His wife, Kelly, suffered severe postpartum depression after the birth of their daughter. Tragically, their infant daughter Emma dies suddenly, apparently of SIDS. This sends Kelly deeper into depression, which leads to her suicide attempt. Only by happenstance does a worried Joel arrive home early enough to discover Kelly bleeding in her bathtub. He calls an ambulance in time to save her life. Teresa Ortiz treats Kelly at that time and she is again at the scene when Cantrel La Fontaine accidentally falls to his death. As Joel uses a garden hose to wash Cantrel's blood off the sidewalk, Teresa asks him how Kelly is doing. This prompts a very troubled Joel to lie to Teresa. "She's good. . . . It was just a freak thing, you know. It was just the shower door breaking . . . The glass . . . She's good." Teresa's laconic reply, "Yeah," tells the whole story. Joel is lying to her. The shower door did not break, causing the cuts on Kelly's wrists. Teresa gives Joel the Look. She knows Joel is lying, and he knows that she knows he is lying. Worse, Joel is lying to himself. He tries to make himself believe that Kelly accidentally cut herself when the shower door "broke." He can't face the fact that she attempted suicide. But his lie, his bad faith, is a failure, and Teresa's Look is an acknowledgment of that awful fact. Joel is simply too honest to practice bad faith.

"Lost Child" (Episode 18) revisits the source of Joel's agony and his failed attempt at bad faith in trying to deal with it. It begins with a search for a kidnapped newborn whose drug-addicted mother, Janice Edwards, is found, like Kelly, unconscious and bleeding to death. Teresa saves Janice's life, as she did previously with Joel's wife Kelly. Joel and Bobby "Fearless" Smith are then assigned the task of discovering what happened to Janice and her baby. They quickly uncover a plot by obstetrician Pamela Donner to steal the babies of drug addicts, and arrest her. These events are only a minor subplot in this episode, however.

The real "lost child" of this episode is Joel's and Kelly's own dead daughter, Emma. A second autopsy was performed on the infant because of suspicion that she had not died of natural causes. Joel has the autopsy results in his locker, but he refuses to look at them because of what he fears they might contain. Not daring to risk the Stare of the autopsy results, he prefers to believe that Emma died due to his neglect, because instead of attending to her needs, Joel had become fixated on watching a very troubled Kelly as she slept. In turn, Kelly believes that she somehow murdered Emma unwittingly while she was under the influence of sleeping medication she was taking for her depression. This suspicion motivated her own suicide attempt. Alll of this somehow comes to the attention of the division of internal affairs and police officer Rich Trumper, who believes that Joel may have murdered baby Emma.

Officer Trumper turns up the heat on Detective Stevens by getting Tom Turcotte to snitch on him. Trumper wants Tom to betray Joel, a betrayal feared by Tom's own father Paul. As Tom's father says to him, "Friends need friends who look out for them." Tom turns the betrayal tables on Trumper and places the copy of the autopsy report into Trumper's files to make it seem as if Trumper has a vendetta against Joel. Tom then snitches on Trumper to the police department's inspector general. Let Trumper himself suffer the Look under the all-seeing eye of the police review board.

After David McNorris tips off Joel about the internal affairs investigation into Emma's death, Joel and Kelly hire Michael Hirsch as their psychiatrist/lawyer. Under the Look of Hirsch's questioning, Kelly hears from Joel that he was watching her during the night of Emma's death and therefore, Kelly could not have caused that death. This revelation liberates Kelly from her feelings of dread and responsibility about unwittingly killing Emma. After Hirsch discusses the results of the second autopsy, Joel also is relieved of his guilt feelings. Baby Emma did not die from neglect or from SIDS, but rather from the rupture of a cerebral aneurysm. There was nothing that Joel or Kelly could have done to save her. This knowledge provides them each with the necessary means for closure by eliminating any further need to practice the bad faith they had each used to assuage their helplessness over Emma's death. Their lives are considerably happier after this revelation.

Joel's partner Fearless also lives a life under the judgment of the Stare, and like Joel, also tries to live up to the expectations of someone who died under his watch. This topic is the focal point of "The Freak" (Episode 6). Fearless is an Army sergeant who served in Iraq during Operation Desert Storm. Serving under him is a wisecracking inner-city kid nicknamed "Freaktown," who has a feckless attitude toward the military life. Freaktown is always trying to get Fearless to loosen up, to enjoy the moment even when confronted with the horrible possibility of combat. But Freaktown is afraid of one thing. He is afraid that he will die in Iraq and he makes Fearless promise to protect his life. "You've got to promise that you'll keep me alive." Fearless makes that promise but is unable to keep it. Freaktown is felled by a sniper's bullet meant for Fearless, and his ghost becomes Fearless's constant companion. "He took a bullet that was meant for me." His partner, Joel, has a different perspective. "It doesn't work that way. That bullet was not meant for you."

Though it appears six times in this episode, Freaktown's spirit does not haunt Fearless in the ordinary sense of that term. Freaktown's Look does not ruin or poison Fearless's existence. As the ghost of Freaktown says to Fearless, "I'm not done teaching you about life yet." Freaktown's ghost, instead, is a reminder to Fearless that he failed to keep a promise, and quite a significant promise at that. On the anniversary of Freaktown's death, Fearless always sings a song to his departed buddy, a lighthearted song that signifies that Freaktown's philosophy about the sheer joy of existence is one to be respected and cherished.

His friend's ghost and Fearless's attempts to come to terms with it provide just one of the story lines in this episode. Another one involves the investigation by Tom and Ray of a dead person whose corpse was shot out of a circus cannon and landed in a hot tub. In a play at slapstick humor to counter the seriousness of the main story line, Tom and Ray discover that Charlie Graham has stolen the body of his best friend, Albert Beechem, from the undertaker, loaded it into a circus cannon, and accidentally fired it into a hot tub while aiming to shoot it into the Pacific Ocean. Charlie is pretty much of a klutz in everything he does, but he jokingly promised Albert that he would shoot him out of a cannon to celebrate Albert's life. Darlene, Albert's wife and the object of Charlie's romantic fantasies, thinks Charlie is a complete goofball, but she is favorably impressed with his dedication to honor the memory of his best friend and accede to his "last wishes." Perhaps Charlie has a chance to romance the fair Darlene after all. How sweet.

The main story line is not so sweet. Russian expatriate mobster Vadim Solonick brutally murders a man in the restaurant where Russian immigrant Katrina and her ten-year-old daughter Lara work. Lara witnesses the crime and her testimony can send Vadim to the chair. Understandably, Katrina does not want to risk her daughter's life by allowing her to testify against Vadim. When Joel and Fearless offer Lara and Katrina protection in exchange for their testimony, Katrina does not know what to do. In her indecision, she seeks advice from Teresa. Was Fearless trustworthy? Can he be counted on to keep the promise that his Look implies? Teresa reassures Katrina. "I know him. I know that he is a man of his word." Fearless promises to protect Lara and Katrina. "If I can keep my word on this one, I just figure somehow I'll make things right, I'll find some peace."

Protecting Lara and Katrina becomes part of the bargain Fearless made with Freaktown. It gives him another swing of the bat, a swing that connects in the climax of the episode as Fearless takes on the Solonick Mob and kills Vadim as Vadim holds a gun to Katrina's head. Fearless' Look trumps Vadim's Look.

Joel listens to Fearless singing Freak's birthday song after all the Russian mobsters are mowed down. "I can see clearly now. . . ."

In response to the imaginary prodding of Freaktown's ghost to "get a life," Fearless makes a list of weird things to do before he dies, a list he carries with him and does his best to satisfy. In "Pilot," Fearless visits a very expensive prostitute, one of the items on his to-do list. When the prostitute asks about Fearless's cigarette lighter, he tells her the story of how he found it during Operation Desert Storm, how bending over to pick it up saved his life from a sniper's bullet. "It just so happens that I like telling stories." Some of those stories allow Fearless to manipulate reality to suit the moment. When Joel asks him how he ended the story this time, Fearless replies, "I let him live," referring to the trajectory of the sniper's bullet. While missing Fearless's head when he bent over to pick up the lighter, the bullet continued on to kill his comrade Freaktown. Fearless rewrites the ending of the story to please the prostitute. "No sense in ruining the moment." Fearless is fully up to the task of being permanently on stage.

As he accomplishes each item on that to-do list, he crosses them off under the watchful eye of either Joel or Freaktown's ghost. One item on that list was to come to terms with a dark and foreboding element of Fearless's childhood, his sexual molestation as a child by Coach Malcolm Barker.

"Fearless" (Episode 16) handles this emotionally powerful issue. It opens on the roof of police division headquarters with Ray telling Fearless how to get away with committing murder. Ray acknowledges that "I've been down that road myself. I don't know what kind of goblins are haunting you. I don't know what sort of peace you're hoping to find." Ray really wants to talk Fearless out of it, so instead of supplying him with a throwaway gun, he gives him a hammer in a bag.

The logic of the episode opens with the shooting death of Trevor Jenkins, a neighborhood pot dealer turned child molester who is killed by one of his victims, ten-year-old James King. When Fearless and Joel threaten to discover that James was the shooter, James's mother, Marvella, confesses to the crime to protect her son from the murder charge.

While trying to discover why a ten-year-old child would purposely shoot anyone, Fearless unearths some personally troubling information. Trevor Jenkins comes from the same neighborhood where Fearless grew up, and both of them had played basketball for Coach Malcolm Barker. Fearless knew that Coach Barker had sexually molested him, a painful fact that he had repressed up until then. When he discovers that Barker also molested Trevor Jenkins and that Jenkins has turned into a child molester as a result of that trauma, Fearless resolves to hunt down Barker and murder him for all the evil he has wrought.

Barker has changed his name to Baxter in order to escape his past, but Fearless has little trouble tracking him down. The Look of revenge, however, proves easier to fantasize about than the real thing proves to accomplish. Accosting Baxter in his home, Fearless pulls a gun on him and deeply wants to kill Baxter for the evil he has engendered in those he had so foully touched. But Baxter has not only changed his name, he has changed his very soul too. Baxter did not practice bad faith. Deeply sorrowful for the pain he inflicted on his young victims, he had turned his life around and was now actively counseling others who had the same sexual desires for children that he once had. Indeed, he was even ready for Fearless to kill him if that was what it took to help Fearless heal from the pain Baxter had caused him. Context is everything. When Fearless sees for himself that Coach Barker is a changed man who really had become Baxter, he realizes that he can't wantonly murder him. He too must reinvent himself, get over it, and get on with the rest of his life. As Fearless tells his girlfriend Katrina, "I guess I'm still a prisoner of something that happened a long time ago." Knowing the truth does not instantly set you free, but it is a start.

Fearless puts down the throwaway gun he planned to use against Baxter and leaves his house, sadder and wiser, only to run into his partner Joel who, unknown to Fearless, was outside waiting for him throughout the confrontation. When Fearless admits to Joel that he could not kill Baxter, Joel acknowledges that he knew all along Fearless would not kill Baxter. "It's not who you are." Fearless also confesses to Joel that the story he told about his brother being molested is a lie. Joel admits that he always knew the truth, but pretended to believe otherwise for Fearless's sake. In turn Fearless had pretended to believe Joel's story that his wife accidentally cut herself with the shower door, and Joel knew that Fearless knew that too. Fearless says, "You knew it wasn't my brother." Joel says, "You knew my wife didn't break our shower door." Each acknowledged the other's Look, and rejecting bad faith, they became better partners.

Regarding Fearless's decision not to murder Baxter, Fearless asked Joel what he would have done had he indeed killed Baxter. Joel responded, "There is a shovel in the car. Had you done it, it would have been the right thing to do."

The Rev. Ronnie Tucker, a friend of Fearless from their days in the 'hood, was a peripheral witness to Fearless's struggles with the torment of his goblins. During a sermon at church following Fearless's confrontation with Baxter, Reverend Tucker raises the problem of evil and the suffering of the innocent. "Where is God when bad things happen to good people? I don't know, but I see God is in a man sharing his strength with a young boy." In the end, Fearless shares with ten-year-old James King the fact that he too had been down the same road James was now traveling, and there really was hope ahead for a ". . . bright, bright, shiny day."

In "All Hallow's Eve," Fearless has an encounter with Andrea Little shortly before raiding the house where the two robber confederates of Holden McKay live. Like both Joel and the Reverend Tucker in "Fearless" and Teresa in "The Freak," Andrea too sees Fearless's essentially good nature. "I guess I'm not as mysterious and unfathomable as I thought," Fearless says to her. No, mysterious and unfathomable Fearless is not, but he was a good man and a good storyteller.

David McNorris, the assistant DA and chief protagonist in this series, was aware of the fact that he too was always on stage, especially in his own eyes. He was both the actor and the audience for all of his mini-dramas. Sometimes this appeared to be simple narcissism. In "Pilot," David staged an on-the-spot news conference at the site of a community center shooting that left one young girl dead and another seriously injured. When reporter Andrea Little put her insightful question to McNorris, "Why are we here? Why a news conference at this particular shooting?" the implied response was that the news conference was staged to watch David McNorris perform before "a live studio audience." Later, when Taylor Gates was tracked down and arrested for the community center shootings, Gate's lawyer asks David, "Where are the cameras? I can't see you making a bust without cameras." But the "cameras" were there; they lay in the eyes of Grandpa La Fontaine, whose grandson Cantrel had died as a result of his participation in the recent shooting when his friend Taylor Gates chose to show off for Cantrel. McNorris showed up at Taylor's arrest not to see himself on camera, but to see justice done in the eyes of Grandpa La Fontaine, a much more significant stage setting.

In "Possession," David worried that Marion was too suspicious of his relationship with Andrea Little. Claiming to be "working out," he lied to Marion that he was at a new gym when she went to his old haunts to check up on him. David was not in a gym at the time, though he was engaged in bedroom gymnastics with Little.

David McNorris had a brief, but very telling, scene in "All Hallow's Eve" that occurs when he and his wife Marion attend a Halloween party sans costumes. Supplied with party masks by their hosts, David excuses himself from Marion's presence to follow the similarly bemasked Andrea to an upstairs bathroom where a corpse lies on an autopsy table (which is about as close to "forensic science" as this series ever got). When David greets Andrea, she asks from behind her mask, "Do I know you, sir?" Yes, biblically, as a matter of fact. Also in a biblical sense, David is troubled by this fact. "Do you think that I want to be the kind of man who cheats on his wife? Look into my eyes and tell me you don't want me. I'm powerless, and I don't like that." In response to these high-wire dramatics, the fake corpse sits up and gives a haunting Look of its own.

David has major problems handling the Look from behind Andrea's mask. So does Marion. After following David into the now deserted bathroom, she spots Andrea's mask looking back at her from the counter where Andrea left it, and she knows in a heartbeat that David is having an affair with Andrea. The Look can kill. It breaks Marion's heart.

In "Reelin' in the Years" Andrea called off her love affair with David, much to his dismay. That episode introduced the TV audience to the beginning of their affair as well as to its apparent ending. Although they are no longer sleeping together, they still need to maintain some kind of relationship. In "Insured by Smith & Wesson," Andrea tells David, "Just because we're not screwing doesn't mean I don't care [about you]," to which he callously replies, "I'd rather be screwing and not have you care."

"The David McNorris Show" (Episode 9) is all about the inner goblins that haunt David, much to his own disgust. David McNorris is a man filled with self-loathing. He is haunted by an inner demon, a demon that drove him to alcoholism as a bad-faith coping strategy. He was afraid he had become just like his own father. In this episode Ron Berman, a bigwig Hollywood producer, promises to advance David's career from that of a mere assistant district attorney to the office of the district attorney for the city of Los Angeles in exchange for McNorris's help in obstructing justice in a case involving Berman's own son Zack. Berman believes his son may have viciously murdered his girlfriend, seventeen-year-old Joy Lam, after an alcohol- and drug-filled party that Ron Berman had hosted.

Ron Berman is a self-made man. Starting out as a member of an Alaska-based fishing boat crew, Berman's first job was to clean and gut the catch of the day. Eventually he worked his way up to ownership of the boat, then the whole fleet. Now he is a mover and shaker in Hollywood. But from McNorris's perspective, "Berman may clean himself up all he wants, but he still smells like the slime line to me." Only now Berman has moved from the fish-gutting slime line to the Hollywood movie business slime line to the murder cover-up slime line. Any way you slice it, he is still at the end of the slime line.

Summoned to the scene of the crime by McNorris's boss, District Attorney Ben Fisher, who hopes to ride Berman's coattails to the office of mayor, David is called upon to be the fixer, the man who makes problems like this one go away. Ben tells David, "Ron wants to do whatever it takes." Fix it he does. David has Zack Berman pretend to flee to Brazil on Ron Berman's private jet while he works on making the Joy Lam murder case go away.

In the meantime Joel and Fearless are the lead detectives in this case. After visiting the Lam home, Fearless notices there were no mementos of the family's previous life in Cambodia. "When I look around your home I see someone who doesn't want to admit where he came from." Indeed, Joy's father had been a bar boy prostitute in Cambodia during the Vietnam War, an experience that seared his soul. Seeing his teenage daughter's infatuation with Zack Berman, Lam adopts a Lamarckian viewpoint about his own nature and mistakenly assumes his daughter had ended up just as he had, a prostitute. "I was afraid that it was something in my genes." Horrified and enraged, he beat his own daughter to death with a fireplace poker. He could kill his own daughter, but he could not kill his own history. He could not stand the perspective of his own Look. Once Zack Berman is cleared by the elder Lam's arrest, Ben Fisher tells David McNorris, "Every town needs someone who gets things done. You are the man. You want something fixed? You call the fixer." Ben thinks that calling David a fixer is a great compliment to him. Didn't he prove Zack's innocence when both Ron Berman and Ben Fisher had assumed otherwise?

Rather than taking it as a compliment to his abilities, McNorris is totally appalled by the label. He is horrified when he tells Ron Berman, "You know what the most amazing thing about this whole mind-blowing day was? Seeing the look on your face when you realized that your kid wasn't a murderer. It wasn't relief. It was surprise. Not all boys turn out like their old man. It's not inevitable." Like Joy's father, Ron Berman also believed that his own child had turned out to be the very sort of wretched person that he knew himself to be. Like father, like child. David McNorris spent his whole adult life running away from that very same identification.

Though Andrea Little tells David in "Possession" that he is "nothing like his father," as he enters a boxing ring to receive his daily dose of humility, the truth of the matter is that Davis is just like his father. Beatings are his problem-solving strategy.

David is deeply ashamed of himself for what he has done, what he has become. Drunk and stumbling, he shows up later at the Berman household and viciously beats Ron Berman, exhibiting the very behavior he so categorically condemned in his own father. Then he staggers to Andrea's house. There he confesses to Andrea what he has willingly become a party to. "Deputy DA helps murder suspect evade capture." Andrea will have none of it. "You're really a drunk," she says. David won't allow his drunkenness to be his excuse. "No. In some ways I'm more clear headed than I've been my whole life. I have become everything that I abhor, everything that my father once was that I swore that I wouldn't be. I've become an adulterer, a liar, a drunk, a *fixer*." Perhaps there was "something in his genes" after all.

Later, in a guilt-racked fit of "the warm blood of honesty," he staggers home and compounds his own horror by confessing to Marion about his affair with Andrea. Like his father before him, the fixer, "deceit comes second nature to me, Jackie McNorris of Dorchester, Massachusetts," he tells her. Marian leaves him. He can't fix that.

"Blackout" (Episode 17) is a continuation of David's self-loathing, self-destructive, love and hate affair with his genetics and the bottle. It opens with a testimonial dinner in honor of David's boss, LA's District Attorney Ben Fisher. Unwisely deciding to make his own impromptu speech in Fisher's honor, David cites the Berman case and recalls how Fisher had ordered McNorris to "pursue this investigation wherever it leads without fear or favor." No matter how brilliant David thought it to be, his drunken encomium to the "virtuous" Fisher comes across as a rambling disjointed embarrassment from the perspective of the audience, which includes David's ex-mistress Andrea Little.

After the dinner, David hitches a ride back to his car from Andrea, and while at his car, a ride home. "I think that I'm too drunk to drive." This prompts a fight about David's alcohol consumption, and, changing his mind, a miffed David decides to go it alone. "No, I'm not that drunk." Then he says sarcastically to a disgusted Andrea, "You're the [real] victim in all of this." Of course David really sees himself as the victim. Fed up, Andrea tells him to "go to hell." To which David responds, "I'll see you there."

The next morning David awakes in Hell on a "bright, bright, shiny day" after passing out in his car, which is parked all catawampus in his driveway. Ominously, one of his car's headlights is broken and there is blood on it. True to the episode's title, David has no memory of what happened to him after he left Andrea. Blackout. It seems David McNorris found a way to practice bad faith and avoid the Stare of others by simply wiping his own memory clean.

In his suit coat pocket he finds a napkin from a strip club with the name "Layla" scrawled on it. Layla is a stripper at this club, where David had gone to lick his wounds after his fight with Andrea. On his way to track down the club's location, David comes across an accident scene involving a disheveled street person who was killed by a hit–and–run driver the night before. Putting two and two together to make five, David immediately jumps to the conclusion that in his drunken stupor he himself had run down the poor victim. In a panic, he asks Tom Turcotte and Ray Heckler, the investigating officers on the scene to "keep me in the loop on this one." Puzzled, Tom and Ray can't figure out the context of why whisky-laden assistant DA David McNorris cares about such a seemingly insignificant case. Where are the cameras on this one?

Totally disconcerted over his failure to remember what transpired the previous night, David finds Layla and has her fill in some of the blanks. In doing so, he forgets about a scheduled afternoon court hearing on a major drug bust case. Back in the station, an angry Joel Stevens confronts David regarding his failure to show up in court. "He [the judge] threw out the whole case. We've been trying to make this case for six months and thanks to you our dealer just walked." Flustered before the Stare of Detective Stevens, David offers to atone for his failure. "Hit me. Go ahead, hit me." Joel is completely taken back. As much as he might want to clobber David McNorris for his failure to do his job, he is not about to physically assault him. The Dirty Look would have to do.

Back home in his garage, a distraught McNorris kneels in front of his damaged car, deciding whether to wipe out evidence. "I know I can fix this one, pop. I made a mistake. The lesson of this will not be lost on me." Then, looking into a mirror at his own hazy countenance, David offers his defense argument to his own self-reflected Stare, which forms his imaginary jury. "You want the truth? The truth is that the defendant is a lying, womanizing, cheating drunk. Sorry, pop, I can't fix this one," he tells the mirror of his soul. Crestfallen though he is, David McNorris still can't sink to the level of covering up the evidence of a crime that he firmly believes he committed.

At this point Ray Heckler shows up at David McNorris's garage. Deciding to teach the haughty McNorris a lesson, Heckler says, "I guess the rules that the rest of us live by don't apply to you." Then Heckler takes McNorris down to the police station and puts him into an interrogation room. When Ray Heckler leaves him in the room, the befuddled McNorris assumes he is there as a suspect. But actually he is there to witness the interrogation of Terry Dinger, whose elderly father had taken John Dinger's truck to "go to work" at a plant that had closed more than twenty years ago. Dinger senior, who suffers from Alzheimer's disease—his own version of a blackout—took the truck and unknowingly and unwittingly ran over the street person. Terry Dinger tied his ill father to his bed to protect him from himself.

McNorris discovers to his own surprise that he is not guilty of vehicular homicide. His bad faith is itself a manifestation of bad faith. Like the elderly Mr. Dinger, David's own conscience was tied down in a bed for its own protection. Echoing the words Marion spat out about Andrea, David's conscience asks him, "Have you ever had a moment in your life that wasn't about your needs, your wants?"

Staggering back to Andrea's house, the Alzheimer's-like memory of David McNorris has an unexpected moment of clarity about that evening. He suddenly remembers that he had run into and killed a stray dog, not the "John Doe" street person who was Dinger's victim. Concerned for his well-being, Andrea says, "David, you don't have to do this alone. There are people that care for you." But David McNorris is not about to accept the help of anyone, let alone "the kindness of strangers." In another alcohol-soaked soliloquy similar to the one he delivers in the episode's opening scene he uses the context of his bourbon-inspired "insight" to declare that "Therein lies the problem—that somehow we are not alone. That somehow we will be there for each other. The truth is that we were born alone and we're going to die alone. Sometimes there's these sweet little moments that we have this illusion that we are connected." Andrea rejects David's bid for solipsism. "All we have are each other, David, that connection." But David refuses to be part of the human community. "There's where you're wrong," he declares. So much for "basking in the warm blood of honesty."

At the end of this somber episode, David McNorris attends the burial of the hit-and-run victim. Fittingly, he is alone in mourning on a day when the heavens themselves open up and pour their sorrows on this solitary individual and the unknown and unknowable victim being interred before him in a potter's field. Before, he was lost; now, he is found.

Suggested Reading

Absolutism in epistemology is defended by Plato in his dialogues *Phaedo, Republic,* and *Theaetetus* (*circa* 380–360 BCE), and by Aristotle in *Posterior Analytics* (*circa* 340 BCE).

Contextualism is defended by Stewart Cohen in "Knowledge and Context" (*Journal of Philosophy,* Vol. 83, 1986: 574–583); and a number of other articles in professional philosophy journals.

Existentialism is defended by Jean-Paul Sartre in *Being and Nothingness* (Paris: Gallimard, 1943); and *Existentialism Is a Humanism* (Paris: Editions Nagel, 1946).

Nietzsche, Friedrich. *On Truth and Lies in the Non Moral Sense* (1873). [Nietzsche defends his views on perspectivism in this work.]

CHAPTER 5

LAW & ORDER: "AND JUSTICE FOR ALL"

"In the criminal justice system the people are represented by two separate, yet equally important groups, the police who investigate crime and the district attorneys who prosecute offenders. These are their stories."

Law & Order opens each episode with these words. As this passage indicates, each of its weekly dramas is divided into two separate components. The first half of each episode is devoted to the presentation of a crime, usually a murder, coupled with the identification and apprehension of the suspect. Following the arrest of the suspect (which occurs just prior to the show's midpoint commercial break), the second half of the episode switches its focus to the district attorney's office for the legal prosecution of the suspect.

The detective work in the series originally focused on the character of Detective Mike Logan, but in Season 6 of the series, he was replaced by Detective Lennie Briscoe, who was assisted by detectives Rey Curtis and later Ed Green. With the actor Jerry Orbach's retirement after Season 14, his Lennie Briscoe character was replaced with Detective Joe Fontana through Seasons 15 and 16. Currently Detective Ed Green has become the series' lead detective. Don Cragen was the captain of detectives for the show's first three seasons and in Season 4 he was replaced by Lieutenant Anita Van Buren, who has remained chief of detectives ever since.

During *Law & Order's* eighteen seasons, the prosecution side also has seen many changes in its lead characters. Adam Schiff was the district attorney (DA) for Seasons 1 through 10, replaced by DA Nora Lewin for Seasons 11 and 12 Arthur Branch took over as DA in Season 13. Several different characters have populated the DA's office, including executive assistant district attorney (EADA) Ben Stone in Seasons 1–4, who was helped by assistant district attorney (ADA) Paul Robinette. Stone was replaced by Jack McCoy as EADA in Season 5, coupled with a changing array of female assistant district attorneys. Either Stone or McCoy generally is charged with the successful prosecution of the culprit apprehended in the first half of the episode.

Episodes are divided equally into two parts at the midpoint commercial break as far as the show's time slot is concerned. Not so for the dramatic focus of the episode, in spite of the opening statement that each criminal justice group is "equally important." Even the most casual viewer of this series will recognize that the second half of each episode consumes the lion's share of the meal. The police detectives prepare the meal and set the table. The district attorneys are there to dine off it. The detectives and the district attorneys receive equal screen time but that does not mean the dramatic weight of the show is parcelled out equally. When the attention of the episode shifts to the courtroom, the break between the two halves of the episode becomes so complete that the audience usually never sees the detectives again. As a rule of thumb, they are rarely brought back to present their evidence on the witness stand.

Law & Order is unique in the history of TV crime fighting. No other series combines the police detection story with the criminal prosecution story. Other TV criminal justice series focus only on one half of the Law & Order equation: either criminal fighting or trial proceedings. They are never about both together. Like a well-oiled relay team, each episode has the detectives seamlessly handing off the prosecution of the apprehended offenders to their colleagues in the DA's office.

While Law & Order stands equally on two legs, as is true of most persons, one leg dominates. Granted, there would be no case if the suspects were not identified and apprehended. Yet Law & Order's detectives represent only the plant foot in each episode. The fact that the arresting detectives seldom appear as courtroom witnesses indicates that as far as the series is concerned, the detectives' primary function is fulfilled with the suspect's arrest. The real kicking is done by the other leg, the members of the district attorney's office. It is no accident that the climax of each episode occurs when the jury reaches its verdict and the camera homes in on the countenance of Ben Stone or Jack McCoy. Their reactions to the trial verdict stand in for the desired reaction of the show's audience—contentment and vindication if the villain has been found guilty, or bewilderment and despair if the jury has (mistakenly) found the offender innocent. There is never any doubt that the accused are guilty. As the opening voiceover puts it, they are "the offenders." Although the usual string of innocent people appear as "red herrings" early in the detectives' investigation for dramatic purposes, they are never put on trial. Agatha Christie-style mysteries have no place here. Though the accused may sometimes get away with their crimes at the end of their trials, or may not be guilty as specifically charged, they are usually guilty of something bad or evil. In one way or another, they all deserve prosecution.

The second half of each Law & Order episode is laden with philosophical issues. It prides itself on presenting cases that are "ripped from the headlines." That it does, in spite of the disingenuous "disclaimer" that appears before some of its episodes. The cases it chooses to lift out of the headlines are chosen because they are multidimensional, complex, newsworthy, and socially controversial. Mercy killing, the death penalty, racism, sexism, gun control, free speech, and the insanity defense are some of the many issues that are examined, all under the guise of a police procedural. Because so many social controversies weave their way into the series' plot lines, the show represents a paradigm for what philosophers call "consciousness raising," or the attempt to educate the audience about the multifaceted complexities of our criminal justice system. *Law & Order* is a TV series that serves up enlightenment gift-wrapped as entertainment.

No matter which controversial social issue is explored in each episode, *Law & Order* as a series exists in a world firmly entrenched in *values dualism*. Viewing the world through the eyes of values dualism is rooted in ancient history for Western cultures. Stemming from the ancient Persians and Hebrews, through the classical civilizations of Greece and Rome, the medieval Christian and Muslim worlds, and right into the twenty-first century, European and American cultures see reality defined by a struggle between the forces of good and evil. Dualism sees things as falling into two distinct and mutually opposing camps. Something is either one thing or its opposite, either male or female, black or white, rich or poor, left-handed or right-handed, up or down, for us or against us. Nothing is both black and white. Everything is one or the other, never both, never neither.

Values dualism applies this dualistic perspective to the assessment and evaluation of human actions. Something is either right or wrong, good or evil, for us or against us. Nothing can be both good and evil at the same time. It is either one or the other. Applying this to "cops and robbers," cops are good and robbers are bad. Prosecution attorneys are good; defense attorneys are bad. Cops and prosecution attorneys are good; crooks and their defense attorneys are bad. As McCoy puts it in "Mad Dog" (Episode 152), "I'm on the side of the angels." As serial killer Mark Brunner responds to McCoy in "Bodies" (Episode 302), "You can't take your eyes off me. Truth is, without me you wouldn't exist. I'm the un-you."

Not only do defense attorneys legally represent wicked clients, some of them are just as evil as their no-good clients. When defense attorney Harold Jensen is accused of murdering his own wife in "Attorney Client" (Episode 275), his lies, evasions, and blatant disregard for professional ethics do more than show his personal corruption; they address the TV audience's prejudices about the legal role of defense attorneys as well. The general perspective about defense attorneys is that they get tarred with the same brush as the wicked people they represent. For example, in "Nowhere Man" (Episode 320), mob attorney William Wachtler does more than provide legal advice for his two clients, "Biscuits" and "Books," when ADA Alan Tenofsky threatens to indict them for the murder of Bobby Parentis. Wachtler helps his clients get their case dropped by blackmailing Tenofsky, who, strangely enough, is the assumed identity of one Jacob Dieter, a man who successfully masquerades as a district attorney for more than a decade, much of which is spent working with Jack McCoy. That Dieter himself is a fraud is overlooked in this strange episode because he is one of the "good guys." He was never a defense attorney.

"Proof" that he was a good guy lies in the fact that for twenty years he did an excellent job as a prosecuting ADA and as an attorney for the Appellate Court. Mob lawyer Wachtler is clearly one of the bad guys, evidenced by the fact that he not only represents Mafia hit men; but blackmails good guy Tenofsky and later arranges for Tenofsky's murder, the crime that opens the episode.

"Divorce" (Episode 173) takes a swipe at another breed of attorneys: divorce lawyers. They are even worse than defense attorneys. As Detective Briscoe describes them, "Divorce lawyers—God's way of telling you to stay single." Paul Redfield and Sheila Atkins are contending attorneys who represent a husband and wife locked in a protracted divorce, which the attorneys themselves turn into a bloody mess, literally. Each attorney has the attitude that, as in baseball, a tie is impossible. For them winning is not the only thing; it is everything. Attorney Atkins is so intent on beating her opponent, Redfield, that she stabs a psychologist to death and attempts to first frame Redfield, then her own client, Molly Kilpatrick, for the psychologist's murder. Redfield says to her in astonishment, "Your own client is going to prison and you're doing a victory dance?"

Not all *Law & Order* defense attorneys are depicted as such shady characters. In "Open Season" (Episode 284), conspiracy defendant Kevin Wilson is accused of plotting the murders of several members of the district attorney's office. He is defended by attorney Danielle Melnick, a long-time personal friend of Jack McCoy's. The viewer's sympathies certainly go out for the feisty attorney, especially when she is shot at the end of this episode by a member of Wilson's wacky clique. The implications of what she does, however, namely, help her clients escape their just rewards, cannot help but cast even this good egg in a bad light. She is portrayed in this episode as serving as an unwitting henchman for Wilson when she conveys his note from his prison cell to another member of his group, a note that helps to arrange the murder of another district attorney. The moral of the story is that even good people like Melnick will inevitably become tainted when they lie down with the devils they legally defend.

Randy Dworkin is another defense attorney who is portrayed positively in the three episodes in which he appears: "Chosen," "Bounty," and "Thinking Makes It So" (Episodes 288, 303, and 367, respectively). He is a wisecracking criminal defense attorney who frequently gets on Jack McCoy's nerves because he often acts in a silly manner, but his legal reasoning is excellent. He presents unusual defense arguments because he understands the theoretical legal dimensions that underlie the basic charges against his clients. He personifies the best image of the defense attorney in this series, a pain in the butt, but when all is said and done, an interesting pain in the butt.

"Bodies" also features a defense lawyer who is played in a sympathetic manner. Young, sincere, legal-aid attorney Tim Schwimmer is in way over his head when he draws ultra-creepy serial killer Mark Bruner for his first death-penalty case. Naively ensnared in Brunner's evil psychological web, he foolishly visits the burial site of some of Brunner's many victims. When knowledge of this visit becomes known, McCoy and many of the parents of these missing girls demand that Schwimmer disclose this location so that at least Brunner's victims can receive a proper burial and their parents can receive a modicum of closure. But Schwimmer refuses to disclose what he knows about the location, citing attorney-client privilege. In order to force him to talk, McCoy charges him with being an accessory after the fact for all of these murders. A young but noble Schwimmer is found guilty by the jury and sentenced to a long prison term because he believed that to violate the attorney-client privilege, no matter how moral the reason, would establish a very bad legal precedent. Schwimmer's loyalty to professional legal ethics is portrayed as noble, though misguided, in this emotionally powerful episode.

Defense attorneys and the criminals they represent are not the only bad guys in *Law & Order*. Occasionally one of the good guys turns evil. In "Jeopardy" (Episode 115), it is a trial judge's turn to go bad. This episode concerns a triple murder at a magazine publishing company in which the publisher's brother is under suspicion for the murder. Peter Nicodos was jealous of and angry with his younger brother and he shoots him and his co-workers in a fit of rage. Peter's mother, Elisabeth, has already lost one son to Peter's anger, and she is not about to lose Peter to a lengthy prison term. Seeking to stack the trial deck in her favor, she manages to get the case listed on the docket of Judge Edgar Hynes, who is in her pocket. Judge Hynes had recently undergone a bloody divorce in which he lost his shirt. Elisabeth Nicodos arranged a favorable loan for Judge Hynes at a bank where she has connections, thereby saving the judge hundreds of thousands of dollars. After the prosecutors rest their case against Peter Nicodos, defense attorney Norman Rothenberg asks for a dismissal of charges. This request is a standard courtroom maneuver for defense attorneys. To McCoy's astonishment and Rothenberg's delight, Judge Hynes grants the motion and dismisses all charges against Nicodos. Back in the DA's office, McCoy suspects that Judge Hynes was corrupted by the Nicodos family fortune. After Briscoe and Curtis uncover evidence of the shady loan deal, McCoy appeals the dismissal verdict to the Appellate Court and succeeds in having the charges reinstated and having Peter Nicodos retried under a different judge. To avoid this retrial and to save his own mother from being charged with bribing a judge, Peter Nicodos pleads guilty to the original charges. Later, word filters back to the DA's office that Judge Hynes has committed suicide. The audience is left with the impression that justice has indeed been served to Nicodos and Hynes alike.

Philosophers, historians, and social commentators long ago recognized that *value dualism* is an awfully simple-minded way of looking at the world. Many things don't easily fall into the twin niches of dualistic metaphysics. From the point of view of popular entertainment, though, it is hard to beat. The *Men in Black* may be good guys, but we all know that good guys really wear the white hats and the bad guys wear the black hats, if not literally on their heads, then deep within their souls. Everyday human existence is a continual struggle between the forces of light and the forces of darkness. That humans are locked in this struggle is tragic. That the forces of darkness and evil may actually win a round or two is doubly tragic. That the forces of darkness will ultimately prevail and vanquish the forces of light and good is unthinkably appalling. It would be like Satan vanquishing God in the Super Bowl.

The criminal justice system is a social problem-solving organization designed to prevent such unseemly and appalling outcomes. When the forces of evil temporarily win a round and prompt people to commit crimes, the detectives of New York's 27th precinct quickly spring into action. Criminals are recognized and apprehended by the likes of Detectives Logan, Briscoe, Green, and Fontana. "Whodunit" is solved through a combination of astute police work, which incorporates eyewitness testimony and forensic evidence, and good old-fashioned scud work. The time-crunching format of this series, however, forces its writers to skate quickly from dot to dot as the detectives round up the usual suspects. Unlike *CSI*, this show does not dwell lovingly on forensics. Unlike *Cold Case*, this show does not focus on the memories of those from the past as the key to cracking a case, even when it happens to *be* a cold case. Past memories and forensics have their place in *Law & Order's* investigations, but that place is strictly subsidiary. As a rule of thumb, twenty minutes into an episode is sufficient time to ascertain who was murdered, who committed the murder, and why the murderer acted as he did. The kinks and wrinkles that bog down many real-life police investigations are barely acknowledged in this series. They would slow down the flow of the plot line.

And then comes the curve ball. After outlining what appears to be a straightforward murder case and winnowing the list of usual suspects, *Law & Order* plot lines frequently take off at odd angles to reveal significant puzzles associated with the original crime. Even though episodes usually open with the discovery of a murder victim, likely as not, that person's death turns out to be peripheral to the real story focus, namely, the moral or legal puzzles arising out of any of a number of complications with the original case. "Bodies" begins by tracking down serial killer Mark Brunner, but takes a left turn in the episode's second half as it focuses on the legal and moral tangles of the attorney-client relationship. After setting up the identification and arrest of Brunner, his subsequent trial, conviction, and death sentence receive barely a passing nod as the focus of the episode shifts to defense attorney Schwimmer's own legal entanglements. "Deep Vote" (Episode 253) begins with the murder of a woman who is killed by mistake. Albert Bennato, her admitted assassin, is never brought to trial. Instead, the episode's story line shifts to questions of voter fraud. In order to protect her election "victory," State Senator Anne Benton hires Bennato to kill crusading newspaper reporter Kate Pierce, who may possibly expose the fact that Benton's people stole thousands of ballots in that election. The woman who is shot at the beginning of the episode was killed by mistake because she was driving the same make and model car that Pierce drove. "Nullification" (Episode 162) appears at first blush to involve a simple robbery of an armored car and murder of its guards, but as the episode unfolds, we learn that the crime was committed by members of The New Sons of Liberty, an illegal militia, whose members claim POW status following their arrest. The real thrust of this episode is on the defendants' Second Amendment right to bear arms.

"Burn, Baby, Burn" (Episode 235) features another set of plot line twists and turns. Lateef Miller, an African American male, is accused of murdering a white police officer. But Miller, formerly a member of the Black Panthers in the 1960s, argues self-defense, and the episode examines concerns that racism still infects the relationship between white police officers and black suspects, even in this new millennium. "Harvest" (Episode 161) raises the question of who is really responsible for the death of Bess O'Neal. Elias Camacho recklessly shoots up the car in which Bess O'Neal is riding, leaving a bullet lodged in her head and O'Neal arguably brain dead. But Dr. Donald Cosgrove removes her heart for an organ transplant. Is he really O'Neal's killer? Was she still alive when her heart was removed, or does the fact that she allegedly failed the apnea test correctly signify that she died prior to having her heart harvested?

Episodes like "Harvest" demonstrate why *Law & Order* is such a viewer's delight. Unlike *Cold Case*, which concerns the completion of life's journey for the resurrected spirits of its murder victims, and unlike *CSI*, which concerns the intricate mechanics of scientific criminal detection, *Law & Order* is all about the legal and moral rectitude of appropriate punishments for those who have soiled the social nest. Episodes start with a murder investigation, but then become a multilayered philosophical tutorial on contemporary social or political problems, all the while masquerading as a straightforward police procedural. In "Invaders" (Episode 371), Jack McCoy is intent on tracking down the murderers of his colleague, ADA Alexandra Borgia. He impatiently insists "Don't wax philosophical on me" to his boss, DA Arthur Branch, who worries that McCoy is becoming too emotionally involved with pursuing a suspect. But "waxing philosophical" is what many episodes in this marvelous series are all about. "Whydunit," "whatdunit," and "whattomakeofit" are far more important to this series then merely "whodunit" or "howdunit."

Section I: "To Protect and Serve"

At the heart of the *Law & Order* series is the search for justice. *Values dualism* implies that all significant human activities are value laden. Once concerns for food, clothing, and shelter are satisfied, there is no value more important to human existence than *justice.* "Justice" is an abstract, philosophical notion. It is an ideal that provides an important service to the community. It has two separate, but overlapping applications, *moral justice* and *legal justice.*

Moral justice is an abstract ideal. It has two components, *distributive justice* and *retributive justice.* Distributive justice concerns the proper sharing of some valuable commodity. Adult children squabbling over who should get deceased

Aunt Mabel's china are arguing over issues of distributive justice. In general, the more valuable an item is perceived to be, the more those who desire it will fight over its possession. They are arguing over what is *fair*, where "fair" is the same thing as "getting what I want." "Unfair" can be quite a serious accusation. How one determines what constitutes being fair in a given situation can be a sticky problem. When Solomon was famously confronted by two women arguing over the possession of a baby, "cutting the child in half" might not have been the ideal solution because the women might have continued to dispute who would get the top half.

Retributive justice is another can of worms, but one that must be opened in order to go fishing for justice. Questions of retributive justice deal with how best to punish or reward those who do certain atypical or unusual things. Those who do what is typically required in a situation usually don't raise questions of retributive justice because rewards for standard behavior are already built into the system. For example, an employee expects to receive an honest day's pay for an honest day's work. It is only when an employee goes above and beyond the call of duty, or underperforms on the job, that questions are raised regarding the appropriate compensation for the extra effort, or lack thereof. Extreme cases raise questions of revenge or "payback." *Law & Order* is all about payback; it is all about retributive justice.

Morally, questions about retributive justice are answered by applying two distinct, incompatible, but intertwining models. First, one can apply the rule "let the punishment fit the crime." Some actions cry out for specific responses. "An eye for an eye" fits this mold. It presupposes that a certain level of response is morally mandated by the degree of atrocity embodied in specific actions. If someone has willfully spiked out the eye of another, only the deliberate removal of the assailant's eye counts as a fitting response. Fitting responses are discovered by matching exactly the level of evil attached to the offense in question to the level of evil inflicted on the culprit. For the loss of an eye, only the loss of one of the assailant's eyes is fitting, not the loss of neither—that would be "getting away with murder"—nor the loss of both eyes—that would be an overreaction. In "Fluency"(Episode 339), con man Mike Bass makes a killing by selling water labeled as flu vaccine to many medical suppliers. Sixteen people die from taking the fake flu vaccine, people who would have lived had the vaccine been real. An outraged Jack McCoy charges Bass with sixteen counts of manslaughter in the second degree for recklessly endangering the lives of these innocent victims. When Bass is convicted on all counts, McCoy argues at the sentencing hearing for the maximum penalty of fifteen years to be served for each count of the indictment, with the sentences to run back to back. The trial judge agrees and sentences Bass to 240 years in prison for killing sixteen people, giving the lie to Stalin's claim that "one death is a tragedy, many deaths are merely statistics."

The perspective of letting the punishment fit the crime is nicely captured by the statue of blind Lady Justice balancing her scales. The appropriate payback response is the one that evenly balances the level of the crime with the level of the punishment. As EADA Stone says in "Mother Love" (Episode 59) "The blindfolded lady has two scales. We should never look like we have our finger on one of them."

But what punishment best fits which crimes? In "Savages" (Episode 114), ADA Claire Kincaid worries about the application of the death penalty to Paul Sandig, a wealthy accountant, who in a fit of panic kills an undercover cop. Kincaid believes that the death penalty is not a morally appropriate response for any crime, but society supported revenge against wrongdoers. "Revenge is sweet," she sarcastically tells McCoy, who insists on applying the death penalty to Sandig. He responds that the desire to seek vengeance "is a natural human instinct and there's no need apologizing for it." For McCoy, an eye for an eye also means a life for a life.

From the point of view of retributive justice, one of the worst moral transgressions is for a guilty person to get away with murder. This is what happens in "Patient Zero" (Episode 304). Married medical doctor Charles Blanchard is doing research on SARS. When his lover, Janine Wilson, threatens to expose their relationship, Blanchard purposely infects her with the SARS virus. She accidentally spreads the virus to twelve other people, including her four-year-old son, who dies. Blanchard, who happens to be the boy's actual father, is charged with second-degree murder for the boy's death as well as the attempted murder of his one-time lover, Janine Wilson. On the witness stand, Blanchard's wife Elaine purposely gives misleading testimony about her knowledge of his affair and the existence of his illegitimate child. Her testimony suggests to the jury that as the scorned woman she herself may be responsible for Janine Wilson's viral infection. But she pretends to be angry with Blanchard in order to provide his defense with a reasonable doubt. The jury believes her false testimony and finds Blanchard not guilty. He gets away with murder, and EADA Jack McCoy and ADA Serena Southerlyn can only watch in disgust as the Blanchards strut out of the courtroom hand in hand.

Concerns about retributive justice also suggest a *utility response*. From this viewpoint, retribution is designed to achieve good results and is justified only by achieving these results. Because moral and legal considerations both aim to achieve a well-ordered society, moral justice and legal justice overlap. The utility saying that "'an eye for an eye' will soon leave the whole world blind" exemplifies this overlap. The utility position on retributive justice maintains that retribution can only be morally or legally justified if it results in a good consequence. Good consequences are understood as benefiting the victim of the original crime, benefiting a subset of a population such as all victims of racism or rape, or benefiting society as a whole. Society may arguably be protected by such punishments as ostracism, fines, imprisonments, loss of social privileges, capital punishment, or life in prison without the possibility of parole. These are both moral and legal responses to serious moral infractions.

A society is civilized when it acknowledges rules that are designed to regulate the conduct of its members. Some rules, like the rules of etiquette and decorum, are designed merely to lubricate social interactions to make them more pleasant and seemly. They produce relatively trivial outcomes and usually have no moral or legal dimensions. Other rules are more fundamental to human interactions. Without them individuals will seriously infringe upon one another's existence. These are the rules that encompass morality and legality. As McCoy says to the jury in his summation in "Nullification," "Without the law there can be no freedom." Without the law there would only be license, the ability to get away with whatever we can for as long as we can, a veritable state of nature à la Hobbes. The rules of morality and the rules of law are fundamental to cultural well-being.

But it would be a mistake to equate the rules of morality with the rules of the legal code. It does not follow that just because something is legal, it is also moral. In "Savages," Judge Albert Parsons tells DA Adam Schiff, "Morality is not now and never has been a significant part of the criminal justice system." This judgment is too severe, however. Legislatures make laws for many reasons: economic, political, cultural, and moral. Murder is both immoral and illegal. It is illegal precisely because it is seriously immoral. Parsons's claim can best be understood as implying that no legal system perfectly captures the moral point of view, not that legal systems have nothing to do with morality. That position is too cynical.

In "Sanctuary" (Episode 85), Joshua Berger, a white Jewish male driver, is not charged with any crime after he accidentally hits and kills a black youth. The failure to indict Berger leads an African American church leader, Reverend Todd Ott, to stir up trouble, claiming that the white Berger is being allowed to get away with killing the child because the victim is black. This leads to a riot in which John DeSantis, a white driver, is beaten to death by a vigilante mob. A member of that mob, Isaac Roberts, is offered sanctuary in Reverend Ott's church. After Roberts is arrested and charged with DeSantis's murder, Shambala Green, his defense attorney, argues that Roberts has a legal right to obtain sanctuary in the church. When the judge rejects that argument, Green argues in Roberts's defense at his trial that cultural racism against African Americans explains and justifies Roberts' participation in the riot. The question raised by this episode is whether institutional racism provides psychological motivation and legal defense for the rioters. EADA Ben Stone argues against this defense, claiming that murder is murder, regardless of the skin color or the religious affiliation of the assailant or the victim. To Stone's disgust, the trial results in a hung jury. While Stone is set to retry Roberts, DA Schiff decides not to retry the case in order to allow the city to heal from its racial strife. The resolution of the case suggests to the viewing audience that in some cases the justice of utility should be allowed to override the justice of retribution.

Racism and politics rear their heads again in "Good Girl" (Episode 137) in which African American college student Charlie Monroe is stabbed to death by his Italian American girlfriend, Danielle Mason. Confronted with her crime by detectives Briscoe and Curtis, Mason denies it at first, claiming that she does not even know the murder victim. When her prints are found at the crime scene, she shifts her story to claim that Monroe raped her after knocking her flat with the date rape drug Rohypnol. When the police can neither verify nor conclusively refute these claims, the Monroe family threatens to go to the media and charge the district attorney's office with racism. They would claim that a white prosecutor was unwilling to bring murder charges against a white girl for killing a African American man. As DA Adam Schiff comments, "This case is completely political." The district attorney's office succeeds in the end by proving to Danielle's racist family that she was Charlie Monroe's girlfriend, and that she did kill him over the fact that Monroe wanted to break up with her. It was not exactly *Romeo and Juliet*, but it was a tragedy all the same.

That the legal system does not perfectly overlap with morality is also illustrated in "Panic" (Episode 218). FBI Agent Dean Tyler uses "psycho-sexual panic" as a (phony) defense against charges that he accidentally murdered the accountant of his wife's lesbian lover. His defense attorney calls it "panic by proxy." McCoy has a different description for Tyler's actions. "When is it just plain old-fashioned murder?" Tyler is really covering for his own daughter, Courtney, who attempted to kill her mother's lover because she threatened to break up their family. Even though McCoy realizes at the end of the episode that Tyler is innocent of the murder charge, he is legally powerless to prevent Tyler from taking the rap for his daughter by pleading guilty to murder in the second degree. The trial judge also realizes what is happening, but says, "I have no choice but to accept a guilty plea." An innocent Tyler is judged to be legally guilty even though everyone knows that he is legally and morally innocent of the crime. He is still guilty of one thing, namely, his willingness to go to jail for twenty-five years or more to protect his daughter from paying the consequences of her crime.

Another example of the crucial distinction between moral and legal culpability was presented in the "Nullification" episode cited above. The "New Sons of Liberty" militia members robbed an armored truck and killed one of its guards. When they are charged with murder, they claim they are really POWs, that they are exercising free speech, and that they have the right to bear arms in defense of their liberty. In their defense they cite an article McCoy had previously written for a law journal, in which he says "a bad law sometimes demands an illegal act." A judge finds them not guilty. Legally they get away with murder; morally they are despicable.

Finally, in "Damaged" (Episode 179), Valerie Maxwell, a mentally disabled high school student, is coerced into having sex with three male students. McCoy charges the teenage youths with aggravated sexual assault on a mentally disabled person through force and coercion because they knew at the time of the act that she was unable to give informed consent for them to have sex with her. They took advantage of her immaturity and naïveté. On the stand, Valerie claims that she knew what she was doing and that she wanted to have sex with the boys. "They said they loved me," she testifies. After the boys are found guilty by the jury, Judge William Wright throws out the conviction because he is unsympathetic to the case's prosecution. Judge Wright believes Valerie wanted to have sex with the boys, and while it may have been morally problematic for them to take advantage of her, it was not illegal because Valerie is past the age of consent.

Sometimes the law can be used to encourage an enhanced society's understanding of morality. An example of this is found in "Gunshow" (Episode 206), which opens with the massacre of fourteen student nurses in New York's Central Park by Denis Trope, who illegally purchases a Rolf Nine shotgun from a gun dealer, which he then uses to shoot the students. Trope easily modified the gun from single shot to fully automatic by purchasing a conversion kit at a gun show. When Detectives Briscoe and Green trace the sale of the gun to the dealer, he says of its illegal sale, "Read the federal statute. Barely a traffic ticket."

In one of its famous right-angle turns so typical of this series, the criminal trial of mass-murderer Trope receives only passing interest. He is allowed to plead guilty to second-degree murder and receives only twenty-five years to life as a sentence for fourteen counts of murder, provided he agrees to testify against Rolf Firearms. McCoy is willing to cut a deal with Trope because he cannot prove with certainty that the gun in question is the murder weapon. Trope messed up the gun barrel prior to abandoning it near the scene of the crime. The prosecutors can't convict Trope without the help of Rolf Firearms, and Rolf Firearms won't help them with the case because it would mean admitting legal responsibility for selling a gun that it knew could easily be converted into an illegal automatic weapon.

An anguished McCoy claims the victims' families are entitled to an eye for an eye, but he can't deliver justice for them because Rolf Firearms got in the way. He charges the owners of Rolf Firearms with manslaughter in the first degree, or criminally negligent homicide, claiming they knew their business practices helped criminals circumvent the laws, and that fourteen women were dead because the design of the Rolf Nine made it easy to modify into an automatic weapon. When Judge Wright rebuts McCoy's attempts at prosecuting Rolf Firearms on the grounds that McCoy is trying to use his court to make social policy, McCoy appeals the negative ruling to the State Appellate Court. At that hearing Rolf's defense attorney argues that since the U.S. Supreme Court upholds the right to bear arms, his client Rolf Firearms has the right to sell them. "Mr. McCoy's problem is with the law."

Waxing philosophical again, McCoy replies, "The courts have always been agents of social change," implying that it is permissible, even mandatory, to use legality to further morality. McCoy's assistant, ADA Abbie Carmichael doesn't buy that position, claiming that McCoy was not after a criminal trial, but was pursuing gun control.

Back at the reinstated trial, McCoy argues against the gun dealer's claims that the enforcement of existing laws are sufficient to stop the likes of Dennis Trope. "You not only armed Dennis Trope, you undermined the very laws that were supposed to protect us from him." Rolf's defense attorney counters that responsible gun ownership is an American tradition protected by the Constitution and that another American tradition is for the prosecution to put the blame where it belongs—on Trope, the assailant. McCoy counters, saying it is a myth that gun ownership is an American tradition and that the framers of the Constitution did not have machine guns in mind when they endorsed the Second Amendment.

The trial jury finds Rolf Firearms guilty of complicity in the fourteen murders, but trial Judge Wright overturns the verdict, saying that until we can cure what ails the human heart, putting gun manufacturers on trial will not end the carnage. "It's not about being [morally] right; it's about doing [what is legally] right." The judge opts for what was legal in overturning the jury's verdict, not for what was moral in the eyes of McCoy.

The rules of law are the product of conscious decisions made by legislatures and other civic organizations whose authority to do so is acknowledged by society. Philosophers call these rules of law "positive laws" to distinguish them from the "laws of nature" or "divine law." Positive laws are the product of human lawmakers and their interpreters. They may or may not accord with everyone's sense of morality. Unlike morality, they exist only because they have been enacted by an appropriate civic body, and they can only be changed or annulled by those same organizations. These laws are openly published and are incorporated into legal codes and court case rulings. Lawyers are people who specialize in studying and working with these codes and rulings.

Positive legal codes define the legal rules of justice. By definition, "legal justice" is whatever the rules of law say it is, no more and no less. Laws are problem-solving devices and, as such, they are general in scope and regulate a whole class of activities. Individual actions, however, are always specific. A murderer, for example, does not commit "murder" in the abstract. She murders a specific person. Police do not arrest an individual for committing murder; they arrest her for murdering John Doe. Police departments and courts systems exist to handle situations in which someone is believed to have violated a rule of law in its specific application to a particular case. Their jobs are to discover and punish those who break the legal codes by committing specific acts outlawed by those codes. The legal system always involves the application of a general rule of conduct to a specific situation. A law must be understood or interpreted as applying in a specific manner to a particular situation, depending on circumstances. There is no getting around this. The application of a criminal statute to a given case always involves the judgment of those who enforce the laws.

By definition, only those who are found guilty of breaking a law can be the appropriate subjects of legal punishment. Punishment involves the intentional infliction of harm on a person, a group of people, or an economic entity such as a corporation because it or they have been properly found guilty of breaking the law. The intentional infliction of harm and evil is morally wrong in itself, so some legal basis must be found to support the notion that intentionally inflicting harm and evil on lawbreakers is not wrong and indeed might even be mandatory in some circumstances.

The criminal justice system is a social organization designed to solve this apparent paradox. Society must respond to harmful deeds by rebounding evil to the original evildoer. Only the fact that a person has been legally determined to have broken the law justifies the imposition of legal punishment on that person. A person who has done something immoral but not illegal may not be penalized for that action through the use of positive law, although that person may rightfully incur moral condemnation for his immoral actions.

Section II: Legal Complexities

Most episodes of *Law & Order* are concerned with felony murder. But not all human deaths are felonies. Some deaths are accidental; others are caused by illness. Such deaths are of no real concern to *Law & Order*. Dispensing justice in cases of felony murder requires the recognition of four levels, or degrees, of murder: 1) murder in the first degree, 2) murder in the second degree, 3) manslaughter in the first degree (manslaughter one), and 4) manslaughter in the second degree (manslaughter two). There are significant legal distinctions between each degree of felony murder.

Though the specific criteria for *murder in the first degree* are established by statutes of the state of New York, which is the location for *Law & Order*, generally murder in the first degree, or first-degree murder, presumes a homicide that is: 1) deliberate and premeditated; or 2) occurs in conjunction with another felony such as rape, armed robbery, or arson; or 3) involves multiple deaths or the killing of certain types of individuals such as children, police officers, witnesses to crimes, prison guards, or fellow prisoners; or 4) utilizes certain weapons such as guns or knives in its commission. The assailant displays an active malice toward the life of the victim. The penalty for first-degree murder in the state of New York is usually life in prison, but the death penalty was added as an additional possible penalty in the late 1990s and it remains in effect today.

The death penalty is highly controversial, and this controversy is well displayed in "Savages." In this episode, Paul Sandig, a wealthy accountant, kills an undercover police officer. EADA Jack McCoy pushes for the death penalty for Sandig, but ADA Claire Kincaid opposes him on this. Kincaid cannot abide the death penalty. She believes it is an unnecessary means for the reduction of crime, and is merely a political football. "[New York Governor George] Pataki rode the death penalty plank all the way to a mansion in Albany." Detective Lennie Briscoe also opposes the death penalty because he thinks it will make criminals more likely to shoot cops. But EADA McCoy is much in favor of applying it in this case. "Paul Sandig is a poster child for the death penalty." Detective Rey Curtis agrees. Anyone who purposely kills a cop deserves nothing less than to be killed in turn.

DA Adam Schiff find's McCoy's and Curtis's positions too rigid. "Any [District] attorney who speaks in absolutes is abdicating his responsibilities [to judge cases fairly]." Schiff's legal friend, Judge Albert Parsons, rejects Schiff's position. "Can anything be moral if it doesn't apply to all things equally?" Legal justice demands that equals be treated equally and unequals unequally. If it is just that one murderer suffers the death penalty for her crimes, then likewise it is just that all murderers suffer the death penalty for their crimes.

Kincaid rejects the death penalty precisely because of questions of equality, in this case the equality of defendants' legal representation. As "Black Tie" pointed out, rich people really can afford to hire the best lawyers, those who are adept at helping them avoid all kinds of punishments, including the death penalty. Kincaid asks McCoy to consider "How many people are sitting on death row because of a bad attorney rather than because they committed a heinous crime?"

McCoy rejects that argument. The death penalty is all about revenge for him, and "Revenge is sweet. It's a natural human instinct and there's no need apologizing for it." Further rejecting Kincaid's argument that life without parole is a fitting enough punishment for a convicted murderer, he argues "The death penalty gives a feeling of control demanded by society. Legal executions are a means of preventing street justice."

Sandig is convicted, but prior to his sentencing hearing, his attorney, Helen Brolin, approaches the Appellate Court to try to get the death penalty judged unconstitutional on its face. In her oral arguments before the Appellate justices she claims the death penalty violates the due process clause of the Fourteenth Amendment of the U.S. Constitution. She argues that the U.S. Supreme Court has recognized the fundamental rights of sex, marriage, childbearing, and child rearing, and she wants the Appellate Court to recognize another fundamental right, the right to life. Brolin claims the due process clause of the Fourteenth Amendment should be applied with "strict scrutiny" to the death penalty question. *Strict scrutiny* is a legal test established by the Supreme Court to test the constitutionality of state laws and other legal practices that seek to regulate basic rights such as the right to marry or have children. To be a constitutionally valid limitation on an individual's freedom of action on matters basic to his self-identity: 1) a state regulation of that conduct must have a *compelling objective*, and 2) the means of obtaining that compelling objective must be *necessary* to obtaining it. Preventing homicides is just such a compelling state objective. But like ADA Kincaid, Brolin argues that the death penalty is not a compelling means of achieving this compelling objective.

In his response before the Appellate Court, McCoy counters that the Fifth Amendment to the Constitution specifically refers to "capital crimes." The

Constitution cannot prohibit what its text explicitly permits. In *Gregg v. Georgia*, the U. S. Supreme Court ruled that the death penalty was permissible if it was administered without being arbitrary or showing prejudice on the part of the jury, and the decision to take a human life was not in itself so subjective that it defied the consistency mandated by the Constitution. Jury members can and do control their prejudices and passions to achieve objectivity when debating about whether to apply the death penalty to a specific individual. The death penalty passes the test of strict scrutiny and it is thereby constitutional.

In its decision, the Appellate Court passes the buck by ruling that "the controversy of the issue has not yet become sufficiently concrete to be worthy of adjudication." In other words, Sandig had not yet been sentenced to death, so the whole debate was a moot point and the court refuses to rule on the constitutionality of the death penalty. After doing a superb job of marshalling the legal arguments surrounding the highly controversial issue of the death penalty, "Savages" arrives at a flat, anticlimactic ending.

"Consultation" (Episode 54) also invokes the death penalty. In this episode a drug runner from Nigeria who ingests condoms filled with heroin dies in New York City when one of the condoms ruptures in her body. Two persons connected to the drug pipeline are arrested and charged with second-degree murder. One of the accused is Ola-Gimju Nwaka, a Nigerian tribal chief who has diplomatic immunity in the United States. His immunity, however, does not apply to serious crimes such as drug smuggling, second-degree murder, or manslaughter in the first degree. The Nigerian consul, Sir Idris Balewa, supplies Nwaka with a duplicate passport during the trial after the court confiscates Nwaka's original passport. This allows Nwaka to escape trial and flee back to his native Nigeria. EADA Ben Stone and DA Adam Schiff are furious over Nwaka's escape from the New York criminal justice system. But a wiser Balewa knowingly assures them that Nwaka has not gotten away with anything. The Nigerian government will prosecute Nwaka for drug smuggling, and will execute him when he is found guilty of that crime. The state of New York only would have punished him with a lengthy prison sentence. "Our culture is not as 'enlightened' as yours," Balewa sarcastically assures EADA Stone. "An eye for an eye is still our way of life. Nwaka thought nothing about purchasing people's lives. He should be made to pay with his own."

"True North" (Episode 190) involves another case of the death penalty and international law. In this episode, Stephanie Harker is responsible for the murder of four individuals, one of whom is a child. She talks Wendy Naughton into killing Harker's husband, and then shoots Naughton herself to cover up her crime. Following the murders she flees to her native Canada. The state of New York charges her with multiple murder and murder for hire.

The Canadian consulate officer worries about extraditing her back to New York City. "Canada has a moral objection to capital punishment," he claims. "Our extradition treaty with the United States says that unless assurances are provided that the death penalty won't be imposed, extradition may be refused." EADA McCoy responds in a huff that it is a bit presumptuous for one country to tell another how to enforce its own laws. In order to secure Canada's cooperation, DA Schiff tells McCoy to tell the Canadians that the death penalty is off the table.

But with Harker back in New York, Schiff needs to be persuaded to change his mind about the death penalty because Harker is a cold-blooded serial killer. He believes that while the death penalty may be allowed by the law, it is not mandated by it. As the district attorney for Manhattan, Schiff must choose which punishment to seek in the case. Do Harker's crimes call for the death penalty? This is a tough decision for Schiff—life in prison without possible parole, or death?

ADA Abbie Carmichael argues that the death penalty is a more fitting punishment for Harker's crimes. "Her crimes fit the death penalty statute. We've got nothing to apologize (to Canada) for." McCoy agrees. "In some cases (the death penalty) really is (called for), Adam. Killing four people. Killing a child. Stephanie Harker isn't pushing my pity button." Still, Schiff perseveres. Reluctantly, he finally agrees with them. "A dirty business, my friend, a dirty business." Seeking justice is not always a pleasant pursuit.

McCoy's philosophical response is that "The truth doesn't always set you free. Maybe we should post warning signs (about the death penalty) at the Canadian border." To which Schiff replies, "Yea, 'ENTER AT YOUR OWN RISK.'"

Murder in the second degree involves a nonpremeditated killing that results from an assault upon the victim in which the victim's death is a distinct possibility. Second-degree murder differs from murder in the first degree in that the death of the victim is not specifically intended by the assailant, but results from the assailant's actions. Also, the assailant should have known that his actions would likely bring about the victim's death. Typically, the assailant does not specifically intend to take someone's life but displays a "depraved indifference" to that life. Murder in the second degree is typically punished by a sentence of twenty-five years to life in prison, but not by the death penalty.

"Harvest" presents a tangled case of second-degree murder. It concerns Marty O'Neal's wife, Bess, who is shot in the head when Elias Camacho recklessly fires his gun into the auto the O'Neal's are driving. When Bess O'Neal later dies at the hospital, Camacho is charged with second-degree murder. During Camacho's trial, his defense attorney argues that Camacho did not kill O'Neal because she was technically alive at the time her organs were harvested by Dr. Donald Cosgrove. So who really killed the victim, Camacho, the gunman, or Cosgrove, who cut her heart out for transplant? A delightful legal puzzle, to say the least.

To solve it, EADA McCoy also charges Cosgrove with second-degree murder, arguing that both men are equally responsible for Bess O'Neal's death. In his defense at the trial, Cosgrove argues that before he harvested her heart,

Bess O'Neal was already dead because she had failed the apnea test. "If she cannot breathe on her own after one minute, she fails the test." Repeatedly failing the apnea test is a condition sufficient for meeting the definition of brain death in New York.

By carefully examining the medical records, McCoy argues against Cosgrove that O'Neal was breathing on her own before her organs were removed. He argues that Cosgrove's decision to harvest her heart was not mercy killing, but a murder for profit. It seems that Cosgrove used O'Neal's heart for transplant into a patient at a different hospital where he was seeking a staff position because his current hospital was going out of the heart transplant business.

On the witness stand, Cosgrove rejects the claim that O'Neal was still alive when he harvested her heart. He says, "According to the medical standards we live by there is no question that she was dead." But there is such a question, because the hospital records show that Cosgrove had given O'Neal morphine before taking her organs. This indicates Cosgrove knew she could still feel pain, which she could only do if she were still alive.

In his theatrical grilling of Cosgrove on the witness stand, McCoy argues that "She was alive. For all of your God-like pronouncements, you knew that, didn't you? That's why you had to pump her full of morphine, so she wouldn't bolt upright screaming in the operating room while you cut her heart out. (Taking her life) wasn't your decision to make, Doctor." A defiant Cosgrove says under his breath, "Of course it was."

If there is a single profession *Law & Order* loves to paint as abjectly evil, it is that of the medical doctor playing God.

Manslaughter in the first degree, a.k.a. manslaughter one, or voluntary manslaughter, involves the unlawful killing of another person without premeditation. The assailant displays an absence of malice toward the victim but behaves in such a manner of reckless endangerment that he causes the victim's unwitting death. *Voluntary manslaughter* includes killing someone in the heat of passion or accidentally killing someone while committing another felony. Typically the punishment for manslaughter one is a prison sentence of ten to twenty years, but sentences can vary widely depending on circumstances.

"Mother Love" presents a convoluted example of voluntary manslaughter. In it, Virginia Bryan shoots and kills her daughter, Dawn, who is addicted to drugs. Dawn Bryan's drug addiction was destroying her once promising life. To feed her habit, she prostituted herself and stole anything of value from everyone she knew, financially destroying her own grandmother in the process. Her life became so wretched that she asked her own mother to shoot her to put her out of her misery. Virginia Bryan acquiesces, and in a long and heart-wrenching soliloquy, confesses her crime to the DA's office. "I killed my baby."

Yet this painful episode is not quite finished. ADA Paul Robinette wants to charge Virginia Bryan with manslaughter one. He believes that failing to do so would be a form of racism. The Bryan family is African American and to not apply the laws equally to their case would be to treat them as inferiors unworthy of full citizenship. EADA Ben Stone is unwilling to charge Virginia Bryan with manslaughter. He is too moved by how this awful tragedy has affected Dawn's family to be interested in pursuing a manslaughter charge against Dawn's mother. But he agrees to present the case to the grand jury. After hearing the facts of the case, the grand jury refuses to indict Virginia Bryan for manslaughter one for her daughter's death. They choose instead to indict her only for possessing an unlicensed firearm, a misdemeanor in the fourth degree. Afterwards a frustrated Robinette asks, "If no one is responsible for Dawn Bryan's death, an African American victim doesn't matter. Is[n't] this a racist issue?"

Manslaughter in the second degree, a.k.a. manslaughter two, or *involuntary manslaughter,* involves causing someone's death while committing an act that is not a felony. A common example of this is reckless driving, or vehicular manslaughter. The victim's death was not intended, but the assailant acted in an illegal and reckless manner such that his actions led to the victim's death. Since it is not considered a felony, involuntary manslaughter typically calls for a prison sentence of probation to less than ten to fifteen years of imprisonment, depending on the characteristics of the case.

In "Consultation," for example, drug smuggler Phillip Marietta is offered a reduction of his original murder charges from manslaughter one to manslaughter two in exchange for his testimony against former Nigerian tribal chief Nwaka. In "Fluency," Mike Bass is convicted of manslaughter in the second degree for causing the deaths of sixteen people by selling fake flue vaccine. He was sentenced to fifteen years in prison for each count of manslaughter.

Plea Bargaining

One of the staple components of each *Law & Order* episode is the arraignment of the accused before a judge. At an arraignment, the charges against the accused are read aloud and the accused is forced to make a plea concerning these charges. There are only three possible plea options: innocent, guilty, or no response. If the defendant refuses to make a response to the preliminary reading of the charges against her, the judge is legally obliged to enter a not-guilty plea. No one ever enters a guilty plea at an arraignment in a *Law & Order* episode. That would obviate the need for a trial and ruin all of the fun.

Occasionally, someone other than the accused will plead guilty to a crime, often while on the witness stand. This happens during the trial scene in "Dissonance" (Episode 232), when Marian Reger pleads guilty while she is on the witness stand to murdering a member of Carl Reger's orchestra. A surprised McCoy assumed she was only going to testify concerning Carl Reger's whereabouts on the night of the murder.

Following a plea of not guilty, the next issue addressed is the question of bail. The assistant district attorney who oversees the proceedings asks the judge either to set a very high bail or to *remand* the accused, which means to hold the accused in jail without bail. The defense attorney will then argue for no bail at all or for a much lower figure than the prosecution requested. Depending on a variety of factors such as the nature of the accusations and the risk of flight, the presiding judge determines whether there is to be any bail at all or sets the bail amount.

During the course of the criminal proceedings, the DA's office may suggest a plea bargain to the defendant. Occasionally a suspect's or defendant's own attorney will take the lead on this and try to arrange a plea with the DA's office. Plea bargains always involve the suggested agreement that the accused plead guilty to a less severe charge than what the DA's office thinks properly fits the crime. Typically, a higher level crime such as murder in the second degree is pleaded or negotiated down to the next lower charge, manslaughter in the first degree. Rarely does the plea go more than one step down. The bargaining never works in the other direction, from a lesser penalty to a greater one. "Let the punishment fit the crime" is a noble saying, but a lesser punishment is often determined to be "close enough for government work."

What is the point of all this? Plea bargaining is the most common problem-solving procedure in the U. S. criminal justice system. It has advantages for both the prosecution and the defense. From the prosecution's perspective there are two chief advantages to a plea bargain. The first, which *Law & Order* never addresses, is convenience. Many more people are arrested and charged with crimes than the court system can possibly process. If everyone who was accused of a crime was actually put on trial for that crime, the court system would immediately choke on a glut of cases. A plea bargain is a laxative to the bowels of the court system. Second, the prosecution can use the offer of a plea bargain as a "bargaining chip" to induce a defendant to tell the police more about the nature of the crime under investigation than the police could discover on their own. Usually a suspect will be forced to *allocute*, to explain how a crime occurred, as his formal part of the plea bargain. This explanation may include the suspect's willingness to testify in court against himself or against others who have been accused of the same crime.

From the defendant's point of view, plea bargaining also offers certain advantages. By agreeing to plead guilty to a lesser crime, the defendant may escape a far harsher punishment than he might have received had he been found guilty at trial. In the court of public opinion, life in prison beats the death penalty, a shorter prison term beats a longer one, probation beats a prison term, and so on. Just as there is a chain of severity in criminal charges, there is a corresponding chain in the severity of sentences. For the defendant, less severe beats more severe every time. For example, by agreeing to testify against State Senator Anne Benton in "Deep Vote," hit man Albert Bennato escapes a charge of first-degree murder that carries a possible death sentence.

In another plea-bargain wrinkle, *"Faccia a Faccia"* (Episode 172) portrays a reputed Mafia crime boss, Alberto Napoli, who is charged, tried, and convicted for first-degree murder for ordering a hit on his own legendary hit man Nick LaGrassa. Jacob Rosen, Napoli's defense attorney, strikes a plea bargain with EADA Jack McCoy. In exchange for Napoli's testimony against a Russian mob, the punishment for his first-degree murder conviction is reduced from life imprisonment to a mere two years in a minimum-security facility. A visibly pleased Napoli declares, "Maybe I'll write a book," echoing LaGrassa's own tell-all book. Indeed, it seems that for Napoli, crime might really pay.

There are drawbacks to plea bargaining. Each side must give a little to get a little. A defendant must acknowledge his guilt of a lesser crime in order to avoid the possibility of being convicted of a greater crime and thus receiving a harsher sentence than that required by the plea bargain. But a lesser sentence is still a sentence. By accepting a plea bargain, the accused forgoes his right to a jury trial, and by thus acknowledging his guilt, he eliminates the possibility of being found not guilty by a trial jury. A not-guilty verdict is a get-out-of-jail-free card. Going to trial involves a roll of the dice. In deciding whether to plea bargain, the accused must make a calculated risk assessment about the likely outcome of a trial. If he calculates incorrectly and is found guilty by a jury, he is in a much deeper world of trouble than he would be if he accepts the prosecution's plea-bargain offer.

From the prosecution's viewpoint, plea bargains have a distinct disadvantage; namely, they allow a guilty party to escape the full legal punishment for a crime she fully admits. In a plea-bargain arrangement, the law settles for less than its pound of flesh, justice for less than its full measure. In a sense it means the bad guy gets away with murder. In *"Faccia a Faccia"* that is literally true. Napoli gets away with murder.

As a legal problem-solving procedure, plea bargaining has significant disadvantages for both defendants and prosecutors. Why is it then so commonplace? Half a loaf, it would seem, is better than nothing. In plea bargaining the certainty of the admission to a lesser charge is balanced against the certainty of receiving a lesser punishment.

In "Bounty," African American reporter Brian Kellogg is charged with murdering a bounty hunter, Robert "Bobcat" Rafelle, who was threatening to expose the fact that Kellogg had made up his story about meeting with a notorious fugitive serial rapist, Robert Mass. Kellogg is defended by Randy Dworkin, a smarmy criminal defense attorney who so gets on Jack McCoy's nerves. Dworkin turns Kellogg's defense into an indictment of a racist social system that promotes African Americans as mere tokens. Such a perspective implies that African Americans have not truly earned their economic or social status. Dworkin argues that in order to sustain the unreasonably high expectations placed upon him by a racist society, Kellogg had to make up interesting stories for his readers. On the witness stand Kellogg claims that, "I had to be superior for people just to think I'm competent." But Dworkin's defense strategy goes up in flames when Kellogg is forced to admit that he is having an affair with a white woman. Knowledge of this by the jury would undercut

Kellogg's whole line of defense. Agreeing to settle out of court, Kellogg cops a plea to manslaughter one and agrees to a sentence of twelve and a half to twenty-five years.

Law & Order also wrestles with the issue of legal nullification. *Nullification* refers to the practice of overturning what the law normally requires in a given case for reasons that are extralegal. There are two common types of nullification—judicial and jury—which are distinguished by the legal function of the person or persons responsible for the nullification.

The DA's office is primarily worried about potential *jury nullification*. A trial jury may refuse to convict an apparently guilty defendant for reasons that have nothing to do with the defendant's legal innocence. Juries that practice nullification do not acquit defendants because they believe the defendant was innocent of the charges lodged against her. They fail to convict defendants whom they believe to be guilty because of extralegal reasons like racism, shared economic or political perspectives, or other philosophical prejudices. When a jury practices nullification, it ceases to act as a jury and acts as a cheerleading body instead.

"Nullification" presents a stunning example of a trial jury's fickle prerogatives. When the members of the New Sons of Liberty militia were accused of murder and armed robbery, the evidence against them was overwhelming. Indeed, at their trial they didn't even bother to deny the charges. Instead, the militia members managed to persuade the jury that vague, unspecified "threats" against their personal liberties were sufficient reasons to murder innocent people, people whom they believed worked for a government that the militia members despised. When the jury found them innocent of the crimes they so blatantly committed, EADA McCoy's reaction of disgust and dismay provided the only proper response to this horrific miscarriage of justice.

A common manner in which a jury may practice nullification occurs when the jury fails to reach a guilty verdict even though the evidence clearly shows the defendant was guilty. This occurs in "Veteran's Day" (Episode 316) in which Gulf War veteran Kenny Silva's son, Matt, is killed while fighting in Afghanistan. Silva believes that antiwar protester Brian Teague is dishonoring the memory and sacrifice of his son, and in a fit of anguish and rage he chokes Teague to death. McCoy charges Silva with both murder in the second degree and manslaughter in the first degree. The trial jury finds Silva innocent of second-degree murder. In spite of the fact that Silva acknowledges on the witness stand that he killed Teague; the jury can't reach a verdict on the manslaughter charge. Legally, the jury's unwillingness to hold Silva accountable for Teague's death nullifies that charge against him. Although Silva could again be charged with manslaughter in Teague's death, the DA's office has no reason to believe that any other jury would be willing to convict given the obvious sympathy Silva's plight invokes.

"Mother Love" presents another view of jury nullification, in this case as practiced by a grand jury. It is part of the American criminal justice system that before a defendant can be *remanded*, or bound over, for a criminal trial, that defendant's case must be reviewed by a state or federal grand jury. In grand jury proceedings, the DA's office presents the evidence it has collected against the accused and seeks to establish that there are sufficient prima facie reasons to bring this case to a criminal trial. Defendants are not allowed to present evidence of their innocence at a grand jury hearing. The only issue at stake is whether there is enough evidence of guilt to justify bringing this case to trial. By a simple majority vote of its members a grand jury determines whether or not to indict a suspect.

In "Mother Love," suspect Virginia Bryan had already admitted that she shot her drug-addicted daughter, Dawn. ADA Paul Robinette sought to indict her for manslaughter in the first degree for the shooting, but after hearing the facts of the case, the grand jury members decided only to charge her with possession of an unlicensed firearm, a misdemeanor. There was plenty of evidence to indict Virginia Bryan for manslaughter, including her own confession to the crime, but the jurors were so sympathetic with the fact that Dawn had ruined her own life with drugs and nearly destroyed the rest of her family that all they could see was Virginia Bryan's pain and suffering. They were not about to cause her any more.

Judicial nullification also gets its turn at bat in *Law & Order*. In judicial nullification it is the trial judge, not the jury, who overturns a legally mandated result for the case in question. The chief practitioner of judicial nullification in this series is Judge William Wright. "Damaged," "Gunshow," and "Dissonance" all illustrate Judge Wright's propensity for nullification.

In "Damaged," teenaged Valerie Maxwell was raped by three of her fellow high-school students. There was no doubt the three had sex with Valerie, and her mental incompetence seemingly made her incapable of giving the boys proper legal consent to have sex with her. After the trial jury found the boys guilty of raping Valerie, Judge Wright threw out the conviction, arguing that Valerie wanted to have sex with the boys, and, well, boys will be boys, after all. In "Gunshow," a jury found Rolf Firearms guilty of complicity in fourteen murders committed by Dennis Trope, who used one of Rolf's weapons illegally modified into an automatic weapon. Judge Wright threw out that conviction because he believed that no matter how horrific Trope's actions, Rolf Firearms was not legally responsible for them. In "Dissonance," a worried DA Norma Lewin felt it necessary to threaten Judge Wright out of court if he should undercut the prosecution of murder suspect Carl Reger by practicing his usual judicial troublemaking.

In this episode, Carl Reger was an orchestra leader and his wife, Marian Reger, was a harpist in the orchestra. He was charged with the murder of a promising young violinist in that orchestra. On the witness stand, Marian confessed to the crime, but there was no way of telling whether she had confessed merely to help win her husband's acquittal. As ADA Abbie Carmichael put it, "We're sure one of them killed her. We're just not sure which one."

Lewin believed Judge Wright had it in for EADA McCoy and would try to wreck his case against either of the Regers.

The Rules of Evidence

Police detectives and district attorneys are the good guys. The bad guys are the ones who commit the crimes. But even the guys wearing the white hats have to follow some rules. Even though their hearts may be pure, the police cannot do whatever they want in their efforts to fight crime. Many episodes of *Law & Order* revolve around the rules and regulations that significantly affect how the forces of "truth, goodness, and the American Way" can go about rounding up and convicting the rascals.

Two kinds of rules govern the work of the detectives and the district attorneys: rules of evidence and ethical standards. Federal and state rules of evidence govern what types of information the prosecution can present to a criminal jury. The prosecution almost always knows more about a defendant and her alleged crimes than it can legally present to the jury. This presents a puzzle for the TV audience. To the layperson, putting legal restrictions on presenting known information to the trial jury, the very body charged with judging the facts of the case, seems silly if not downright contradictory. It would seem self-evident that the opposite should be the case. If anything, the body of relevant information available to a jury concerning the crime scene, the defendant, and the defendant's actions ought to be as absolute as possible. There should be a requirement for total evidence. The more relevant information the jury has about the facts of the case, the more accurate its judgment. The jury's first job is to determine the truth about the case under review. Omitting key facts can lead a jury to draw incorrect conclusions, which inevitably may lead to mistakes about the defendant's guilt or innocence. No one wants to convict the innocent or release the guilty. What purpose do these evidential limitations serve?

Jury trials in the American system of criminal justice are zero-sum games. A zero-sum game is one in which for every winner there must be a loser. Baseball and basketball are zero-sum games; ties are impossible. Chess and football are not zero-sum; there are ties in football and stalemates in chess. To make a contest "fair," rules of play are adopted that are designed to prevent either side from achieving an improper advantage. These rules are known to the players and spectators alike. There are penalties attached to violations of the rules. In sports, umpires and referees determine whether the game's rules have been violated and when to assess penalties for their violations. In the criminal justice system, trial judges and appellate judges take the place of referees and umpires. They determine when the rules have been violated and also are obliged to assess penalties for those violations. One of the major penalties that judges can apply to the prosecution is the suppression of illegally gathered evidence. Without such a restriction, the prosecution could pretty much convict anybody it fingered, be they guilty or innocent.

In general, the criminal justice system rejects evidence when its value for establishing the guilt of the accused is outweighed by its likeliness to inflame the jury unduly against the defendant, making a fair trial impossible. Graphic information about the defendant's previous criminal problems and emotional outbursts by the victim's family are prohibited in courtrooms. Such information or behavior could so poison the mindset of the jury that it would be incapable of giving the accused a fair trial.

As previously noted, *Law & Order's* TV audience is prone to regarding criminal defendants as guilty as charged. After all, the show's opening sequence describes them as "the offenders." Real-life juries are also prone to seeing the accused as *offenders*. In spite of the legal system's best attempts to empanel an impartial jury, a truly impartial jury is a noble fiction. There is a poisoned mindset at work in the legal system. It is human nature to see things from a certain mindset or point of view. The legal system is all about rounding up the rascals; not about playing around. The application of the law is serious business. That is why defense attorney Randolph Dworkin gets on EADA Jack McCoy's nerves so much. He wants to introduce a note of levity into what is not a laughing matter. Criminal accusations are serious business. Police detectives would not arrest someone they did not believe firmly to be guilty. The office of the district attorney would not charge someone whom they did not believe firmly they could convict. The defendant on the docket was arrested and charged. Do the math. Guilty! Guilty! Guilty! The task of defense attorneys is a daunting one. If they represent crooks, they must be crooks too, right?

To keep the task of defending alleged criminals from being completely impossible, the American legal system established as its cornerstone the presumption of innocence. In theory, a suspect is presumed to be innocent of the crime with which he is charged. The burden of proof rests on the shoulders of the prosecution, whose job is to overcome that presumption of innocence and prove the suspect's guilt. To prevent the overly hasty conviction of the guilty and innocent alike and keep the playing field level, the prosecution is restricted from introducing illegally obtained evidence to the jury. This would make it too easy for the prosecution to overcome the burden of proof and it is the reason why police cannot torture a suspect into "confessing" to a crime and then offer that "confession" as proof of the suspect's guilt. The fact that the TV viewer presumes the accused is guilty makes it easy to forget that the burden of proof is still with the prosecution. Without severe limitations on their conduct, the police and prosecutors could paint anyone guilty of anything, and the burden-of-proof issue would become the joke that it is in countries ruled by dictators. Stalin's show trials of the 1930s provided ample evidence of this. Because the police and the district attorney's office usually have so many methods at their disposal to prove the defendant's guilt, there would be no practical way to establish a defendant's innocence unless the prosecution was forced to meet very high standards of proof.

Evidence is also rejected if it was obtained without a search warrant or by means of an objectionable search warrant. Before the police can legally invade someone's private property, they must secure a valid search warrant. Search warrants are issued by judges when detectives outline to the judge details about the exact location of the search and the sought-for items believed to be connected to criminal activity, things such as murder weapons, DNA evidence, illegal drugs, or counterfeit money. In the absence of a search warrant, the district attorney, during trial, may submit evidence that was in plain view of the detectives at the time of an arrest, evidence that would have been discovered inevitably in the process of a normal search, or evidence that was uncovered while the detectives sought to prevent another crime from taking place.

Virtually every episode of *Law & Order* has a segment in which a suspect's defense attorney files a legal motion with a judge to rule out items of evidence obtained by the detectives in the first half of that episode. These are called *motions to suppress*. Trial judges frequently grant these motions when they believe the evidence has been obtained illegally. Suppressed information will not be shown to the trial's jury. Nor will a trial judge allow the admission of any evidence that, by a logical train of discovery, can be linked to the excluded evidence. Of course, the TV audience has already seen this evidence and come to a reasonable conclusion about how it helped show the guilt of the accused.

"Fluency" aptly illustrates a case of suppressed evidence. Suspect Mike Bass sold saline solution masquerading as flu vaccine to the medical community. When individuals with a variety of health impairments randomly received the fake vaccine, many died from flu-related complications. Bass's middle man, Sklar, was caught by detectives Fontana and Green. Sklar cops a plea and tells police where the fake vaccine is stored. But Sklar incorrectly describes the location of the vaccine, so that the police have the wrong address on the search warrant. Even though they search the correct warehouse and find the fake vaccine, Bass's defense attorney moves to exclude the evidence because the police obtained it by an illegal search. After some deliberation, Judge Donald Karan agrees with Bass's attorney and rules that the evidence of the fake vaccine was inadmissible, thereby ruining the case against Bass. Happily for the prosecution, the warehouse belongs to Bass's aunt, who has not given him permission to use it to store his fake vaccine. Upon hearing this, Judge Karan reverses his original ruling, accepting McCoy's argument that Bass had no legal right to the expectation of privacy because he had no permission to use the warehouse in the first place.

"Thinking Makes It So" illustrates issues about discovery and the chain of evidence. Bank manager Howard Grant's daughter, Julie, has been kidnapped by Mitchell Lowell, a smooth-talking con man who threatens to harm her unless Grant helps him rob his own bank. When Detective Fontana tracks down Lowell, he brutalizes Lowell into telling him where Julie is hidden. At his trial, Lowell's defense attorney, Randolph Dworkin, seeks to have most of the evidence against Lowell thrown out of court, including the eyewitness testimony of young Julie Grant, the kidnap victim. Dworkin argues that Julie was rescued only because of the information that Fontana illegally beat out of Lowell. As with any other "fruit from the poisoned tree," her testimony is legally inadmissible. McCoy claims that independent of roughing up Lowell, Fontana would have searched his ex-wife's boat, moored at the home where Julie was found, because he had captured Lowell at her house and her boat was parked in plain view. Trial Judge Mildred Kurtzman rules that Julie's testimony is admissible evidence, and the jury convicts Lowell of her kidnapping.

The old-fashioned use of eyewitness testimony serves as the cornerstone of criminal trials in *Law & Order*. While *Law & Order* may make use of the same forensic science that has pride of place in *CSI*, it usually does so only to establish certain facts, for example, that "the victim was shot with a nine-millimeter Glock automatic, the bullet of which had six striations with a right-handed twist" or "the defendant's fingerprints were found on the shell casings and inside the victim's belt-buckle." Important information, but incidental to the drama of the trial scene. In *Law & Order*, there is nothing like good old-fashioned eyewitness testimony when it comes to presenting the case for the prosecution. When defense attorneys cross-examine eyewitness testimony, they are usually characterized as complete ninnies in their foolish and vain attempts to bleach the blood stains out of the truth.

In "Gaijin" (Episode 323), Japanese playboy Hiroji Yoshida hires Hiroji Ito, a punk Yakuza hitman, to murder Yoshida's wife in New York so that he can collect three million dollars of her life insurance and pay off his gambling debts to the Yakuza mob. Yoshida then turns around and, following the trail blazed so brilliantly by the real Susan Smith, sends the police on a wild goose chase by claiming that his wife's assailant was an African American. Following his wife's death, he beats a hasty retreat back to Japan and lambastes New York as a hotbed of danger.

Detectives Briscoe and Green locate Lucy Chen, a waitress at a restaurant where Yoshida and Ito had met to seal the murder deal. On the witness stand, Chen identifies Yoshida as the man she saw with Ito. Yoshida's defense attorney tries to shake Chen's story by claiming that to a Chinese person like Chen, all Japanese people look alike. Yoshida's defense attorney would have been better off questioning Chen's memory. But he does not do this. The jury doesn't buy it either. They convict Yoshida of first-degree murder. Good old-fashioned eyewitness testimony nails the lid on Yoshida's coffin.

Probably the most famous, or infamous, limitation on the police's ability to gather information about a suspect is the U.S. Supreme Court's 1966 *Miranda* ruling. The court's *Miranda* ruling mandates that police detectives must verbally apprise an arrested person of his "right to remain silent" and his right to request the presence of an attorney. Any evidence obtained from a suspect who has not been properly "Mirandized" is inadmissible in a court of law. Defense attorneys are forever presenting motions to suppress evidence they believe was illegally obtained from their clients owing to *Miranda* slip-ups. They call this evidence "fruit from the poisoned tree."

Arguments about *Miranda* issues fill the episodes of *Law & Order*. In "Ill-Conceived" (Episode 311), Miguel Camacho twice admits to Detectives Briscoe and Green that he killed Helene Zachary's husband in a fit of jealous rage. Camacho's girlfriend Maria Villanueva had agreed to act as a surrogate mother for the Zachary's child, but her pregnancy left her boyfriend Miguel upset and confused. The *Miranda* wrinkle in this case centers on the fact that Miguel Camacho, an illegal immigrant who speaks English poorly, is worried about being deported back to Mexico by the arresting officers. Because neither Briscoe nor Green speak Spanish, they read Camacho his *Miranda* rights in English. Camacho's defense attorney, Vanessa Galiano, succeeds in getting his confession thrown out when she convinces Judge Grace Larkin that Camacho did not sufficiently understand English to wave his *Miranda* rights. Of course the audience jolly well knows that Camacho is guilty.

"Monster" (Episode 181) turns on the question of whether Detectives Briscoe and Curtis have browbeaten Owen Stokes into confessing that he raped a ten-year-old girl and put her in a permanent coma. "Ten years old and she's finished." Stokes is an acknowledged pedophile, and Briscoe and Curtis firmly believe he is responsible for the crimes in question. Lt. Anita Van Buren tells Briscoe and Curtis to "take him into a room and don't come out until you have a statement from him." But Stokes really is innocent of this crime. After he is badly beaten by a vigilante mob, the detectives deny Stokes needed medical attention until he "confesses" to the crime. When Stokes asks to go to the hospital, the detectives keep him under interrogation. He asks "What about the lawyer I asked for this morning?" The detectives won't let him leave. Rey Curtis tells him that "an innocent man has nothing to hide." They were "waiting" for a doctor. They claim that he won't clear his name if he asks for a lawyer, as if the detectives have any real interest in clearing Stokes's name.

EADA McCoy is perfectly willing to use this extorted "confession" to convict Stokes. Even when Judge Gary Feldman raises concerns about the validity of Stokes's interrogation under *Miranda*, McCoy plays slippery with it. "It's OK for the police to lie to the accused. The police are allowed to use cunning, even deceit in an interrogation. If he's not guilty of this, he's still guilty of something." Damn that pesky *Miranda* ruling! Recognizing the hanky-panky involved in Stokes' interrogation, Judge Feldman tells McCoy, "Another fast one, huh McCoy?" Another fast one? No. Unlike the criminals they seek to apprehend and convict, the police department and the district attorney's office do not pull "fast ones." As McCoy tells his staff in "Judge Dread" (Episode 252), "It's called prosecutorial discretion."

When does the use of "prosecutorial discretion" to obtain needed information to convict the accused become mere lying? Ethical standards form the second set of rules that limit official conduct in the criminal justice system. Can the police and the district attorneys use immoral means to further moral ends? If the end justifies the means, then the so-called immoral means would not really be immoral if they were harnessed in pursuit of moral ends. They would only be immoral if they were put in the service of immoral ends. From *Law & Order's* point of view, one which it shares with viewers, the police and the district attorneys can morally do things that would be immoral for others to do. Indeed, they may be morally and legally obligated to use "immoral" means in their efforts to enforce the law.

"Open Season" starts with the death of Vance Grodie, a defense attorney who just won a big case by securing a not-guilty verdict for a cop killer. Standing over Grodie's gunned-down corpse Briscoe says of him, "I guess every adversarial system needs a bad guy. He argued for the wrong people, the guilty." Good riddance to bad garbage. But murder is murder, so McCoy prosecutes Grodie's assailant, Kevin Wilson, a certified gun-nut. In order to prosecute Wilson successfully, McCoy lies to him about the evidence available to the police. At first McCoy worries about the ethics of this tactic, but DA Arthur Branch comes to McCoy's defense. "Told a couple of whoppers, did you? Well, the Constitution is not a suicide pact." McCoy replies, "What's a whopper when it helps convict a bad guy?"

In "Mad Dog" (Episode 152), EADA McCoy comes especially close to crossing the moral line. In this episode the legal system is seen initially as preventing justice. Lewis Darnell was long ago convicted of multiple counts of rape and was sent to jail for those crimes. But at his parole hearing, he manages to song and dance his way past the parole board. Not fooled by his false display of repentance and piety, McCoy insists that Darnell be recognized for the sexual predator that he is. While he is out on parole, McCoy does just about everything possible to hound Darnell into breaking his parole so that he can send him back to prison where he belongs. McCoy is so ruthless in his pursuit of Darnell that Adam Schiff warns him off. "I won't let you drag the law through a sewer to catch a rat." Even McCoy's assistant Jamie Ross thinks he has gone overboard in his Captain Ahab-like attempt to harpoon "The Great White Whale," Lewis Darnell. Ross argues that "even the rights of a disturbed social rapist are protected" by the U.S. Supreme Court.

McCoy will have none of that. "Until the Nine Supremes rule otherwise, I'm having Darnell locked up." Even the court's own psychiatrist, Dr. Elizabeth Olivet, is disturbed by McCoy's attempts to nail Darnell, claiming he wants to misuse psychiatry "the same way the Soviets filled up the Gulags, using psychiatry to punish people."

McCoy's insistence that "I'm on the side of the angels here" seems as unconvincingly single-minded as Darnell's own daughter's naïve defense of her father. In a hearing to determine Darnell's potential for danger to others, Janeane Darnell defends her father's collection of violent pornography. "Experts can make mistakes. Witnesses lie.... You can't lock people up for their fantasies." How ironically this saga ends. In a setting out of Greek tragedy, Janeane Darnell bashes her father's brains out with a baseball bat when she catches him in the act of raping her best friend. McCoy was right all along.

Diminished Capacity (or Responsibility)

When *Law & Order* homes in on the trials of the accused, many of the attorneys defending the alleged perpetrators offer versions of the "I did it, but not really" defense. This legal defense strategy does not try to exonerate the accused from the charges against them; instead, it seeks to moderate the accused persons' full participation in these deeds by appealing to extenuating circumstances. Ordinarily, individuals are held accountable for their actions. In some circumstances, however, individuals may correctly argue that they did not act of their own free will. Because of some factual contingency, they somehow were coerced into acting in a way that they typically would not, except for the coercing agent. Blame the coercing agent. Do not blame the accused. They were victims themselves.

The complex episode "Thinking Makes It So" presents an interesting example of coercion. The episode opens with a bank robbery in which a security guard kills one of the bandits. A second bandit, Mitchell Lowell, has kidnapped Julie Grant, the daughter of bank manager Howard Grant and threatens to kill her unless Grant helps to rob his own bank. Thinking this is an inside job, detective Joe Fontana initially charges Grant with bank robbery and murder. But Grant is released and the charges are dropped when Fontana realizes why Grant was withholding cooperation with the police. It is not because he was in on it from the start, but because of fear for his daughter's life. Lowell indirectly held a gun to Grant's head to get his cooperation with the robbery. Although Grant did it, he really did not "do it" after all.

In "Veteran's Day," for example, Kenny Silva does not dispute the fact that he strangled Brian Teague. But in Silva's defense, his attorney claims that he did not kill Teague "willfully." Silva had snapped emotionally. He killed Teague in anger that had boiled over when he thought that Teague was "dissing" Silva's dead son Matt, who had died as a hero fighting in Afghanistan. Silva did it; he strangled Teague, but he did not really "do it." And in "✳" (Episode 285) baseball star Kevin Seleeby claims he murdered Norman Pratt, his limousine driver, in a "steroid-induced psychosis" and not because Pratt had threatened to blackmail him as his gay lover and expose his illicit drug use. Seleeby did not "really" do it; the demon drugs made him do it.

Diminished capacity (or diminished responsibility) can be applied in two ways: 1) Either the accused should not be held fully liable for criminal action because he was incapable of controlling himself at the time of the crime, or 2) the accused should not be made to stand trial because he is currently incapable of assisting in his own defense. In *"Faccia a Faccia,"* accused mobster Alberto Napoli tries to avoid standing trial by having his lawyer argue that he suffers from a variety of disorders, any one of which so diminishes his capacity to mount a legal defense that it would be wrong to prosecute him for anything, let alone the first-degree murder charge the DA's office wishes to hang on him. He has suffered a stroke; he has Alzheimer's; he has dementia; he is too old and too rickety. Yada, yada. In reality he was none of these things, so his prosecution is allowed to proceed as scheduled. But what if circumstances really had rendered him incapable of assisting in his own defense?

Many episodes of *Law & Order* wrestle with the puzzle of diminished capacity or diminished responsibility. While criminal defendants are seldom nice people, most have voluntarily committed the crimes with which they have been charged, and most are considered legally capable of mounting a defense against these charges. But under what conditions do either of these presumptions of competence break down?

Stupidity is not a defense. Plenty of defendants make really stupid decisions while committing crimes or while attempting to defend themselves against the legal charges attached to these crimes. That is how Logan, Briscoe, and Green can catch them so easily; that is how Stone or McCoy can prosecute them so easily. It is amazing how many accused persons babble on about their misdeeds even after their arresting officers have read them their *Miranda* rights or while they are on the witness stand "defending themselves." Shutting up seldom seems to be an option. It is not uncommon for a defendant to talk the jury into a guilty verdict while attempting to show her innocence. No, sheer stupidity is not a legal excuse.

Being the child of Nazi concentration camp survivors just might mitigate one's actions, or at least help explain them to a sympathetic jury. In "Survivor" (Episode 138), Judith Sandler is an art restorer whose parents were imprisoned by the Nazis. Sandler believes that before his imprisonment, her father had owned a collection of rare coins. With the collusion of certain Swiss bankers, this collection was stolen by the Nazis right out of the bank. It apparently just resurfaced in the possession of a New York art dealer who intends to use it as collateral for a bank loan. An addled Sandler kills the art dealer in an attempt to recapture her father's long-lost collection. Ironically, the coin collection never existed. Sandler's psyche was so twisted by the wrongs done to her parents by the Nazis that she became delusional. During Sandler's trial for the murder of the art dealer, evidence is presented in court concerning the complicity of many Swiss banks in the wartime atrocities of the Third Reich. It was true that Sandler's father had deposited certain assets in a Swiss bank to keep them out of the Nazis' reach. It also was true that this attempt failed when the Swiss allowed the Nazis to get their hands on these assets for a share of the loot. These events occasioned Sandler's delusional tale of woe and the death of the innocent art dealer. On the witness stand, Sandler completely breaks down when McCoy proves to her that her father had never really owned a coin collection. Sandler killed the art dealer for nothing, yet her frail psyche had predisposed her to see the innocent actions of the art dealer as complicit with the Swiss bankers who conspired with the Nazis to defraud her family of its rightful possessions. As Adam Schiff says of the bankers, "Our Swiss banker friends, what refugees are they taking deposits from now as they yodel their way to the bank?"

"Sheltered" (Episode 299) represents an example of how a person can be corrupted by his companions. In this episode teenager Justin Capshaw kills four people, one of whom is the man whom he believes is about to fire his "father," Herman, who had kidnapped Justin from his real family when Justin was five years old. In Justin's defense, his attorney presents a version of the battered wife syndrome or the Stockholm syndrome. Either would absolve Justin from his evil deeds. Herman Capshaw had so brainwashed young Justin that he was incapable of acting on his own or even reuniting with his real mother after his proper identity was established. The trial jury finds him not guilty because of diminished capacity.

Certain forms of mental illness present real problems for the prosecution. In "Disappeared" (Episode 176), Matthew O'Dell is too mentally ill to be capable of even acknowledging his illness. He brutally murders three people while under the delusion that they are somehow conspiring to violate his imagined property rights to inhabit a building in which he never actually lived. He is turned in to Briscoe and Curtis reluctantly by his brother Ben. Ben recognizes the style of a pamphlet Matthew had produced denouncing urban renewal. On trial for first-degree murder, Matthew O'Dell refuses to mount an insanity defense or even to allow any mention of his mental illness. The problem for the prosecution is that in the absence of extenuating circumstances, Matthew O'Dell would take a one-way walk into the execution chamber. As DA Adam Schiff describes O'Dell, "He's too crazy to say he's crazy."

EADA McCoy worries that a successful prosecution of O'Dell will amount to "legally assisted suicide." The prosecution doesn't want to convict O'Dell of the three murders because that would amount to sentencing him inappropriately to death. By acting as his own attorney, O'Dell refuses to allow the prosecution to attach any sort of insanity judgment to his case, even though that recognition is the proper assessment of O'Dell's behavior. After he is convicted of murder, ADA Jamie Ross manages to insert questions about O'Dell's mental health into his sentencing hearing. She is appalled that the death penalty might be invoked in this situation. Over O'Dell's most strenuous objections she succeeds in getting questions about his mental instability on the record, the results of which are that O'Dell is not sentenced to death for the murders, but instead to the very mental treatment he so desperately needs.

In "Shrunk" (Episode 305), famous songwriter John David Myers kills aspiring actress Carrie Underwood. Under police interrogation, he confesses to the crime, yet his defense attorney, Lisa Cutler, changes his plea to "not guilty because of mental defect." As a teenager, the young John David witnessed his mother brutally stab his father to death. When he is not "self-medicating" with alcohol, cocaine, or psychotropic drugs prescribed by his psychiatrist, Dr. Frederick Barrett, the adult Myers harbors a latent hatred for his mother. Carrie Underwood unfortunately triggers that latent hatred during her one-night stand with Myers, who kills her for her efforts, believing that Carrie is really his mother. In one of those plot twists so beloved by *Law & Order* fans, Meyers was purposely put in the proximity of Underwood by Dr. Barrett, who had an affair with Underwood and sought to remove her permanently from his life by inducing Meyers to kill her. When EADA McCoy presents these facts to Myers, he is too addicted to his relationship with Barrett to turn on him. Myers pleads guilty to manslaughter in the first degree and accepts a sentence of fifteen years to life. Dr. Barrett, the real villain of the case, walks away free as a bird. While Myers may have had a diminished capacity, Barrett's capacity for evil was in no way inhibited.

"Switch" (Episode 110) features another twisted scenario involving mental infirmity. Psychiatrist Lillian Hampton is murdered in her office by her patient, Megan Nelson. Nelson suffers from multiple personalities, "Megan," "Bobby," and "Nancy," one of which "witnessed" the murder. McCoy says of her recollection of the crime that "she seems more confused than anything." To which DA Adam Schiff replies, "With three personalities at the wheel, who wouldn't be?"

It seems that Nelson "remembers" that as a three–year-old she witnessed her father push her mother down the stairs, killing her. But her mother really fell down the stairs because she was drunk, not from being pushed by her husband. Nelson has a false memory belief that is the origin of her multiple personalities. Nelson's persona "Bobby" initially confesses to killing "their" psychiatrist, but as a male persona, his job was to protect Megan at all costs. Her persona Bobby could not have committed the crime because he did not know key elements of the murder. McCoy claims "'Bobby' was trying to protect Megan by confessing."

Is Megan Nelson so insane she should not be held accountable for committing the crime? Did she do it, but not really? Her persona "Bobby" can form and remember impressions and can talk about them intelligently. That is the gold standard for legal competence in the state of New York. But is Bobby's "confession" credible? Court psychiatrist Elizabeth Olivet rejects the reliability of Bobby's testimony. "Like testimony derived from hypnosis or truth serum, it was from a hypersuggestible state."

Megan Nelson's third persona, "Nancy," turns out to be Dr. Hampton's murderer. ADA Kincaid declares that "If we ever need to justify letting people plead insanity, Megan Nelson fits that bill."

"Pride and Joy" (Episode 72) offers another perspective on psychological illness. Sean McKinnon murders his father, staging the crime to make it look like his father was killed during a break-in. Apprehended through the efforts of Logan and Briscoe, Sean claims in his defense that he is a long-suffering victim of his father's abuse. He claims that he was goaded into killing his father in self-defense. Unhappily for Sean's defense strategy, the diminished capacity argument is simply a smoke screen. He really is a sociopath who killed his father because his father's job as a building superintendent was a constant reminder to Sean that he was being forced to live with "inferiors."

After the court psychiatrist, Dr. Elizabeth Olivet, examines him she declares, "This kid doesn't want to be who he is. Sean McKinnon has enough anger to blow this office apart." Sociopath that he is, Sean is still capable of distinguishing right from wrong and acting accordingly. The jury is unconvinced by his defense that "social superiority" made him do it and convicts him of murder in the second degree.

"Double Blind" (Episode 140) begins as a free-speech case in which a publisher prints an assassin's handbook, which later is used by Alan Sawyer in his murder of a building janitor. But the case transforms into one involving mental illness. It seems Alan is not legally guilty by reason of mental illness, or schizophrenia. Alan heard voices encouraging him to kill the janitor. As long as he took his experimental medicine T489 he did not hear the voices, but the medicine's effectiveness wore off and his illness returned. Dr. Christian Varick, his psychiatrist, knew that and ignored it. Varick is arrested and charged with manslaughter in the second degree. It is discovered that Alan really has a brain tumor, not schizophrenia, which Dr. Varick knew about and tried to cover up. His reckless behavior constitutes a substantial and unjustifiable risk with his patient's life. So Alan Sawyer is found not guilty of the murder of the janitor because he had been acting under the compulsion of his brain tumor, the very tumor that would take Alan's own life in short order.

Law & Order deserves high marks for tackling another form of diminished capacity or diminished responsibility—crimes motivated by religious conviction. "Disciple" (Episode 196), focuses on a troubled teenager, Kira Grayson, who dies during an exorcism. Her mother, Margo Grayson, and Sister Rosa Halacy are charged with murder in the second degree based on their "depraved indifference" for Kira's life. Sister Rosa says Kira had a spiritual problem; there was evil inside Kira and she knew a ritual to drive it out. She believes Kira was possessed by the devil and that an exorcism would drive it out.

Sister Rosa believes she heard the voice of St. Michael, who was a messenger between her and God. "St. Michael revealed to me that Kira had been taken by a demon." DA Adam Schiff can't believe Sister Rosa's claim. "A voice is a voice. Nobody is that naïve. People see the Devil as an allegory." But Sister Rosa truly believes the Devil is real and controlling young Kira. Sister Rosa believes that she and Margo Grayson did not commit a moral offense by accidentally killing Kira. On the witness stand she claims, "God resolved (us) of the responsibility. I can only take comfort in saying that this terrible thing was God's will."

Her defense attorney argues to the jury that "What the law asks you to do is to judge my client's actions by the state of her mind when the tragedy occurred. In Ms. Halacy's mind it was holy." She did it, but because she thinks the action was holy she did not really do it.

EADA McCoy raises the key issue in his summation before the jury. "What do you make of Rosa Halacy and her calling? Can a righteous person commit a wrongful act? We cannot let Rosa Halacy assert for herself the power we invest in our Supreme Being. She may hear God, but she may not play God. Just because she may have a divine mission, it does not exempt her from the code of human behavior. She is responsible for the consequences of her convictions." She did it, plain and simple.

The jury finds Sister Rosa Halacy guilty of second-degree murder. She may have been motivated by her sincere religious convictions, but when those convictions inspired her to act in a manner that showed a depraved indifference to the human consequences of her actions, she was legally accountable for them.

"Angel" (Episode 119) provides an even more extreme example of the legal consequences of religious convictions. Leah Coleman smothers her baby and incinerates the dead infant in her apartment building's furnace, claiming that God wanted her to do these things. Prior to these actions she had consulted her parish priest, Father Michael Carner. On the witness stand Father Carner testifies that he had told the troubled Coleman that everything that happened was for the best and that her baby was now in heaven with God. In Father Carner's opinion, the only conceivable way to rationalize such horrific actions and go on in the face of such misfortunes is to believe that God gave man free will, and because of that, we are responsible to Him for our actions.

McCoy understands Father Carner's words to Leah as an attempt to reconcile a benevolent God with all of the evil in the world, but Leah drew a different meaning from them altogether. "I wanted the best for my baby. What kind of evil world do we live in? Now baby Rachel is in heaven with God. He has my Rachel. It's what He wanted." From Leah Coleman's perspective she did her baby daughter a favor by strangling her and incinerating her body. Now baby Rachel is out of harm's way, safe in the hands of God.

McCoy rejects this theology. "So now do you know what you did was wrong? Is God happy about what you did? I'd say that was pretty selfish of Him, wouldn't you? The God that you describe sounds like He's sitting around heaven. He got bored, so He arranged for you to kill your child. You know what you did and you knew it was wrong. That means you're guilty as sin."

DA Adam Schiff is impatient with the theological complexities of this case. "This is a murder trial, not a theodicy seminar." But Schiff has it backwards. It is a theodicy seminar masquerading as a murder trial. If Leah Coleman's theology is correct, she had indeed done her daughter a favor. To turn a phrase, "God made her do it."

Alas for the *Gospel of Leah Coleman*, the jury finds her guilty of murder in the second degree. Leah Coleman's theological beliefs are judged to be an insufficient defense of infanticide. Perhaps God made the jury find her guilty of murder two.

"Haven" (Episode 193) offers a completely different type of diminished capacity argument. Like "Sanctuary" and "Bounty," "Haven" has a plot line that plays on race issues. In this episode, college student Jerome Warren kills community activist Randy Chase. Warren's guilt is obvious, but his defense attorney takes a shot at jury nullification and claims that Warren killed Chase because Chase had hounded Warren to do well in college. Warren is a beneficiary of his college's affirmative action policies, which in his case was a misfortune because it put an academically ill-prepared African American student at risk by throwing him into an academic environment for which he was unsuited. His resulting failure causes anger and frustration, especially when do-gooder Chase constantly holds him up as a role model to the African American community. Warren's defense attorney arguess that "Affirmative action is what put my client in harm's way." He then calls a parade of expert witnesses who claim that while it has the best of intentions, affirmative action frequently backfires by placing poorly prepared students into situations that almost guarantee their academic failure. The affirmative action devil made Warren do it.

Judge David Wilcox aborts the defense's analysis of affirmative action. "This is a murder trial, not a political debate." Alas for the good judge's attempts to narrow the focus of the trial, he presides over a political debate disguised as a murder trial.

"Night and Fog" (Episode 57) presents the case of David Steinmetz, a Polish Jew who cooperated with the Nazis during World War II. At the beginning of the episode, detectives Logan and Briscoe are called to his apartment where his wife lays dead on the bedroom floor. Steinmetz claims that his wife was old and in failing health, and that to free herself of further suffering, she asked him to help her commit suicide. He claims he helped her take a lethal dose of sleeping pills and then left the apartment so that he did not have to be with her when she died. But an autopsy shows that she does not have sufficient drugs in her system to kill her and that Steinmetz had really smothered her with a pillow. It seems to the viewing audience that this case will turn on the question of whether Steinmetz is guilty of assisting in a suicide or is guilty of murder. These issues, however, take a back seat to the discovery that Steinmetz cooperated with the Nazis during the war. The Polish government has uncovered information about Steinmetz's brutal treatment of his fellow concentration camp inmates, when he had used his original name of Schulmann, and it is seeking to bring criminal charges against him. Steinmetz's wife discovered her husband's true identity and argued with him heatedly about his wartime activities. When she threatens to reveal his past, he kills her. The U.S. State Department wants to extradite him to Poland where he faces trial for his war crimes but DA Schiff wants to try him for murder first. EADA Ben Stone opposes Schiff. "I'm helping a mass murderer cover up his crimes." Schiff is adamant that Steinmetz be tried for murder in New York and serve out the requisite prison sentence before he is extradited to Poland. Schiff says of this legal mess, "We are not in the evil business; we're in the crime business."

But Schiff is wrong about that. The office of the district attorney is in the crime business because criminals themselves are in the evil business, the business of wrecking other peoples' lives and seeking to profit from the wreckage.

As serial killer Mark Bruner said in "Bodies," "Without me, you would have no reason to exist" Were it not for the evil perpetrated by the bad guys, the good guys—the usual suspects—would indeed have no reason to exist and TV viewers would have to look elsewhere for first-class entertainment.

Suggested Reading

Courrier, Kevin and Susan Green. *Law & Order: The Unofficial Companion.* Los Angeles: Renaissance Books, 1998.

Dwyer, Kevin and Juré Fiorillo. *True Stories of Law & Order: The Real Crimes Behind the Best Episodes of the Hit TV Show* New York: Berkley Trade, 2006.

The legal issues briefly presented here were first laid out in a philosophical examination by John Austin in *The Province of Jurisprudence Determined* 1832. Reprint, New York: Pronetheus Books, 2000. Further refined by H. L. A. Hart in *The Concept of Law.* Oxford: Oxford University Press, 1961.

The specific question of legal responsibility is discussed by H. L. A. Hart in his essay "Negligence, *Mens Rea*, and Criminal Responsibility" (*Oxford Essays in Jurisprudence.* Edited by A. G. Guest. New York: The University of Oxford Press, 1961).

Theodicy is discussed by Gottfried Wilhelm Leibniz in his *Theodicy* (1710) [Translated by E.M. Huggard. New York: Biblio Bazaar, 2007.] and Immanuel Kant in his essay "On the Failure of All Philosophical Essays in Theodicy" (1791) [*Religion and Rational Theology.* Translated by Allen W. Wood and George di Giovanni. Cambridge University Press, 2001].

Values dualism is defended by Plato in his *Phaedo* and *Republic* (*circa* 370 BCE). Complete Works, edited by John M. Cooper. Indianapolis: Hackett Publishing, 1997.

GLOSSARY

Absolutism: An epistemology that says there is only one possible right answer for any question and that any competing answer must be wrong. Opposed to perspectivism and contextualism. *Boomtown* rejects absolutism; *Cold Case*, *Without a Trace*, and *CSI* embrace it.

Algorithm: A problem-solving methodology such as a mathematical formula or deductive argument. As long as no "counting mistake" is made, the conclusion follows invariably from the application of the laws of science to the crime scene evidence. DNA fingerprinting illustrates this methodology. Championed by *CSI*.

Amnesia: The inability to recall a memory that one knows he has (partial or temporary amnesia) or the complete loss of one's event memory (total amnesia). Partial or total loss of event memory is usually not accompanied by the corresponding loss of emotional, factual, or habit memories. A concern for *Cold Case*.

Bad Faith: The only sin in Jean-Paul Sartre's existentialist view—the rejection of self-honesty. Lying to yourself and claiming that you had no choice about something. You always have a choice. A frequent focus of *Boomtown*.

Catharsis: A storytelling technique in which the author first creates psychological tension and distress in the eyes of the audience by depicting terrible events, only later to produce a sensation of relief in the audience when the terrible events are resolved through a happy ending.

Closure: The resolution of the psychological distress that criminal activity causes for the victim or his survivors, friends, and family members; or the arrest and conviction of the criminal by the police forces and the law courts of society. The focus of *Cold Case* and *Without a Trace*.

Coherence Theory of Truth: True claims are true because they fit consistently into the story line's other claims. Akin to perspectivism and contextualism and opposed to the correspondence theory of truth. *Boomtown* adopts this theory of truth.

Contextualism: An epistemology that emphasizes the manifold factors, assumptions, and prejudices that each knowing individual brings with her to each knowledge situation. Changes in any of these factors, like the movement of a kaleidoscope, reformulate what counts as knowledge for that person in that situation. Akin to perspectivism and opposed to the correspondence theory of truth. *Cold Case*, *Without a Trace*, and *Boomtown* depict this approach to crime fighting; *CSI* rejects it.

Correspondence Theory of Truth: True claims are true because they correspond to or point to things in the world that exist just like the claims say they do. Opposed to perspectivism and contextualism. *CSI* adopts this position.

Diminished Capacity: The "I did it, but not really" legal defense in which a defendant tries to avoid legal responsibility for his actions by arguing that these actions sprang from any number of causes, which the courts have traditionally found to be legally acceptable excuses for such actions.

Distributive Justice: That part of the moral and legal theory of justice that attempts to answer the question of how limited goods and services are correctly to be divided when the demand for these goods and services exceeds their supply. Whose turn is it to ride shotgun? *Law & Order* focuses on this issue.

Epistemology: A central component of philosophy that studies and seeks to understand what knowledge is and what are the proper subjects of knowledge. Modern science and modern crime fighting evolved from epistemology.

Essentialism: The metaphysical position that maintains in general that all Xs are Xs because they share the same set of properties (e.g., all triangles have only three sides and three angles, etc.) and specifically, that each person is the person he is because he has a specific set of character traits throughout his entire lifetime. Essentialistic world views are tragic because many people will fail to live up to social standards that conflict with their essential nature. Opposed to existentialism and queer theory. *Without a Trace* adopts an essentialistic view of human nature.

Existentialism: A metaphysical view that says that there is no such thing as a fixed human nature, nor do individuals have fixed personalities. Instead, persons are what they make themselves to be. Existentialistic world views are comic because personal failure to live up to a standard set by that individual is his or her own fault. Opposed to essentialism. *Without a Trace* and *Boomtown* feature existentialist concerns.

False Memory Syndrome: The mistaken belief that one's memories are accurate when actually they are not. Opposed to veridical memory. A threat to the crime-fighting methodology of *Cold Case*.

Foundationalism: A model of scientific crime fighting originating in the epistemology of French philosopher René Descartes according to which criminals can only properly be apprehended through the application of scientific laws and algorithms to the scene of the crime. *CSI* uses this crime-fighting model exclusively.

Heuristic: A rule of thumb applied to the crime scene evidence, which does not infallibly guarantee an irrefutable conclusion but succeeds frequently enough in practice to provide a usable guide. Accepting the validity of eyewitness testimony is a heuristic problem-solving rule of thumb. Rejected as inadequate by *CSI*, but endorsed by *Cold Case, Boomtown, Without a Trace*, and *Law & Order*.

Howdunit: A police procedural that focuses on the means used to commit the crime in order to uncover the identity of the criminal. *CSI* champions this model.

Imagination: The faculty of the mind that allows a person to formulate missing or absent data (pieces of the puzzle) and recognize the role those missing data might play in making a coherent picture of the world. Used by the detective to formulate an educated guess about whodunit, howdunit, and whydunit.

Justice: A synonym for what is fair or right. Divides into distributive justice and retributive justice. Of major concern in *Law & Order*.

Lamarckian View of Human Nature: Adopting the view of the French naturalist Jean-Baptiste Lamarck, this metaphysical theory maintains that within an individual's lifetime, her experiences may change her nature, giving her a new essence.

Leibniz's Law: If X (the murderer) really equals Y (the defendant), then everything true about X is also true about Y. The source of the defendant's alibi: Something is not true about Y (e.g., she was not at the scene of the crime) that is true of X, the murderer; therefore Y could not have been the murderer.

The Look: A component of Sartre's existentialism. Being on stage before the eyes of the whole world. Have you got the guts to act like that with everybody watching? Also called the Stare. *Boomtown* uses this notion extensively.

Memory: The mind's capacity to recall information (factual memory), emotional states (emotional memory), events of one's own past (episodic memory), and the ability to perform routine activities (habit memory). *Cold Case* uses memory as a crime-fighting heuristic.

Metaphysics: Any theory about the ultimate nature of reality.

Miranda Ruling: The U.S. Supreme Court's famous 1966 decision that dictates that an arrested defendant must have certain legal rights specifically read to her by the arresting officer immediately upon her arrest.

Morality: A synonym for ethics. The branch of philosophy that seeks to determine what actions and policies are right or wrong and why they are right or wrong.

Motion to Supress: A legal maneuver made prior to a trial in which the defense attorney attempts to get evidence against her client excluded from the trial because the evidence was obtained illegally or because its admission at the trial would so inflame the jury that the defendant could not get a fair trial. A frequent concern in *Law & Order.*

Murder: First-degree murder constitutes any illegal homicide in which the murderer willfully intended the death of the victim. Second-degree murder constitutes an illegal assault upon the victim in which the death of the victim was a distinct possibility. First-degree manslaughter (or voluntary manslaughter) involves the unintended death of a victim when the assailant was also committing a separate felony. Second-degree manslaughter (or involuntary manslaughter) involves the unintended death of the victim when the assailant was not otherwise committing a felony. Of prime concern to *Law & Order.*

Nullification: A legal twist in which the trial jury or the trial judge rejects the conviction or overturns the conviction of a clearly guilty defendant for any number of philosophical, political, or ideological reasons. A nightmare for the prosecution in *Law & Order.*

Perspectivism: An epistemology that insists that the viewpoint (perspective) of the knowledge seeker inevitably colors what that person counts as knowledge and that there is no such thing as a "view from nowhere," a position-less viewpoint. Akin to contextualism and opposed to the correspondence theory of truth. *Cold Case, Without a Trace,* and *CSI* reject this position; *Boomtown* adopts it; *Law & Order* grapples with it.

Philosophy: The love of wisdom. Historically developed by the ancient Greeks, philosophy had three major subdivisions: epistemology, metaphysics, and value theory.

Plea Bargaining: A legally binding deal worked out between the defendant and the district attorney in which the defendant agrees to plead guilty to a lesser charge in order to avoid being convicted of a greater charge at his trial. Of concern to *Law & Order.*

Police Procedural: A detective story that focuses on the crime-fighting methodology used by the police or the courts of law.

Problem of Grue: A form of skepticism about Foundationalism. How can we be certain of any empirical law of nature? Just because emeralds so far have always been green does not mean that they can never become blue at some future date.

Problems: Recurring difficulties in discovering the identity of criminals or proving criminals' legal responsibilities. Adequate solutions for these difficulties require the development of a crime-fighting methodology.

Puzzles: Difficulties in discovering the identity of criminals or proving criminals' legal responsibilities that the common crime-fighting methodology seems to be incapable of solving.

Queer Theory: A metaphysical theory formulated by the contemporary American philosopher Judith Butler according to which essentialism is an ideology imposed on its victims by a dominating social system that seeks to extinguish a varied and diverse range of human beings and their lifestyles in the name of an imaginary uniformity. Queer theory is akin to existentialism in rejecting any essentialistic account of human nature and adopting a comic view of human nature.

Realistic: The height at which the audience sets the bar in terms of which it judges fictitious events as factually close enough to be acceptable for the purposes of enlightenment or entertainment.

Reductionism: The translation of a macro class of phenomena into its microcomponents, which are thought to be responsible for the phenomena's macro characteristics. For example, the macro characteristics of a person's appearance are reduced to that person's DNA, which causes that person to have curly, red hair and blue eyes. The cornerstone of the crime-fighting methodology adopted by *CSI*.

Remand: To be held in jail without bail. A legal issue for *Law & Order*.

Retributive Justice: Payback. A legal or moral theory that attempts to answer the question, What is the correct response to infractions? "Let the punishment fit the crime" embodies the question of retributive justice, but which punishment "fits" which crime is highly debated. Of great concern to *Law & Order*.

Romantic World View: Any view of the word that portrays the solitary individual as incomplete and unhappy in the absence of her missing "other half." The missing other half of a person may be another person, a vocation, a cause, or even a career, but in all cases the romantic story is that of the struggle to overcome the void left by the missing part of the self and the anticipation of the "and they lived happily ever after" ending that would accompany the uniting of the missing pieces. *Cold Case* depicts criminals as destroying the romantic unity of their victims.

Skepticism: The rejection of the claim that someone knows some supposed fact in a given situation. More generally, the rejection of Foundationalism and thus any possible foundational criminal science. In legal terms, this appears as an appeal to "reasonable doubt" in jury trials. Of great concern for very different reasons for *CSI* and *Law & Order*.

Theory: An explanatory model composed of evidence, algorithms, and heuristic practices, which combine to form a subject such as chemistry or biology into a science. Evolutionary theory or Einstein's theory of relativity are examples of this sort of model. *CSI* aims at producing just this sort of model of scientific crime fighting.

Time Line: The "ticking clock" that seemingly provides the tension in *Without a Trace*. If the missing person cannot be found within 48 hours of her disappearance, then she is usually "gone for good."

Tipping Point: A form of skepticism regarding Foundationalism. The point at which all Xs change over into Ys. Water freezes into ice at 32 degrees Fahrenheit, its tipping point. What if DNA has an undiscovered tipping point? Of concern to *CSI's* crime-fighting methodology.

Utility Theory of Justice: Any distributive or retributive theory of justice that maintains that it is only the good consequences of an action or a social practice that provides its moral or legal justification. "The end justifies the means."

Values Dualism: A metaphysics that sees each specific event as completely good or completely evil, never both and never neither. Of concern to *Law & Order*.

Value Theory: A systematic account of the nature and origin of moral duties and obligations which explains their relationship to legal rights and duties. Of concern to *Law & Order*.

Veridical Memory: Accurate memory beliefs. Opposed to the false memory syndrome. Of concern to *Cold Case*.

Whodunit: A police procedural that focuses on uncovering the identity of the person responsible for the crimes highlighted in its story line.

Whydunit: A police procedural that focuses on the motives and mindset of the criminal in order to uncover the identity of the criminal.

Willing Suspension of Disbelief: The decision of the audience to allow the storyteller to invent fictitious elements of a story line simply for the sake of the story.

INDEX

About the Author

RAYMOND RUBLE has taught philosophy for over thirty-five years at Appalachian State University and is the author of *The Theory and Practice of Critical Thinking* as well as various essays on philosophical issues contained within popular culture topics.

The *CSI* crew (left to right): Captain Jim Brass, Dr. Al Robbins, Criminalists Warrick Brown, Gil Grissom, Sara Sidle, Catherine Willows, Nick Stokes, Greg Sanders. Courtesy of Photofest.

The cast from *Without a Trace* (left to right): FBI Special Agents Danny Taylor, Samantha Spade, Jack Malone, Vivian Johnson, Martin Fitzgerald. Courtesy of Photofest.

The *Cold Case* squad (left to right): Police Detectives Lilly Rush, Will Jeffries, Nick Vera, Scotty Valens, Police Captain John Stillman. Courtesy of Photofest.

The cast of *Boomtown* (left to right): Detective Bobby "Fearless" Smith, Detective Joel Stevens, A.D.A. David McNorris, Paramedic Teresa Ortiz, Policeman Tom Turcotte, Reporter Andrea Little, Policeman Ray Heckler. Courtesy of Photofest.

The cast of *Law & Order*, Season 4 (left to right): A.D.A. Claire Kincaid, Exec A.D.A. Ben Stone, Police Detective Lennie Briscoe, Police Detective Mike Logan, Police Lt. Anita van Buren. Courtesy of Photofest.

The cast of *Law & Order*, Season 7 (left to right): Police Detective Rey Curtis, Police Detective Lennie Briscoe, Police Lt. Anita van Buren, A.D.A. Jamie Ross, D.A. Adam Schiff, Exec. A.D.A. Jack McCoy. Courtesy of Photofest.

The cast of *Law & Order*, Season 17 (left to right): A.D.A. Connie Rubirosa, D.A. Arthur Branch, Exec. A.D.A. Jack McCoy, Police Lt. Anita van Buren, Detective Ed Green, Detective Nina Cassady. Courtesy of Photofest.